# Getting Started in Futures

# Getting Started in Futures

**TODD LOFTON**

**WILEY**

JOHN WILEY & SONS

New York • Chichester • Brisbane • Toronto • Singapore

*Library of Congress Cataloging in Publication Data*

Lofton, Todd.
  Getting started in futures.
  Bibliography: p.
  Includes index.
  1. Futures market.     I. Title.

HG6024.A3L64  1989       332.64'4        88-37856
ISBN 0-471-61492-0
ISBN 0-471-61493-9 (pbk.)

Printed in the United States of America

10  9  8  7  6  5  4  3  2

To my wife, Barbara, who bought one contract of silver coin futures 15 years ago, sold it 3 weeks later for a $750 profit, bought a color TV, and retired from the markets

# Preface

Y ou're talking with guests at a wedding reception or college reunion, and a graying well-dressed man whom you don't know says, "Boy, did I take a bath in cocoa."

Now you've heard of milk baths but not cocoa baths. While you're trying to figure it out, he explains that he was referring to his losses in the cocoa futures market. With no prompting, he launches into a story about the wild price movement, the phone calls, and how he lost thousands of dollars in just a few days. While he is telling his tale, he watches you carefully for signs of awe or sympathy. If he sees neither of these, the story will be better the next time he tells it. The loss will be greater, the time less.

People who wouldn't admit they lost $5.00 in the Vegas slots will tell you willingly about their real or imagined travails in the futures markets. Participation in futures puts them in the company of the Hunt Brothers and hooded Arab sheiks.

Their stories also create misconceptions, and one of the purposes of this book is to undo some of those. Another is to give you a chance to decide for yourself whether you or your company should be utilizing these highly efficient economic markets.

Futures offer knowledgeable speculators a unique high-risk, high-return investment medium.

Futures offer prospective hedgers opportunities that were unheard of as few as 15 years ago. You don't have to grow corn, raise cattle, or grind flour. Today's futures markets enable you to:

- Establish now the price you will pay for U. S. Treasury bills next year.

- Ensure that the major foreign currency you will receive in 6 months will be worth as much then as it is now.

- Protect the value of your large stock portfolio while you systematically increase or reduce your holdings.

- Immunize your inventory of fixed-income securities against rising interest rates.

- Set the return now on a market-rate loan your bank will make next quarter.

This book is intended to be easy reading. There is no economic jargon. There are no formulas or mathematics. Examples are given for every important point, sometimes more than one. When you finish it, you will understand how futures and options work.

The first few chapters introduce you to the players. Along the way you'll also find out what some of the unfamiliar words mean. Next come discussions of price forecasting, money management, and financial futures. A separate section is devoted to the newest game in town, options on futures. The last chapter presents a profile of each major futures market. Only masculine pronouns have been used throughout, to avoid the constant repetition of the phrase "or she." There is no intention to slight distaff readers or practitioners.

I would like to be able, as other authors do, to thank several people for their help in making this book possible. But I can't. This book is truly a product of the electronic age. I have no secretary or typist; the words were pecked out on my trusty Macintosh. I'm self-employed, so I can't thank my boss for his indulgence. The research I did myself, and in that regard I do have something to say. I called most of the exchanges and many professional organizations to gather information. They not only provided me with what I needed, they were unfailingly friendly and cooperative. I thanked them then, and I want to thank them again here.

There are three people whose support should be acknowledged. Perry J. Kaufman and Mark J. Powers read all or part of the manuscript and provided me with several valuable comments and suggestions. It's a better book because of their efforts. Karl Weber, my editor at Wiley, conceived the idea of a primer on futures, encouraged me while it was being written, and suggested the design of the book.

TODD LOFTON

_McLean, Virginia_
_March 1989_

# Contents

# 1

# Introduction

Suppose that you and I lived in rural Iowa. I raise beef cattle. You have a corn farm about 15 miles down the road. Each fall, when your corn comes in, you truck the entire crop to me, and I buy it to feed to my steers. To make things fair, we agree that I will pay you the cash price for corn on the Chicago Board of Trade on the day I take delivery.

Corn is important to both of us. It is your principal crop; it is my main cost in feeding cattle. I hope for low corn prices. All summer long you are praying that something benign—an unexpected Russian purchase, for example— will send corn prices up.

One spring day you come to me with a suggestion. "Let's set our corn price now for next fall," you say. "Let's pick a price that allows each of us a reasonable profit and agree on it. Then neither of us will have to worry about where prices will be in September. We'll be able to plan better. We can go on about our business, secure in the knowledge of what we will pay and receive for the corn."

I agree, and we settle on a price of $2.25 a bushel. That agreement is called a forward contract—a "contract" because it's an agreement between a buyer (me) and a seller (you); "forward" because we're going to make the actual transaction later, or forward in time.

It's a good idea, but it's not without flaws. Suppose the Russians did announce a huge surprise purchase, and corn prices went to $3.00. You would be looking for ways to get out of the contract. By the same token, I would not be too eager to abide by our agreement if a bumper crop caused corn prices to fall to $1.50 a bushel.

There are other reasons why our forward contract could fail to be met. A hailstorm could wipe out your entire corn crop. I could sell my cattle-feeding operation, and the new owner not feel bound by our agreement. Either one of us could go bankrupt.

Futures contracts were devised to solve these problems with forward contracts, while retaining most of their benefits. A futures contract is simply a forward contract with a few wrinkles added.

# 2

# Basic Terms and Concepts

There are some basic concepts that you should
understand if you are going to deal with the
futures markets. The first is the futures contract
itself. We said in Chapter 1 that a futures
contract is simply a forward contract with some
added wrinkles. One of those wrinkles is
*standardization*.

A forward contract can be for any commodity.
It can also be for any amount or delivery time. If
you want to make a deal to buy a 1400 bushels
of silver queen corn for delivery to your
roadside stand next July 2, you can do it with a
forward contract. You can't in the futures
market.

A futures contract is for a specific grade,
quantity, and delivery month. For example, the
futures contract for corn on the Chicago Board
of Trade (CBOT) calls for 5000 bushels of No. 2
yellow corn. Delivery months are March, May,
July, September, and December. There are no
other delivery months and no other contract
sizes available. All futures contracts are

**A futures contract is a standardized forward contract that can be broken by either party with simply an offsetting futures market transaction.**

standardized in this way. That's done to make specific futures contracts interchangeable. Grade, quantity, and delivery months are specified by the exchange when they design the contract. Only the price is left to be determined.

Another difference is where business may be done. A forward contract can be drawn up anywhere. Futures contracts are bought or sold only on the exchange trading floor by members of the exchange.

## Money

Three other differences between a forward contract and a futures contract involve the important matter of money. If two parties make a forward contract, no money need change hands until the cash transaction is completed at a later date. If you buy a futures contract, you will have to put up *margin* money. This is not a down payment, and no money is borrowed, as in stocks. It is a good faith deposit, or "earnest money," to demonstrate your intention to pay for the commodity in full when it is delivered.

If you take a long futures position and cash prices go up, so will the price of your futures contract, as they tend to move together. In that event you would have an *unrealized profit* in your futures account. Without closing out the futures position, you may withdraw this profit in cash and use if for whatever you wish. This is not possible with a forward contract.

You will have to pay your broker a *commission* for handling the futures transaction for you. There is no commission in a forward contract.

## An Exit

One of the most important qualities of a futures contract is its *escapability*. If you enter into a forward contract and later decide you want out, the other party would also have to agree to break the contract. If he won't, you're stuck. If you buy a futures contract and later decide that you don't want to be a party to it any more, you can close out your position and wipe the slate clean by simply selling the same futures contract. (Now you can see why it is important that futures contracts be interchangeable.)

Futures provide other, broader economic benefits that probably won't affect you directly. Because they trade actively, futures markets are constantly "discovering" the current price for the particular commodity. These prices are disseminated around the world within seconds. If you want to make a futures transaction, there's no need to search for a buyer or seller. There are virtually always buyers and sellers (or their representatives) waiting on the exchange trading floor; the only question is price. The futures markets, by providing for alternate delivery of the actual cash commodity, also provide a "safety valve" for producers who for some reason cannot deliver their actual commodity through normal supply channels.

## THE LONG AND SHORT OF IT

Before we talked only about buying a futures contract. That's known as being *long*, or having a *long position*. The holder of a long futures position will receive delivery of the actual commodity if he holds the futures position into the delivery period.

You may have also heard the term *short*. The rules surrounding futures trading allow you to sell a futures contract before you buy it. When you do, you are said to be short futures, or have a *short position*. You will be expected to deliver the actual commodity if you hold a short futures position into the delivery period. To close out a short futures position, you buy an identical futures contract on the exchange. You would then be out of the market altogether.

**In futures there is a short position for every long position.**

The idea of a short position may be confusing because it involves selling something you don't have. Actually, you may have participated in a short sale. If a car dealer doesn't have the car you want on his lot and orders one for you from the factory, he has sold the car short. Furniture is often sold (short) by a retail store before the items are manufactured.

Why would someone want to sell a futures contract short? To establish his selling price, because he believes the market is headed lower and that he will be able to buy the futures contract back later at a lower price. Regardless of which transaction came first, the profit or loss in a futures trade is the difference between the buying price and the selling price.

Who's long and who's short is one of the biggest differences between the futures markets and the stock markets. Most stock investors buy shares. They hold them for dividends and price appreciation. Only the most sophisticated investors sell stocks short. It is conceivable, therefore, that everyone who owns a certain stock has a profit in it. For example, let's say that General Motors stock advanced from $68 to $69 in today's trading. If there are no short positions in the stock and no present stockholder paid more than $68 a share, everybody involved with GM stock would have a profit. And they would all have just seen their profits increase by $1 per share.

That's not true in futures. In futures, there is a short position for every long position. If you are out of the market and decide to buy a futures contract, another market participant must take the other side and sell it to you. If

**If you gain a profit in a long futures position, a short somewhere has lost the same amount.**

you sell a futures contract short, somebody somewhere must take the other side and buy it from you. That's the only way a futures contract can be created. Gains on one side of the futures markets therefore come out of the pocket of someone on the other side of the market; what the longs win, the shorts lose, and vice versa. It

may serve as a sobering thought: If you take
money of the futures markets, it's not coming
out of thin air; you're taking it from another
player.

# PRICES

## Cash versus Futures

The *cash* or *spot* price of a commodity is the
price at which the actual commodity is
presently being bought or sold in the
marketplace. The *futures* price is the price at
which futures contracts are changing hands.
Cash and futures prices for a particular
commodity do not stray too far from each other.
If the cash price of a commodity goes up or
down, its futures prices tend to follow. But cash
and futures prices do not all necessarily move
together, penny for penny. The reason is that
different forces are at work on the two prices.

Cash prices respond to the present supply of
and demand for the actual commodity. If there
is an immediate shortage of a certain
commodity, its price will be bid up by
processors, distributors, and others who use it in
their course of business. If the commodity is in
abundant supply, its cash price will fall.

Futures prices respond to changes in the cash
price. The futures price most affected by a
change in the cash price is that of the nearest
delivery month because it will soon be virtually
the same as the cash price. Distant futures
months are less responsive, perhaps because
traders feel that whatever is affecting the cash
price now may not be a factor later on.

However, these are not the only winds
blowing on futures. Futures prices are also
driven by traders' *expectations*. The mere threat
of drought or crop disease or labor strike can
send futures prices up long before the actual
event materializes. An example of the power of

**Cash prices
respond to the
supply of and
demand for the
actual commodity.
Futures prices
respond to changes
in the cash price
and to traders'
expectations.**

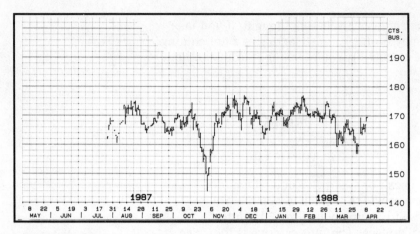

**FIGURE 1.** The power of traders' expectations can be seen in this actual chart for July 1988 oats. In mid-October, prices suddenly fell from 174 to 144, a loss of 17%. Two weeks later prices were right back up where they started. There was no dramatic change in the supply/demand picture for oats. The move was caused by traders' expectations, which were obviously not fulfilled. Reprinted with Permission, © 1988 Commodity Perspective, 30 South Wacker Drive, Suite 1820, Chicago, Illinois 60606.

traders' expectations can be seen in Figure 1, which is an actual chart for July 1988 oat futures.

## Price Charts

The oat chart in Figure 1 is called *bar chart*. To take a more complete example, Figure 2 shows a daily action bar chart for the June 1988 Treasury bill futures contract. Each day's price activity is represented by a vertical line; the top of the line marks the day's high price, the bottom of the line the day's low price. The closing or settlement price is denoted by a short "tick" mark extending to the right of the vertical line. Futures prices are on the right-hand scale, and the corresponding T-bill yield is on the left-hand scale.

The calendar across the bottom shows only weekdays; that is, the weekends are omitted, so the price action has a continuous appearance.

The vertical bars extending upward from the
bottom are daily trading volume, read on the
lower right-hand scale. The two horizontal lines
wandering across the chart from left to right
represent open interest (the number of
outstanding futures contracts) and are read on
the lower left-hand scale. The broken horizontal
line is the 5-year average open interest in T-bill
futures. The solid horizontal line below shows
current daily open interest.

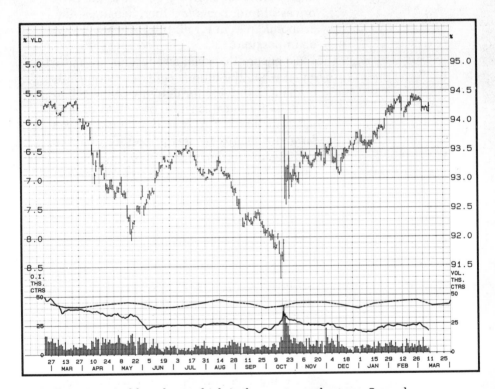

**FIGURE 2.** A typical bar chart, which is the most popular type. Several
months of price activity are shown, enabling a ready comparison between
today's prices and past prices. Shown at the bottom of the chart are daily
trading volume and open interest, the latter comprising the number of
outstanding futures contracts in that market. Reprinted with Permission, ©
1988 Commodity Perspective, 30 South Wacker Drive, Suite 1820, Chicago,
Illinois 60606.

Price charts are economic shorthand, enabling you to compare several weeks or months of past price action at a glance. Most traders use price charts at one time or another, and some key their entire trading strategy to the interpretation of price movements.

## THE NECESSARY ARBITRAGE

For a futures market to do its job, the cash price and the futures price of a given commodity must meet during the delivery period. If the two prices did not come together, hedging—the economic reason for all futures markets—would be impossible.

To ensure that cash and futures are virtually equal when the futures contract matures, the exchanges provide for delivery of the actual commodity in satisfaction of a short futures position. Then, if cash prices should range too far above nearby futures prices, for example, arbitrageurs in the trade would buy the nearby futures, take delivery against the futures contract, and sell the cash commodity thus received in the spot market for a certain profit. This action by arbitrageurs would put downward pressure on cash prices and upward pressure on futures, moving the two prices back together again.

Conversely, if nearby futures prices move far enough above the cash price to make it profitable, arbitrageurs would sell the futures, buy the cash commodity, store it, and deliver it against the futures contract. This action would continue until cash and futures prices moved closer together, erasing potential arbitrage profits.

An example from the world of agriculture may make this arbitrage process easier to understand. We'll use the (fictitious) Breadstuff Grain Company of Omaha, Nebraska. The vice-president of the company is always on the lookout to turn a penny, particularly when he happens to have some idle storage space. He knows that the total cost for Breadstuff to store actual wheat is 8 cents per bushel per month. That includes transportation, insurance, warehouse rent, interest on the money involved, and an allowance for possible spoilage. His commission on a futures transaction is 1 cent per bushel. And he has decided that he wants at least 3 cents per bushel profit for his trouble.

He watches futures prices carefully for arbitrage opportunities. In fact, he has his desktop computer programmed to track futures and cash prices and to buzz him when the spread reaches a point where the cost of storage, commissions, and a 3-cent minimum profit would all be covered.

One morning his computer sounds off, and he sees that wheat futures 1 month distant are at a premium of 13 cents a bushel to cash wheat. It would cost him 8 cents storage + 1 cent futures commission = 9 cents per bushel to carry the hedged cash wheat for that month. The futures price thus offers a potential arbitrage profit of $13 - 9 = 4$ cents per bushel, a windfall. He immediately sells the 1-month wheat futures, placing a limit on the price he will accept. That done, he buys an equivalent amount of cash wheat and has it delivered into his warehouse.

With these actions he has, for all practical purposes, locked in a profit of 4 cents per bushel. One month later he delivers the cash wheat in satisfaction of his short futures position and is paid in full for it.

How can there be such price distortions? Why wouldn't everyone take advantage of an opportunity like that? For several reasons. Breadstuff Grain Company had the storage space available. They also had good access to the cash grain market, allowing the actual grain to be moved in and out without excessive cost or delay. Breadstuff Grain was also paying attention. Other members of the trade may not have been aware of the situation. Breadstuff's computer not only displayed up-to-the-second prices, it was programmed to alert the company when conditions were favorable.

## VOLUME AND OPEN INTEREST

*Trading volume* is the number of futures transactions that took place during a certain period. For example, if you bought a futures contract today, you would add 1 to today's trading volume. One contract would have changed hands, from the seller to you. If later today you decided to sell it, you would add another unit to today's trading volume. When you pick up the newspaper tomorrow morning and see that trading volume in that commodity was 2105 contracts, you know that you were personally responsible for two of them.

Open interest is the number of *outstanding* futures contracts, or the total of short and long positions that have not yet been closed out by delivery or by offsetting futures markets transactions. Your two transactions could have changed the open interest, but not necessarily. As you will see later on, it depends on who took the other side of your trades. The idea of open interest is unique to the futures and options markets. There's nothing comparable in stocks or bonds.

## THE CLEARINGHOUSE

Each futures exchange has its own clearinghouse. Some are separate and distinct from the exchange itself; others are departments within the exchange. Membership is available only to members of the exchange. In addition, clearinghouse members must meet very strict financial requirements.

The functions the clearinghouse performs are vital to the efficient operation of the futures markets. It is the clearinghouse that makes it possible to close out a futures position with simply an offsetting futures market transaction. It does so by breaking the tie between the original buyer and seller. At the end of every trading day, the clearinghouse becomes the buyer to every seller and the seller to every buyer. Either party can therefore close out his futures position through the clearinghouse, without having to locate and obtain the agreement of the original second party.

The accounts of the clearinghouse show the numbers of long and short positions held by each clearing member, not by individual customer name. If you sell to get out of a long position, the clearinghouse balances your sale with a purchase made that day. You'll never know (and don't care, really) who was on the other side of your transaction.

The clearinghouse also has other important responsibilities, including supervising the delivery of actual commodities against a short futures position and guaranteeing the financial integrity of each futures contract it clears.

**It is the clearinghouse that makes it possible to close out a futures position with simply an offsetting futures market transaction.**

## Suggested Reading

*Economics of Futures Trading*, by Thomas A. Hieronymus. Commodity Research Bureau, New York City, Rev. 1977.

# 3

# Futures Markets Today

There is a wide variety of active futures markets today, many of which are for "commodities" that could not possibly have been envisioned when the first futures contract for corn was traded in Chicago in the early 1800s. For ease of discussion, it's best to group them.

Grains: Wheat, corn, oats, soybean complex (soybeans, soybean oil, soybean meal).

Meats: Live cattle, feeder cattle, hogs, pork bellies.

Metals: Platinum, silver, copper, gold.

Foods and fibers: Coffee, cocoa, sugar, orange juice, cotton.

Interest rate futures: Treasury bonds, Treasury bills, Treasury notes, Eurodollars.

*Foreign currencies:* Swiss franc, Deutschemark, British pound, Japanese yen, Canadian dollar.

*Index futures:* S&P 500 Stock Index, NYSE Index, Value Line Index, Major Market Index, Municipal Bond Index, CRB Futures Index, U. S. Dollar Index.

*Petroleum futures:* Crude oil, heating oil No. 2, unleaded gasoline.

*Wood:* Lumber.

Following is a typical report of one day's trading in one futures market, such as you might find in the financial section of your daily newspaper. As you can see, it contains a great deal of information.

### Wheat (CBOT); 5,000 bushels; cents per bushel

| Delivery | Open | High | Low | Settle | Change |
|----------|------|------|------|--------|--------|
| December | 308½ | 311 | 308¼ | 310 | +2½ |
| March | 313½ | 316 | 307 | 316½ | +3 |
| May | 309½ | 311½ | 309½ | 310¾ | +2¼ |
| July | 298 | 299½ | 297 | 287¼ | +1¾ |
| September | 302½ | 302¾ | 302 | 302 | +1¾ |
| December | 308¼ | 310 | 308¼ | 310 | +1¾ |

Est. sales 6,000  Prev. sales 3,317  Open int. 29,816  Change +299

The top line identifies the commodity and provides information about the futures contract. It shows the exchange where the futures contracts are traded (CBOT stands for the Chicago Board of Trade). It also shows the size of the futures contract (5000 bushels). The last item in that line explains that prices in the table are expressed in cents per bushel.

The second line identifies the columns. In the far left column are the delivery months. Chicago wheat futures are traded for delivery in March, May, July, September, and December. Notice also that delivery months extend out to 1 year ahead. Each futures market has its own delivery months and schedule of longevity. U. S. Treasury bond futures, by comparison, mature in March, June, September, and December and come on the board 27 months before maturity.

The second column shows the opening price for each contract that day. In the next four columns are the day's high price, the day's low price, the day's settlement price, and the change from yesterday's settlement price.

The bottom lines shows today's estimated trading volume; yesterday's actual trading volume; yesterday's total open interest in Chicago wheat; and, the change in open interest from the previous day.

To interpret the prices, you add a decimal point. A price of 310, for example, means $3.10 per bushel. The minimum price change is ¼ cent per bushel. To calculate a change in equity caused by a price change, you must take into consideration the contract size. For example, if you had been long one futures contract of nearby December wheat that day, the value of your equity would have increased 2½ cents per bushel; 2½ cents × 5000 bushels = $125.00. If you had been short one futures contract of December wheat, you would have had an unrealized loss of $125.00. If it's easier for you, you can simply remember that 1 cent = $50.

The size of the futures contract for all grains and for soybeans is 5000 bushels. Prices of all grains and soybeans are expressed in cents per bushel, and 1 cent equals $50 in equity.

Let's take a look at the meats.

## Cattle (CME); 40,000 Pounds; Cents per Pound

| Delivery | Open | High | Low | Settle | Change |
|----------|------|------|-----|--------|--------|
| December | 65.30 | 65.57 | 64.95 | 65.42 | +1.35 |
| February | 62.00 | 62.57 | 61.87 | 62.47 | +1.35 |
| April | 64.50 | 65.00 | 64.35 | 64.67 | +.80 |
| June | 64.40 | 65.15 | 64.40 | 64.72 | +.62 |
| August | 62.10 | 62.65 | 62.00 | 62.07 | +.45 |
| October | 61.50 | 61.90 | 61.30 | 61.40 | +.45 |
| December | 62.45 | 63.00 | 62.45 | 62.90 | +.60 |

Est. sales 19,858  Prev. sales 16,260  Open int. 77,110  Change −748

The cattle futures contract on the Chicago Mercantile Exchange (CME) is for 40,000 pounds of live cattle, and prices are expressed in cents per pound. A price of 61.87, for example, means 61.87 cents per pound. If you had been long one contract of February cattle that day, you would have had an unrealized profit of 1.35 cents per pound, or $540 ($.0135 times 40,000 pounds). For shorthand, simply remember that a 1 cent change in cattle futures prices causes a $400 change in equity.

Futures prices for live cattle, feeder cattle, hogs, and pork bellies—which comprise the meat futures—are all expressed in cents per pound. However, the minimum "tick" (price change) is 2½ cents per pound. The prices of 65.52 and 65.57 are really 65.52½ and 65.57½. The "½" is omitted in the table to reduce clutter. The last digits of all meat futures prices are therefore always 0, 2, 5 or 7.

Here are prices for the most well known of the metal futures contracts:

## Gold (COMEX); 100 Troy Ounces; Dollars per Troy Ounce

| Delivery | Open | High | Low | Settle | Change |
|----------|------|------|-----|--------|--------|
| December | 501.00 | 502.30 | 497.00 | 495.50 | −1.60 |
| February | 506.30 | 507.40 | 499.80 | 500.40 | −1.60 |
| April | 513.50 | 514.00 | 506.50 | 507.10 | −1.50 |
| June | 519.80 | 521.00 | 514.00 | 513.60 | −1.40 |

COMEX stands for Commodity Exchange, Inc., which is in New York City. The futures contract calls for delivery of 100 troy ounces of pure gold, and prices are expressed in dollars per troy ounce. A futures price of 495.50 thus means $495.50 per troy ounce. The minimum price change is 10 cents per troy ounce, which represents a change in equity of $10 per futures contract ($.10 × 100 = $10).

Metal futures contract sizes and prices are not uniform, as the following list shows:

*Copper:* 25,000 pounds; cents per pound.

*Platinum:* 50 troy ounces; dollars per troy ounce.

*Palladium:* 100 troy ounces; dollars per troy ounce.

*Silver:* 5000 troy ounces; cents per troy ounce.

Prices for futures in U. S. Treasury bonds are expressed in an entirely different way.

**Treasury Bonds (CBOT); $100,000; Points and 32nds of 100%**

| Delivery | Open | High | Low | Settle | Change |
|---|---|---|---|---|---|
| December | 84-20 | 85-07 | 84-20 | 85-05 | +14 |
| March | 83-19 | 84-07 | 83-16 | 84-05 | +14 |
| June | 82-19 | 83-09 | 82-19 | 83-07 | +14 |
| September | 81-29 | 82-13 | 81-27 | 82-12 | +13 |

Treasury bond futures are traded on the Chicago Board of Trade. The asset underlying the futures contract is $100,000 worth of T-bonds. T-bond futures prices are expressed in points and 32nds percent of par. The digits after the dash are therefore not decimals but number of 32nds. A price of 83-20, for example, means 83 percent of $100,000 plus $20/32$ of 1 percent of $100,000.

The minimum price change is $1/32$ of 1 percent, which equals $31.25 ($1000 divided by

32). A trader with a long position in March T-bonds, for example, would have had an unrealized gain of $^{14}/_{32}$ on this day or 14 × $31.25 = $437.50. A short somewhere would have had a mirror image unrealized loss of $437.50. Prices for 10-year Treasury note futures and municipal bond index futures are expressed in the same way.

Foreign currency futures are also irregular. The table shown here is for the Deutschemark, one of the most widely traded foreign currency futures contracts.

**West German Mark (IMM); 125,000 Marks; Dollars per Mark**

| Delivery | Open | High | Low | Settle | Change |
|----------|------|------|-----|--------|--------|
| December | .6158 | .6158 | .6149 | .6156 | +.0025 |
| March | .6228 | .6233 | .6195 | .6206 | +.0004 |
| June | .6290 | .6296 | .6293 | .6272 | +.0004 |

Futures contracts in the West German mark are traded on the International Monetary Market (IMM), an affiliate of the Chicago Mercantile Exchange. The futures contract size is 125,000 marks. Futures prices represent dollars per mark; that is, prices shown are the cost of one unit of the foreign currency in U. S. dollars. Deutschemarks were at this time selling at about 62 cents apiece.

The other active foreign currency futures and their specifications are

| Currency | Contract Size | Prices Expressed in |
|----------|---------------|---------------------|
| Swiss franc | 125,000 francs | Dollars per franc |
| British pound | 62,500 pounds | Dollars per pound (sterling) |
| Canadian dollar | 100,000 dollars | Dollars (U. S.) per dollars (C) |
| Japanese yen | 12.5 million yen | Dollars per yen (.00 omitted) |

Of these, the last could give you trouble in interpreting, so let's take a closer look. The

following are representative futures prices for
the Japanese yen.

| Open | High | Low | Settle | Change |
|------|------|-----|--------|--------|
| .7608 | .7637 | .7600 | .7603 | −.0010 |

In Japanese yen futures prices, two zeros are
omitted right after the decimal point to keep the
numbers manageable. The approximate cost of 1
Japanese yen in U.S. currency is not 76 cents,
but 76/10,000 of a cent, or $.0076. The change of
.0010 that day was really a change of $.000010
per yen. That number multiplied by the contract
size of 12.5 million yen equals a change in
equity of $125 that day, a modest move.

The final prices we will show you in this
chapter are for S&P 500 Stock Index futures.

**S&P 500 Index (CME); $500 Times Index**

| Delivery | Open | High | Low | Settle | Change |
|----------|------|------|-----|--------|--------|
| December | 235.40 | 244.40 | 235.20 | 244.00 | +8.55 |
| March | 235.90 | 245.00 | 235.90 | 244.80 | +8.65 |
| June | 237.05 | 247.25 | 237.05 | 246.35 | +9.05 |

Futures contracts in the S&P 500 Stock Index
are traded on the Chicago Mercantile Exchange
(CME). Because all stock index futures are
settled in cash, the size of the futures contract is
not fixed but is equal to $500 times the present
value of the index. Each 1.00 change in the
futures price therefore represents a $500 change
in the total value of the futures contract.

This table shows price activity about 2
months after the precipitous 508-point decline
in the Dow Jones Industrial Index on October
19, 1987, and prices are obviously still
unusually volatile. A speculative long position
in the March 1988 delivery month, for example,
would have earned a unrealized gain of $4325
that day!

The futures contracts we have presented in this section are those that represent large groups of futures or that are irregular. There are several other futures contracts that we have not mentioned here, including the minicontracts traded on the MidAmerica Commodity Exchange and those traded on overseas futures markets. Specifications for each active U. S. futures contract, along with a description of the fundamental factors that influence its price, may be found in Chapter 16.

## NORMAL AND CARRYING CHARGE MARKETS

**Futures prices for different delivery months of the same commodity do not always move together. Although there are other causes, the major reason for the divergence is seasonality.**

Futures prices for all delivery months of a particular commodity tend to move together. After all, the same commodity underlies December T-bills and March T-bills; February cattle and April cattle; March corn and May corn.

Nevertheless, different delivery months of the same commodity do not always move in lockstep. One reason for the difference, which we alluded to earlier, is seasonality. Wheat provides an example. The harvest for winter wheat in the United States takes place in late May and June. May wheat futures contracts mature before the harvest, when cash prices depend on old-crop supplies; July wheat futures mature after the harvest, when a new supply of the actual grain will be on hand. As a result, a rally in the May wheat might not be matched in the July wheat.

Petroleum futures provide another example. Because the demand for heating oil is greater in winter, cash prices tend to firm then; futures traders anticipating this effect may drive the prices for January and February futures contracts up above those for the warmer months.

Livestock are a special case. Live cattle and hogs cannot wait around long after they have

reached marketable weights; they must be sold.
The futures price for each delivery month in
these two markets therefore anticipates the
pending supply of live animals for that
particular time period. A delivery month with a
large pending supply will tend to be relatively
weaker than one with a fewer number of
animals in the pipeline.

Trading tactics may also cause a divergence.
Some traders buy one delivery month of a
commodity and simultaneously sell another
delivery month of the same commodity. Their
actions cause the delivery month bought to gain
on the delivery month sold.

Certain delivery months of a commodity
simply attract a large following. December
cotton shows high volume and open interest
even in the spring, when December is a distant
month. The U. S. Treasury refunding cycle can
make certain delivery months of Treasury bond
futures more in demand than other delivery
months.

**Futures prices are
considered to be
"normally" arrayed
when each
succeeding delivery
month is higher
priced than the
preceding delivery
month.**

## Normal Market

Futures prices are considered to be "normally"
arrayed when each succeeding delivery month is
higher priced than the preceding delivery
month. A normal futures market in wheat, for
example, might look something like this on any
given day:

| Wheat Futures Contract | Price (per Bushel) |
|---|---|
| September | $2.95 |
| December | 3.05 |
| March | 3.12 |
| May | 3.12 |
| July | 2.94 |

December wheat is higher priced than the
September, the March higher priced than
the December, and so on until anticipation of

the coming harvest pushes July wheat below all the other delivery months.

The difference between price of September wheat and December wheat is 10 cents. That difference represents the cost of carrying the actual wheat for that 2-month period. It includes, among other things, the cost of warehouse space and the cost of insurance against loss from dampness or rodents.

**Arbitrage brings cash and futures prices together in or near the futures delivery period.**

If the price difference between the 2 delivery months were to become much greater than the actual carrying charge, arbitrageurs in the trade would see a sure profit. They would buy the (lower priced) nearby future and sell the (higher priced) distant future. When the nearby future matured, they would take delivery. They would store the grain and deliver it against the more distant futures contract when it matured. In effect, the futures market would pay them more for storing the wheat than it actually cost them to do so. Their actions would put upward pressure on the nearby futures price and downward pressure on the more distant futures price, driving the two prices back into line.

This phenomenon requires that the commodity concerned be storable because storage is necessary to make the strategy work. It also requires that there be a good supply of the commodity on hand.

## Inverted Market

When an agricultrual commodity suffers from short supply, people do what they have done for centuries: they hoard it. This causes the cash price of the commodity to rise. Nearby futures prices are also affected, for reasons we have already seen, and an "inverted" futures market develops, where succeeding delivery months are lower in price.

An inverted market in soybean meal, for example, might look like this:

| Futures Contract | Price (per ton) |
|---|---|
| July | $266.20 |
| August | 262.50 |
| September | 258.70 |
| October | 257.70 |
| December | 255.20 |
| January | 252.00 |

August meal is lower than July, September is lower than August, and so on. There is virtually no limit as to how far the cash and nearby futures price can go above the price of the more distant futures contract. The arbitrage possible in a normal market doesn't work in an inverted market; to buy the (higher priced) cash commodity and deliver it against a (lower priced) distant futures contact would lock in a loss, not a profit.

**If futures prices become successively lower as they go out in time, the market is said to be "inverted."**

It should be noted that the situation is different in the financial futures. No warehouse is needed to store a Treasury security or a foreign currency bank balance. The carrying charge for these cash assets is figured in a different way, and the price relationship between delivery months depends on different factors. We will talk more about this subject later, when we take a closer look at the financial futures.

## Suggested Reading

_Economics of Futures Trading_, by Thomas A. Hieronymus. Commodity Research Bureau, New York City,
Rev. 1977.

# 4

# The Speculator

Commodity speculators get blamed for many of the economic ills that befall mankind. Speculators cause runaway high prices, and prices so low that agricultural producers cannot survive. Gluts are their doing, as are shortages. They are accused of manipulating markets, fixing prices, and disrupting normal supply channels, all for their own nefarious ends.

Most of these accusations arise from ignorance. Futures markets are complicated mechanisms, and an understanding of how they work is not exactly common knowledge.

A futures market without speculators would be like a country auction without bidders—and would work just about as well. In most markets, speculators are many times more numerous than any other participants. It is the speculators who create a liquid market. Their activities cause prices to change often, and by small increments, enabling relatively large orders to be filled without sending prices sharply higher or lower.

When a speculator buys or sells a futures contract, he is voluntarily exposing himself to the risk of price change. The speculator accepts the risk because he expects to profit from the price change.

Here's an example of a successful speculative trade.

|  |  |  | Margin |
|---|---|---|---|
| May 15 | Bought 1 contract December copper at | 65.25 | |
|  |  |  | $1,500 |
| June 4 | Sold 1 contract December copper at | 71.70 | |
|  |  | +6.45 | |

The speculator made a profit of 6.45 cents per pound, or (6.45 × $250) = $1612.50, less commissions. That's a gain of 107 percent on his original margin of $1500, and it was earned in about 3 weeks. However, losses can accrue equally fast.

|  |  |  | Margin |
|---|---|---|---|
| May 15 | Bought 1 contract December copper at | 65.25 | |
|  |  |  | $1,500 |
| June 4 | Sold 1 contract December copper at | 59.25 | |
|  |  | −6.00 | |

When a speculator buys or sells a futures contract, he is voluntarily exposing himself to the risk of price change. The speculator accepts the risk because he expects to profit from the price change.

The decline of 6 cents caused the loss of $1500, or 100 percent of the original margin.

Most speculators have no truck with the actual commodity. In fact, inadvertent delivery of the commodity against a long futures position—which, despite the stories you may have heard, very rarely happens—would be a financial gaff for most speculators. This would be particularly true in the agricultural markets. You can imagine someone who wouldn't know soybeans if he saw them being told by his broker that he is now the proud owner of 10,000 bushels in a grain elevator in Illinois.

Speculators are drawn to the futures markets by the opportunity for profit and by the game itself. It is not unusual for $20,000 equity in a futures trading account to become $100,000—or $5000—within a few months. The game is not difficult to play. An account can be opened in a few minutes; after that, your telephone connects you indirectly with every futures exchange in the world. It's certainly not dull. As a speculator, you are pitting your judgment and trading skill against some of the best financial minds in the world.

Speculators come from every walk of life. They may be private individuals, informal groups like commodity trading clubs, or corporate members of the trade. Their goals are the same: to earn trading profits from futures positions by being long when prices are rising and short when prices are falling.

Speculators also use *spread* positions. A simple spread involves two positions, one long and one short. They are taken in the same or economically related commodities. Prices of the two futures contracts therefore tend to go up and down together, and gains on one side of the spread are offset by losses on the other. The spreader's goal is to profit from a change in the *difference* between the two futures prices. He is virtually unconcerned whether the entire price structure moves up or down, just so long as the futures contract he bought goes up more (or down less) than the futures contract he sold.

One of the most popular spreads involves the end of the crop year in wheat. As we mentioned earlier, May wheat is the last futures contract before the harvest, and July wheat is the first futures contract after the harvest. Prospects for a good harvest will therefore weigh more heavily on July wheat than on May wheat.

A spreader who expected a bumper crop would buy the potentially stronger contract (May) and sell the potentially weaker contract (July). Some time later he would "unwind" the spread (close out both positions) by selling the May and buying back the July.

**A simple spread involves two positions, one long and one short. They are taken in the same or economically related commodities. Prices of the two futures contracts therefore tend to go up and down together, and gains on one side of the spread are offset by losses on the other.**

**The spreader's goal is to profit from a change in the *difference* between the two futures prices.**

An example will help you understand how it works.

|  |  |  |
|---|---|---|
| *May Wheat* |  | *July Wheat* |
| Buy at   $2.85 per bushel | February | Sell at   $2.80 per bushel |
| Sell at   $3.20 per bushel | April | Buy at   $2.90 per bushel |
| Gain +$ .35 |  | Loss −$ .10 |

Net result + $.25

The spread was put on in February and taken off in April. During that time, the effect of the coming harvest held the price of July wheat down, while May wheat registered a fair gain. The end result was profit for the spreader because the futures contract he bought went up more than the futures contract he sold.

Prices don't have to go up for the spread to earn profits. Suppose that right after the spread was established, Brazil and Canada announced unexpectedly large wheat crops.

|  |  |  |
|---|---|---|
| *May Wheat* |  | *July Wheat* |
| Buy at   $2.85 per bushel | February | Sell at   $2.80 per bushel |
| Sell at   $2.35 per bushel | April | Buy at   $2.10 per bushel |
| Loss −$ .50 |  | Gain +$ .70 |

Net result + $.20

Both futures prices went down in expectation of the flood of wheat. The long side accrued losses; the short side earned profits. But the short position lost more ground than the long position, so the spread still generated gains.

A spread incurs market losses when it moves in a direction opposite to that which the spreader anticipated:

|  |  |  |
|---|---|---|
| *May Wheat* |  | *July Wheat* |
| Buy at   $2.85 per bushel | February | Sell at   $2.80 per bushel |
| Sell at   $3.20 per bushel | April | Buy at   $3.25 per bushel |
| Gain +$ .35 |  | Loss −$ .45 |

Net result − $.10

Although both prices advanced, the long position went up less than the short position. This resulted in a net loss.

Examples of other spreads would include

Long wheat/short corn

Long hogs/short pork bellies

Long gold/short silver

Long cattle/short hogs

Long Deutschemark/short Swiss franc

In each case, the prices of the two commodities tend to go up and down together, and that's a basic requirement for a spread. Long silver/short coffee and long cattle/short cotton are examples of multiple positions that do not qualify as spreads because the two commodities are not economically related. The two prices move independently.

Because a loss on one side tends to be offset by a gain on the other, the market risk in a spread is categorically less than the risk in a net short or long position. This fact, coupled with relatively low margin requirements, makes the spread an attractive trading vehicle to smaller traders. However, it is still possible, by taking on too many contracts, to establish a total spread position with overall market risk just as high as that of a single net long or short position.

How well do speculators do? That depends on to whom you talk. The conventional wisdom is that some 95 percent of private individual speculators lose. A more reliable indication may be found in a study done by Thomas A. Hieronymus, an agricultural economist at the University of Illinois. He analyzed 462 speculative trading accounts of a major brokerage firm over a period of 1 year (1969). The accounts traded the full gamut of commodities at the time. Over the year, 164 accounts showed profits, and 298 accounts showed losses; or, nearly twice as many people lost money as made money.

On the assumption that one trade does not a speculator make, Hieronymus then divided the accounts into two groups: those who entered the market, made one or two trades, and went away; and those who stayed to play the game. The latter group he called *regular* traders; a regular trader was defined as one who made at least 10 trades *or* who had made or lost $500.

Here the results were different. Forty-one percent of the regular traders made money during the year. Most won or lost $3000 or less, although a few made or lost substantial sums. For the group, net (after commission) profits were about the same as net losses.

Among the one-time traders, some 92 percent lost money.

His conclusion from the 1-year sample: the game is played and won by some people; but, for the most part, the regular players take money from the nonregular players and give it to the commission house to pay for the cost of playing.

Granted, the evaluation was made some 20 years ago, and there have been many new futures markets added since then. But human nature has not changed.

What does the average speculator look like? Some data have been gathered on that, too. He is male, 45 years old, a professional, has more than 4 years of college, and a median income above $60,000. He tends to be a small trader (only one or two contracts at a time) and holds a futures position for less than 1 month.

**The "average" speculator is male, 45 years old, a professional, has more than 4 years of college, and a median annual income above $60,000.**

## Suggested Reading

The Commodity Futures Game: Who Wins? Who Loses? Why? by R. J. Teweles, C. V. Harlow, and H. L. Stone. McGraw-Hill, New York City, Rev. 1984.

The Complete Guide to the Futures Markets, by Jack Schwager. John Wiley & Sons, Inc., New York City, 1984.

# 5

# The Hedger

You've heard the phrase "hedging your bet." If you put $100 on the Los Angeles Lakers to win tomorrow night and later find out that two of their starters have the flu, you could hedge your bet by putting $100 on their opponents.

A hedge in the futures markets operates on the same general principle. A hedge is a futures position that is roughly equal and opposite to the position the hedger has in the cash market. A better definition may be that of Holbrook Working, a Stanford University economist. He defines a hedge as a futures transaction that acts as a substitute for a later cash transaction.

What makes a hedge work is the fact that cash and futures prices for the same commodity tend to go up and down together, so the losses on one side are canceled out by gains on the other. If you are long (own) the cash commodity, your hedge would be a short futures position. If prices decline, the money you lose on the cash commodity would be offset by the profits in your short position.

> A hedge is a futures position that is roughly equal and opposite to the position the hedger has in the cash market. It is also defined as a futures transaction that acts as a substitute for a later cash transaction.

# SHORT HEDGE

Let's take an example. Assume you are a dealer in Treasury bonds. You buy them and sell them at a markup. Between the time you buy the bonds and the time you find a customer, the bonds are, in effect, sitting on your shelf. If bond prices go down while you are holding them, you would have a loss on your inventory.

You know that a short position in Treasury bond futures would accrue gains if prices decline, offsetting the loss. So you hedge your bonds as soon as you buy them.

### Short Hedge in T-Bond Futures

| Cash Market | | Futures Market |
|---|---|---|
| Buy cash bonds at 95-07 | Now | Sell T-bond futures at 95-17 |
| Sell cash bonds at 94-18 | Later | Buy T-bond futures at 94-28 |
| Loss 0-21 | | Gain 0-21 |

Net gain or loss = 0

**Short hedgers comprise those who grow, store, process, or distribute a cash commodity and who would be hurt by a decline in the cash price.**

This example is oversimplified, but it demonstrates the point. If the bond dealer had not hedged his inventory, he would have lost $21/32$ ($6.56) on each bond. The gain of $21/32$ on the futures position fully offset the decline in the market value of the cash bonds while he held them.

Another example: it is fall, and a farmer plans to plant his winter wheat soon. It will be harvested next May. The price for cash wheat now is $2.85 cents per bushel. He'd like to be able to "lock in" that price for his wheat for that price next May. With futures, he can.

### Short Hedge in Wheat Futures

| Cash Market | | Futures Market |
|---|---|---|
| Wheat price $2.85 | Fall | Sells wheat futures at $2.90 |
| Sells wheat at $2.44 | Next May | Buys wheat futures at $2.49 |
| Opportunity loss $ .41/bushel | | Gain $ .41/bushel |

Net Gain or Loss = 0

In May, the farmer received $2.44/bushel for his actual wheat plus an 41-cent gain in his futures hedge. The sum of $2.44 and $.41 is $2.85, which is the cash price he wanted. If it were not possible to hedge, or if for some reason he had chosen not to hedge, the farmer would have gotten only $2.44/bushel as the fruits of his labors.

In this case, the loss on the cash side is referred to as an "opportunity loss," which means that it's not actually money removed from the farmer's pocket, but what he might have earned under other circumstances (e.g., if he had had the cash grain in the fall and sold it then).

There's something else different about this particular example. Notice that the farmer put the hedge on (took the short futures position) even before he planted the wheat. An _anticipated_ position in the cash commodity can be hedged just as effectively as an existing position.

Short hedgers comprise those who grow, store, process, or distribute a cash commodity. A U. S. oil importer with a tanker of crude on the high seas would use a short hedge to protect his cargo from a price decline. General Mills would use a short hedge for the wheat stored in their warehouses. The common denominator is risk of loss due to a decline in the cash price.

For the short hedge to be effective, the hedger has to be dealing with the basic commodity, or something very close to it. A manufacturer of cotton shirts, for example, would probably find hedging in cotton futures of limited value because there are so many other, more important costs in the making of a shirt.

## LONG HEDGE

It is also possible to use a long hedge in futures. To help you understand it, bear in mind Holbrook Working's definition: a futures transaction that substitutes for a later cash transaction.

Let's assume you are an exporter of grains. You have sold 1 million bushels of corn to China for delivery 3 months from now. The agreed price is today's cash price in Chicago— $1.85 per bushel. You could buy the cash corn today, store it for 3 months, and then deliver it. But you have no warehouse. Instead you buy corn futures.

### Long Hedge in Corn Futures

| Cash Market | | Futures Market |
|---|:---:|---|
| Cash corn at $1.85/ bushel | Now | Buy corn futures at $1.96/bushel |
| Buy cash corn at $2.10/ bushel | 3 Months Later | Sell corn futures at $2.21/bushel |
| Loss $.25/bushel | | Gain $.25/bushel |
| | Net gain or loss = 0 | |

You paid $2.10 per bushel for the cash corn to ship to China; however, the gain of $.25 in your long futures position lowered your effective cost to only $1.85 per bushel, which is the price on which you planned.

**A long hedge would be taken by someone who has promised to deliver the cash commodity later and is concerned that cash prices will go up in the interim.**

These examples do not reflect brokerage commissions or certain other costs such as storage and insurance. These costs are intentionally omitted to keep things simple. Also, you may have observed that each hedge we described worked perfectly, which is seldom true in actual practice. We'll take a closer look at these important financial transactions in a later chapter.

# Suggested Reading

*Economics of Futures Trading*, by Thomas A. Hieronymus. Commodity Research Bureau, New York City,
  Rev. 1977.

*The Complete Guide to the Futures Markets*, by Jack
  Schwager. John Wiley & Sons, Inc., New York City,
  1984.

# 6

# The Green Stuff

**W**e mentioned earlier that the margin for a futures position is not a down payment, as in stocks. A futures position confers no rights of ownership to the underlying asset. The owner of a futures position does not gain any income or benefits from the asset. A futures contract is really just a pair of promises: one to deliver the underlying commodity and another to receive and pay for it.

Futures margin is a good-faith deposit. The balance of the value of the futures contract is not borrowed, so no loan interest is paid by the holder of a margined futures position.

The purpose of futures margin is to ensure contract performance and to protect the financial integrity of the marketplace. Margin is required of both the buyer and the seller of a futures contract. Each futures contract has its own minimum margin levels, set by the exchange where the contract is traded. The margin put up when a futures position is first

**The purpose of futures margin is to ensure contract performance and to protect the financial integrity of the marketplace.**

opened is called *original* margin. Depending on the requirements of the particular exchange, original margin may comprise cash, a transfer of funds from another one of the customer's accounts, U. S. government securities, a letter of credit, or a negotiable warehouse receipt.

If a futures position generates unrealized losses as a result of adverse price movement, additional margin may be called for. This is referred to as *maintenance* margin. Its purpose is to restore the financial protection that margin provides, so the amount of maintenance margin required is that needed to build the margin back up to the original level. The requirements for maintenance margin are more stringent, requiring either (1) deposit of the necessary cash or (2) a reduction in the number of futures positions held.

In addition to prescribing minimum margin levels, the exchange sets the levels at which maintenance margin will be called for. This varies from exchange to exchange, but the 75 percent level is a common benchmark; that is, if the margin level drops below 75 percent of its original value, a margin call would be triggered.

Delivering margin calls to market participants and following up to see that they are met is the responsibility of the futures broker (technically, an *associated person*). If you receive a margin call and for some reason do not meet it within a suitable period of time, the brokerage firm is empowered to raise the necessary cash by (1) closing out the position that created the margin call, (2) closing out any other futures position you might have, or (3) transferring funds from another of your accounts that the firm holds—your stock account, for example—into your futures account to cover the shortfall. This authority is given to them by you in the forms you sign when you open your futures account.

**Futures margin is a good-faith deposit. The balance of the value of the futures contract is not borrowed, so no loan interest is paid by the holder of a margined futures position.**

## CAPITAL LEVERAGE

Futures prices have the reputation of wild volatility that is generally undeserved. There are common stock issues that fluctuate more in price than many commodities. The apparent volatility of futures prices is derived; it is result of extremely low minimum margin requirements.

Most futures margins range from a fraction of a percent to 10 percent of the value of the underlying futures contract. A small change in the value of the commodity therefore causes a big change in the equity in the futures account.

### Example

Cash cotton and cotton futures are both 80 cents a pound. You are long one contract of cotton futures. Your original margin is $2000. The contract size for cotton is 50,000 pounds, so the total value of the cotton itself is 50,000 pounds × 80 cents = $40,000.

Cash and futures prices of cotton both advance 1 cent, from 80.00 to 81.00 cents a pound. The value of the cash cotton has thus gone up $500 ($.01 × 50,000 pounds), or from $40,000 to $40,500; that's an increase of 1¼ percent. The value of your equity in the futures contract has also gone up $500; but that's from $2000 to $2500, a jump of 25 percent.

This effect is called *capital leverage*, and it is a two-edged sword. If cotton prices were to fall, your losses would be magnified on the same scale. If cotton prices fell 3 cents per pound, for example, three-fourths of your original margin would be wiped out.

| | Old Price | New Price | Percentage Change in Price | Change in Value | Equity | Percentage Change in Equity |
|---|---|---|---|---|---|---|
| Cash | | | | | | |
| Cotton | 80.00 | 77.00 | −3.75% | −$1,500 | $40,000 | −3.75% |
| Futures | | | | | | |
| Contract | 80.00 | 77.00 | −3.75% | −$1,500 | $2,000 | −75% |

## MARGIN

The setting of margin levels is a chain reaction that begins with the exchange. The exchange sets the *minimum* amounts required to support a futures position. Next in the chain is the clearinghouse. It is responsible for the financial integrity of the market and may ask more margin from its clearing members than the exchange minimums. The final link in the chain is the brokerage firm (technically, a *futures commission merchant*, or *FCM*). If the FCM considers it necessary, it may ask more margin from their public customers than the clearinghouse requires.

The flow of actual margin money is the reverse. The public customer writes a check to cover his margin requirement and gives it to his FCM, who holds the funds in the customer's name in a segregated account. The FCM posts margin with the clearinghouse for the FCM's open positions. In most exchanges, the FCM's countervailing long and short positions are offset, and only the net exposure is margined. The balance of the customers' funds are retained by the FCM.

Original and maintenance margins may be changed at any time by the appropriate exchange. In the past, exchanges have used changes in margin levels as an effective means to control price volatility. When a futures market becomes overheated, margin levels are raised significantly. Fewer futures positions can then be supported with any given amount of capital, and trading slows. Margin requirements may also be routinely increased during the "spot month," or the period of time when delivery of the actual commodity can be made against the futures contract.

On most exchanges, changes in margin levels are retroactive. That is, the changes apply immediately to both old and new futures positions. If margins are raised and the new maintenance level is above the old maintenance level, the change could trigger margin calls in existing positions. If margins are lowered, capital committed to existing positions would be freed and the owner of the futures accounts could withdraw the excess funds in cash or use them to margin additional futures positions.

Only funds in excess of the original margin level are free and available for withdrawal or other use. That increment of margin between the original level and maintenance level is part of the original margin and must be on deposit as long as the futures position is held.

For example, suppose you buy one contract of gold futures at 483.00. Your original margin is $2700; the margin maintenance level is $2100.

| End of Day | Gold Futures Price | Equity in Account | Remarks |
|---|---|---|---|
| 1 | 483.00 | $2,700 | Opening transaction. |
| 2 | 479.00 | 2,300 | Equity has been eroded, but margin is still above the maintenance level. |
| 3 | 474.50 | 1,850 | Margin below $2,100 maintenance level. Margin call would be issued for $850, to build margin back up to original level of $2,700. |
| 4 | | 2,700 | $850 margin call deposited in A.M. |
| 4 | 484.10 | 3,660 | $960 (3,660 − 2,700) is now available for withdrawal in cash or to use to margin other futures positions. |
| 5 | 493.90 | 4,640 | $1,940 (4,640 − 2,700) is now available for withdrawal in cash or to use to margin other futures positions. |
| 6 | | 3,640 | You withdraw $1,000 in cash in A.M. |

| End of Day | Gold Futures Price | Equity in Account | Remarks |
|---|---|---|---|
| 6 | 490.70 | 3,320 | No change in status. |
| 7 | 484.20 | 2,670 | Margin is below original level but still above $2,100 maintenance level; no action required. |
| 8 | 485.70 | 2,820 | You close out the position at end of trading day. |

**Only funds in excess of the original margin level are free and available for withdrawal or other use.**

Your accounting in the preceding transaction: You paid an original margin of $2700 and maintenance margin of $850. That totals $3550. You withdrew $1000 on Day 6 and had an equity of $2820 after the closing transaction. That totals $3820. You therefore received $270 ($3820 − $3550) for your efforts.

A shorter route to the same answer is simply to compare the opening and closing gold futures prices. The closing price of 485.70 minus the opening price of 483.00 equals $2.70 per ounce. For 100 ounces, that's $270.

When setting minimum margin levels, the exchange also countenances the kind of futures position involved. Speculative short or long positions present the highest risks and so have the highest margins. At the other end of the spectrum are hedges, which generally have the lowest margins. The reason: hedgers hold offsetting cash and futures positions in the same (or similar) commodity, making the overall economic effect similar to a spread.

## DAILY MARK TO MARKET

The clearinghouse member deposits original margin with the clearinghouse when the opening transaction is cleared. Outstanding futures contracts are marked to the market by the clearinghouse at the end of each trading day. That is, gains are credited and losses are debited on all open positions. The settlement price is used as the benchmark for these calculations.

If a clearinghouse member's account has a credit balance as a result of the daily marking to market of his positions, he may withdraw that amount of cash overnight. If the clearing member owes money, it must be deposited before the opening of trading the next business day. This is called *variation* margin.

In most clearinghouses, a clearing member's margin requirements are based on his net holdings, after his offsetting long and short positions have been canceled out. The two exceptions are the Chicago Mercantile Exchange and the New York Mercantile Exchange, which require that clearing members margin their long and short positions separately, without netting out offsetting positions.

Exchanges are also empowered, during times of emergency, to call for variation margin during the trading day. This is generally due in the clearinghouse within 1 hour. On October 19, 1987, the day the Dow Jones Industrial Stock Average fell more than 500 points, the Chicago Mercantile Exchange made two such extraordinary calls for variation margin for long positions in S&P 500 Stock Index futures.

## COMMISSIONS

The FCM performs a variety of services for its public customers. These services include safekeeping their funds; apprising them of current market conditions; taking their orders and reporting back the fill prices; issuing periodic written statements of trading activity, profit and loss, and account balances; and publishing market research reports. For providing these services, the FCM charges a commission on each trade its customer makes. This commission is for a "round trip." It is paid only once, when the position is closed.

Futures commissions are not uniform. They vary from commodity to commodity, with the type of futures position, and from one FCM to another. By law, commissions on futures trades on U. S. exchanges are negotiable between FCM and customer. As a practical matter, only the biggest customers have enough clout to negotiate. FCMs publish "recommended" commission schedules for the guidance of their brokers, and most customers pay these amounts without question.

The lowest commission is for a position that is opened and closed during the same trading session because it does not have to be taken up fully into the FCM's accounting system. Also at the low end of the scale are commissions on spreads, which are less than the commissions would be on the two positions if they did not comprise a spread. Commissions are highest on net long or short positions that are held overnight.

The greatest difference in commissions is between FCMs. A major brokerage firm might charge $100 for a trade that a discount broker would handle for $25. The difference is in the amount of support you receive. At the major firm, you would have your own personal broker to help you with your trading decisions. The firm would provide you with printed research reports from time to time, pointing out potentially profitable situations. The firm would likely conduct business in all kinds of markets, so your money could be moved easily from equities to bonds to futures to a money market account.

There are also several large discount futures brokerage operations in the United States. Many of them specialize in futures only. They have no research departments and acknowledge that they are for the person who makes his own trading decisions. When you call to place an order, you talk to the Associated Person who answers the phone. For giving up the ancillary benefits of a

**In most markets there is a limit on how far prices can move in one day. The daily limit is measured from the previous day's settlement price and applies in both directions.**

**The daily price limit is set for each commodity by the exchange on which the commodity is traded.**

full-service FCM, you receive futures
commissions that are sharply reduced.

## PRICE LIMITS

From time to time, unexpected news galvanizes
a futures market, sending prices up or down
sharply. In most markets there is a limit on how
far prices can move in one day. The purpose of
these daily price limits is to force a "cooling-off"
period, to allow market participants time to
reevaluate the news and its impact on their
holdings.

The daily limit is measured from the previous
day's settlement price and applies in both
directions. It is different for each commodity.
For soybeans, for example, the normal daily
price limit is 30 cents. If beans close at 5.50
today, their maximum trading range tomorrow
would be 5.20 to 5.80. If they closed at 5.48
tomorrow, their maximum trading range the next
day would be 5.18 to 5.78.

When the price reaches a limit during a
trading day, market activity tends to slow, and
may even stop, because of the same economic
forces that caused the price move. If prices have
hit limit up, for example, it means there are
many buyers and few sellers. If there are no
sellers at the limit price, trading could literally
cease in that market. However, no one goes
home. Transactions may still take place at or
within the limit. It is even possible that later
news or a reevaluation could bring sellers
suddenly back into the market, prices could
back away from the limit, and active trading
could resume.

The daily price limit is set for each
commodity by the exchange on which the
commodity is traded. Exchanges also have
standing rules to deal with exceptionally strong
or weak markets. Limits are, after all, artificial
constraints. Despite their benefits, they block the

free operation of economic forces in the marketplace. In an effort to mitigate the adverse economic effects of limits, exchange rules allow for automatic expansion of price limits when prices have closed at the limit on consecutive days. There are also standing rules for returning the daily price limit to its normal value when the market has quieted down again.

## Suggested Reading

*Economics of Futures Trading*, by Thomas A. Hieronymus. Commodity Research Bureau, New York City, Rev. 1977.

*The Complete Guide to the Futures Markets*, by Jack Schwager. John Wiley & Sons, Inc., New York City, 1984.

# 7

# What Happens after You Hang Up the Phone

**W**hen you place an order to buy or sell a futures contract, your local broker fills out an order form. He fills in your name, your account number, what it is you want to buy or sell, and any special instructions. This form is then hand delivered to an order room in the brokerage office, where it is time-stamped and electronically transmitted to the trading floor of the appropriate exchange.

At the exchange, your order is transcribed onto another piece of paper. A runner delivers it to the floor broker who represents your brokerage firm. The floor broker enters the trading pit, executes your order for you, notes the price, and drops the slip of paper on the floor behind him. A runner picks up the order slip, returns it to the telephone station on the trading floor, and the communication process is reversed. At the last step, your local broker phones to tell you the outcome. The entire process takes place in a very short time.

Although typical, the foregoing order process is not utilized in all firms. Some firms have dispensed with the local order room altogether, providing their individual brokers with direct telephone lines to the trading floor. Some use hand signals instead of runners on the exchange floor.

# ORDERS

A futures order consists of five elements:

1. Whether to buy or to sell.
2. The quantity.
3. The delivery month.
4. The commodity, including the exchange, if the commodity is traded on more than one exchange.
5. Any special instructions, such as a time or price limit.

The first element—whether to buy or to sell—is not as self-evident as it might seem. You and your local broker are aware of whether your order is for an opening or closing transaction. It's not an issue after that. The floor broker who executes your order doesn't know or care. To the clearinghouse, your trade is just another purchase or sale to be processed.

Except in a few instances, it is not legal to be both long and short the same futures contract in the same account. When you buy a December T-bond, for example, your broker's computer checks your account to see if you are already short a December T-bond. If you are, the trade is treated as a closing transaction. If you are not presently short the December T-bond, your trade is logged in as an opening transaction.

The rule against being both long and short the same futures contract is quite specific. Chicago wheat and Kansas City wheat are *not* considered the same; nor are New York silver and Chicago silver, even though the contract sizes are the same and the underlying commodities identical.

The exceptions to the general rule are day trades, where you open and close the transaction within the same trading session; a futures position taken to meet the exercise of a futures option you have sold short; a bona fide hedge; the sale of futures during the delivery period for the purpose of making delivery; and, in certain circumstances where different independent money managers control separate accounts for the same investor.

Your order must also specify the number of futures contracts you want to buy or sell. Here again there is more than meets the eye. Most futures contracts are sold as contracts; that is, you would buy or sell one June cattle or three March T-bills or two December copper. The grains and soybeans are exceptions. They are ordered by number of bushels, with the three zeros omitted. The futures contract size for wheat, for example, is 5000 bushels. In a futures market order it would be referred to as "5," as in "Sell 5 December wheat." Contract sizes for corn, soybeans, and oats are also 5000 bushels, and their orders are expressed in the same way.

The delivery month must be included in your order because, as we will see later, different delivery months of the same commodity may vary considerably in liquidity and price behavior. The year should also be specified in the order if there is any possibility of confusion between a nearby contract and the same delivery month a year away. Likewise, it may be necessary to indicate the exchange on which the commodity is traded.

Futures market orders differ most in the possible contingencies they may contain. We will discuss these in the context of actual representative orders.

**A market order authorizes the floor broker to take the best price he is offered, without qualifications. In a thinly traded market, that price could be several cents away from the previous price.**

**A limit order to buy may be filled only at or *below* the limit price.**

## MARKET ORDER

The simplest order is called a *market order*. It would take the form of:

"Buy one June cattle at the market."

This order would be filled by the floor broker at the best price obtainable at that moment he receives it. The price you paid for your June cattle will not be known to you until the actual fill is reported back to you.

The market order is executed without delay and is used in situations where that is desirable. For example, suppose that you had been short June cattle for 3 weeks, had a trading profit, and felt that the market was about to rally sharply. You would not be interested in finesse but would want to be out as soon as possible. You would use a market order in this instance.

The price you get on a market order depends largely on the liquidity of that particular futures contract. Futures markets are very efficient. The spread between the bid price and the asked price in an active futures trading pit may be as little as one-tenth of 1 percent. By comparison, the bid/asked spread for most common stocks is about one-half of 1 percent; in real estate, it is not unusual for a buyer to bid 15 to 20 percent below the original asking price.

**A limit order to sell may be filled only at or *above* the limit price.**

Care must be taken, however, in futures markets where there is little trading activity. A market order authorizes the floor broker to take the best price he is offered, without qualifications. In a thinly traded market, that price could be several cents away from the previous price. You have no recourse if the price you receive on a market order is an unpleasant surprise.

## CONTINGENT ORDERS

All other futures market orders are contingent orders; that is, they contain some condition that must be satisfied before the order can be executed. The most commonly used is the *limit order*. It would take the form of:

"Buy one June T-bond at 89-20."

This is called a limit order because you have placed a limit on the price you will pay. It resolves the biggest problem with the market order, that of price vulnerability. The floor broker can fill your buy order at less than 89-20 but not at more than that price. The words *or better* are sometimes added to the limit order, but they are unnecessary. If the market is trading below 89-20 when your order reaches the floor, the floor broker will get you the best price he can. With a limit order, however, you have no assurance of execution. If the limit price is never reached, your order will never be filled.

Orders that are placed at prices well away from the current market are defined broadly as resting orders. There are two kinds: *stop orders* and *market-if-touched* (MIT) orders.

An MIT order is used enter or leave a market at a price somewhat more favorable than the present price. An MIT buy order is therefore placed below the current price, and an MIT sell order is placed above the current price. To take an example, suppose December T-bill futures were trading at 94.50. You want to take a new long position in that futures contract but don't want to pay more than 93.90. You would tell your broker:

"Buy one December T-bill at 93.90 MIT."

When this order reaches the trading floor, the floor broker puts it in his deck of resting orders, which are organized by price. If December T-bills later trade at 93.90, your order would become a market order at that instant and would be treated by the floor broker like any other market order.

At what price would you buy your December T-bill future? It depends. Remember that an MIT order becomes a market order when the

> **Orders that are placed at prices well away from the current market are defined broadly as resting orders. There are two kinds: *stop orders* and *market-if-touched* (MIT) orders.**

specified price is hit, and market orders are filled at the best price obtainable at that moment. If the market rallied after touching 93.90, you could legitimately pay 94.00 or even more for your December T-bill.

MIT orders are used when there is no particular urgency in entering or leaving a market. As with all orders that specify price, however, there is the chance that the MIT order will not be filled. In the specific example just given, if December T-bills never traded at 93.90 but instead rallied to 95.00 and beyond, the resting MIT buy order would remain unexecuted. Some experienced traders, who have developed a knack for forecasting daily price trading ranges, are willing to risk the chance of not getting filled to try for the possible price advantage.

Stop orders may also be used to enter or leave a market, but they perform a different function than MIT orders. The simplest way to avoid confusion between the two is to remember that the most common use of stop orders is to curtail losses. If you are long, falling prices generate losses; any sell order intended to curtail those losses must therefore rest *below* current price levels. Conversely, any buy order to curtail losses in an existing short futures position must rest *above* current price levels.

Let's take a specific example. Suppose you have held a long position in December S&P 500 Index futures for a month. You bought it at 245.70, and it is now trading at 274.10. You have a good gain, but you feel prices may not go much higher; you decide that if the market falls below 272.50, you will get out. The order you would give your broker is:

"Sell one December S&P 500 at 272.45 stop."

The December S&P 500 is trading at 274.10 when you place this order. If prices continue to advance, the stop price will never be touched, and your order will not be executed. However, if

you were correct in your assessment of the
market and prices start to slip, your stop order
automatically converts to a market order when
the stop price of 272.45 is reached, and your
long position will be closed out.

To understand the significance of the word
*stop* in the order, look at what happens if you
take it out:

"Sell one December S&P 500 at 272.45."

If this order were entered when December
S&P 500 futures were trading at 274.10, it could
legally be executed immediately, as the price
limit is long since passed. As a practical matter,
a floor broker who received such an order would
most likely suspect a mistake and query the
brokerage firm before he acted on it.

As with the MIT order, there is no guarantee
of receiving the stop price when the order is
filled. The stop order becomes a market order
when the stop price is hit; if prices are moving
quickly at that time, the price you receive could
be several "ticks" away from the stop price.

The *stop limit* order combines the qualities of
both the stop order and the limit order. It would
take the form of:

"Buy one September Deutschemark at .6158
stop, limit .6175."

Nothing would be done on this order until
the stop price is reached. At that point,
however, it becomes not a market order but a
limit order. The floor broker can legally fill it
only at a price of .6175 or lower. If prices were
to jump above .6175 immediately after the stop
price was hit, the order could remain
unexecuted.

The purpose of the stop limit order is, of
course, to preclude the possibility of getting an
unfavorable price. The stop limit order is not
widely used. It is employed mainly in thinly
traded markets or those that, even though liquid,
are quite volatile.

Many practitioners feel that the closing prices at the end of the trading day are the best consensus of the market. After all, these are the prices that buyers and sellers are willing to take home for the night. There is a futures market order designed to obtain the closing price. It takes the form of:

"Sell one March Eurodollar MOC."

The *MOC* stands for "market on close." This order would be held by the floor broker until a minute or two before the closing bell, at which time he will simply treat it as a market order. The price you receive will not necessarily be the exact closing or settlement price, but it will be somewhere in closing range, which is loosely defined at the last 60 seconds of trading.

Orders may also be executed at the opening of the market. The letters *MOO* would be added to the order; they stand for "market on opening." MOO orders can be utilized to take advantage of the overnight buildup of market orders. For example, if a short-term trader suspected that there was a bulge of overnight orders to buy and that once these orders were assimilated the market would settle back, he might sell short on the opening in the hope of buying his contracts back at a lower price later in the day. MOO orders are not as widely used as MOC orders.

Any order that does not mention time is considered a day order. That is, it will expire at the end of the trading session during which it was entered. GTC stands for *good 'til canceled* and may be added to any resting order. Most brokers prefer to use day orders, reentering them order each morning if necessary. There isn't a broker who's been in the business more than 2 years who hasn't returned from vacation or a business trip to learn that a forgotten GTC order was triggered in his absence. The resulting position is rarely a gain.

We talked about commodity spreads in Chapter 4. A spread involves a long position in one commodity and an offsetting short position in the same or economically related commodity. There is a special order that can be used to establish these dual positions. Because a spread trader is interested only in the price difference between the two sides of the spread, he loses nothing by placing his order in that context. For example:

> "Spread buy 5 Chicago May wheat/sell 5 Chicago July wheat, May 5 cent premium."

**Any order that does not mention time is considered a day order.**

An order entered in this fashion gives the floor broker latitude. He can elect to execute each side separately, taking whatever prices are available; or he can deal directly with a floor trader who specializes in spreads. If the same order were entered as two separate transactions— for example, buy 5 Chicago May wheat at 2.75 and sell 5 July wheat at 2.70—your floor broker would be handcuffed. He has two orders, with two different limits, and somehow has to execute them both at the proper time.

There are other possible orders that can be used in the futures markets. They are known more for their exotic qualities than their value in obtaining a desired price or time of execution. The exchanges publish lists of orders that they will accept. Generally speaking, no contingent orders are accepted on the last day of trading in a futures contract because trading activity may be too hectic to allow their orderly handling.

## Suggested Reading

*Futures Trading Course,* Futures Industry Association, Washington, DC, 1987.

# 8

# The Arena

There are three major organizations involved in futures trading. They are the exchange, the clearinghouse, and the futures commission merchant (FCM).

## THE EXCHANGE

There are a dozen or so major futures exchanges in the United States. Most are private, nonprofit organizations owned by their members. The oldest futures exchange in the United States is the Chicago Board of Trade, founded in 1848. The newest is the New York Futures Exchange, a satellite of the New York Stock Exchange, which first opened its doors in 1978.

The exchange provides the arena where buyers and sellers of futures contracts meet to conduct business. The trading floor, where the actual buying and selling takes place, is divided into several large circular trading "rings" or "pits." Each pit is designated as the trading site for one or more commodities, depending on the level of activity. If a commodity trades only a few hundred contracts a day, it may share a pit with another relatively inactive market. If a commodity has a large following, the entire pit will be devoted to it.

Trading is done by open outcry. That is, orders to buy or to sell are shouted out for anyone who might be interested in doing business. Hand signals are also used because it is sometimes difficult to hear above the din. Each completed trade is recorded by the individual traders on cards they carry for that purpose. These cards are later turned in to the clearinghouse, where the trades are matched and recorded. Each transaction in the pit is also noted by an observing price reporter, who transmits the information to an electronic display on the exchange floor and to price reporting services who flash the data around the world.

Only exchange members may buy and sell futures contracts on the trading floor. Persons in the pits break down into two broad categories: *floor brokers* and *floor traders*. Floor brokers are agents; they transact trades for third parties, for which they receive a small commission. Virtually all floor brokers are affiliated with one or more FCMs.

**Only exchange members may buy and sell futures contracts on the trading floor.**

A floor trader uses his exchange membership primarily to buy and sell futures contracts for his own account. His advantages over off-floor trading include immediate access to new market information and very small commission costs. Under present rules, a member may act alternately as a floor broker and floor trader at any time, and there are regulations to preclude his taking advantage of a public customer.

The exchange determines, with approval of the Commodity Futures Trading Commission (CFTC), what futures contracts will be traded on its floor. The exchange specifies the underlying commodity, the contract size, delivery months, how prices will be expressed, and daily price limits. The exchange also sets original and maintenance margin levels for its futures contracts; however, this activity is, as of this writing, expressly exempt from CFTC purview.

The exchange establishes and enforces the rules under which its futures contracts may be traded. The rules are designed to ensure free and orderly markets and to protect both the public customer and the commodity professional from damage. The exchange does not own any commodities.

Only individuals may be members of a futures exchange. When a major brokerage firm states that it belongs to the Chicago Mercantile Exchange, for example, it means that an individual member of the CME has conferred his membership privileges on that firm. Exchange memberships are sold by the exchange when it is first established and whenever new memberships are made available, which is not often. Otherwise, a new member must buy his or her "seat" from a present member. Seat prices on the two major futures exchanges in Chicago have ranged from $200,000 to $350,000 in the 1980s.

## THE CLEARINGHOUSE

Each exchange has its own clearinghouse. At the end of each trading day, the clearinghouse takes the other side of every trade it clears. This action breaks the link between the original buyer and seller, making it possible for a trader to close out a futures or options position with simply an offsetting market transaction. There is no need for the original two parties to relocate each other or for both original parties to agree to undo the trade.

The clearinghouse serves two other vital functions. It warranties the financial integrity of each futures contract it clears; and it supervises deliveries made against futures contracts by holders of short positions.

To create the funds necessary to guarantee the financial stability of the futures markets it clears, the clearinghouse requires that each of its clearing members post a guaranty deposit. The amount required is substantial. It may be in cash or letter of credit. If a member defaults, these funds may be drawn on to ensure that no public futures customer loses money as a result of the default. If the total of the guaranty deposits on hand are still not enough to cover a defaulting member's debits, the clearinghouse is authorized to levy a special pro-rata assessment on its members to make up the difference.

## Mark to Market

Rules for the payment of variation margin to the clearinghouse are quite strict. There is no maintenance level or trigger point. Clearinghouse members' accounts are marked to the market at the end of each trading day, and all deficits must covered before a certain time the next business morning. The clearinghouse is also empowered to issue calls for additional margin during the trading day if market conditions warrant and has done so on many occasions.

**Traders who hold futures positions beyond the last trading day must settle their futures contracts by delivery.**

**The delivery process is initiated by the short position holder, who may choose any day during the delivery period.**

**Only individuals may be members of a futures exchange.**

## Delivery

The last day of trading in a futures contract is specified by the exchange; it will be a day during the delivery period, which is usually a calendar month. The last day of trading in December T-bond futures on the Chicago Board of Trade, for example, is the eighth business day from the end of December. After that date, the December T-bond futures contract for that year expires and is gone forever.

Traders who hold futures positions beyond the last trading day must settle their futures contracts by delivery. Shorts will be expected to deliver the actual commodity to an exchange designated delivery point; longs will be expected to take ownership of the actual commodity and pay for it in full.

The delivery process is initiated by the short position holder, who may choose any day during the delivery period. The exact procedure differs from exchange to exchange, but it generally starts when the short asks his broker to prepare a delivery notice. This notice is presented by the broker to the exchange clearinghouse, who assigns it to one of their clearing members with a long position still open on the clearinghouse books. The clearing member in turn assigns the notice to one of its customers who is still long.

On some exchanges, the assigned long may decline the notice by selling the equivalent number of new futures contracts short and passing the notice along, via the clearinghouse, to another long. On others, a delivery notice cannot be passed along; it must be accepted and the cash commodity received and paid for.

The form of delivery varies with the commodity. Evidence of delivery in the grains may be a warehouse receipt for actual grain stored in some distant location. Cotton can be delivered into any one of five licensed southern warehouses. "Delivery" of stock index futures involves only the transfer of cash. A trader who accepts delivery against a long position in Deutschemark futures receives a credit for Deutchesmarks in a West German bank designated by the clearinghouse. Delivery against a short position in T-bond futures results in a book-entry transfer of ownership of the cash bonds; no actual bond certificates change hands.

In some instances, more than one grade of the commodity is deliverable against the futures contract. The epitome is the T-bond futures contract. Much has been written on the selection of the optimum cash bond to deliver because it may be chosen from among all outstanding Treasury bonds with at least 15 years to maturity.

Delivery against a futures contract was a relatively rare occurrence in the past. Producers, processors, and distributors of foods, metals, and fibers used the futures markets to hedge against price risk but continued to conduct their normal day-to-day cash business with their regular customers. With the advent of financial futures, delivery against futures contracts has become more common. In fact, some financial futures traders take their positions for the express purpose of making or taking delivery.

Delivery procedures vary, and a close examination of them is beyond the scope of this book. If you intend to become involved with the making or taking of delivery against a futures contract, be sure to acquaint yourself beforehand with the intricacies of that particular market.

## THE FUTURES COMMISSION MERCHANT (FCM)

FCMs are the most visible members of the futures industry. They have names like Merrill Lynch, Prudential-Bache, and Shearson Lehman Hutton. The FCM is the private individual trader's link to the futures and option markets. The FCM carries the public customer's account. It accepts and holds margin money for the customer. It executes his or her trades, reports back on the outcome, and maintains a complete record of the customer's open positions, cash balance, and profit and loss. It provides current market information and research reports on historical price activity.

### Opening an Account

When you open a futures or options account with an FCM, you will be required to fill out and sign several forms. One form is personal information. Another concerns your income and net worth and asks many of the same questions you would find on a loan application. Your broker is required by law to have these data, as it is his responsibility to qualify you under a "know-your-customer" rule. If he considers that you do not have the financial wherewithal to take on the risks associated with futures or options trading, he should refuse to open your account.

The most important form, from the standpoint of your broker, is usually called something like "Commodity Account Agreement." It identifies whether the account is for hedging or speculating. It identifies the owner of the account, which can be a single individual, two or more parties in joint form, a partnership, or a corporation.

The Commodity Account Agreement also contains a "Transfer of Funds Authorization." This paragraph gives your broker an advance okay to move your money around if you are on margin call and for some reason do not meet it. The actions he is authorized to take include closing out the futures position that created the margin call; or, transferring money from another of your accounts with the firm to your commodity account to cover the deficit.

## Suggested Reading

*Economics of Futures Trading,* by Thomas A. Hieronymus. Commodity Research Bureau, New York City, Rev. 1977.

*The Complete Guide to the Futures Markets,* by Jack Schwager. John Wiley & Sons, Inc., New York City, 1984.

# 9

# Fundamental Analysis

If you could buy a copy of next week's *Wall Street Journal*, there would soon be buildings with your name on them. Correctly assessing where prices will be in coming days or weeks is an important element in successful futures trading. No player is exempt. Price increases generate gains for the longs and losses for the shorts. When prices decline, the shorts gain what the longs lose.

If you exclude tea leaves and Gypsy fortune-tellers, there are two approaches to futures price forecasting. The first involves evaluating the supply of and demand for the actual commodity, on the premise that a short supply or high demand will cause prices to rise, and vice versa. This approach is called *fundamental* analysis.

The other major school of thought is referred to as *technical* analysis. The pure technical analyst studiously disregards any information about the supply of and demand for the actual commodity. He focuses his attention instead on the futures market itself, on the assumption that no matter what the fundamentals portend, the effects will show up in the behavior of price, trading volume, and open interest.

We'll look at both approaches.

## FUNDAMENTAL FACTORS

Every significant commodity price move in the history of futures trading has been rooted in fundamental factors. Unless there is a true shortage or surplus of the actual commodity, unusually low or high prices cannot be maintained. Remember the oat chart we showed you in Chapter 2; prices collapsed and then just as abruptly returned to where they started, all in a period of a few weeks. That was an example of a price move fueled entirely by traders' expectations.

There have been some spectacular sustained futures price moves when fundamental factors were the engine. Blight sent corn prices from $1.40 to $3.90 a bushel in 1973 and 1974. Bumper corn crops in the following 3 years finally drove prices back down to $1.80 again.

After hovering between 2 cents and 10 cents a pound for 9 years, sugar prices responded to a worldwide shortage by soaring to 67 cents a pound in 1974.

**Every significant commodity price move in the history of futures trading has been rooted in fundamental factors. Unless there is a true shortage or surplus of the actual commodity, unusually low or high prices cannot be maintained.**

The combination of reduced world supply and growing industrial demand propelled copper futures prices from 60 cents to $1.40 a pound in 1987. More recently, grain and soybean prices soared to new 11-year highs on news of crop-threatening drought in growing regions.

Deutschemark, Japanese yen, and Swiss franc futures staged a virtually unbroken rally from early 1985 to late 1987, more than doubling in price. The cause: not short-term expectations but an inexorable world demand for the foreign currencies from buyers spending U. S. dollars.

## Fundamental Analysis

The fundamental analyst tries to estimate how much of the commodity will be around in coming months, and how much demand there will be for it. The supply of a commodity comprises imports, current production, and any carryover from previous years. Consumption is the sum of domestic use and exports.

For example, for an agricultural field commodity the fundamental analyst would consider planting intentions, yield per acre, forecast weather in growing areas, probability of crop disease, the prices of competing commodities, government loan levels, and current supplies on hand. These same data would also be considered for foreign growing areas, to evaluate potential U.S. exports.

Fundamentals for cattle, hog, and pork belly futures include farmers' farrowing intentions, expected litter size, the number of animals presently on feed, prices for competing red meats, trends in consumption, and the present status of the livestock price "cycle."

A trader of copper futures would be interested in the level of mining activity, housing starts, the amount of copper presently resting in the London Metal Exchange (LME) and other storehouses around the world, and the potential for political unrest in foreign producing areas. Platinum traders keep an eye on automobile production. Gold has a dual role: in jewelry and as a worldwide store of value when rampant inflation or armed conflict creates a temporary mistrust of paper currencies.

Frozen Concentrated Orange Juice (FCOJ) is the futures market most susceptible to weather. Even the hint of a coming winter freeze in the Florida growing area will send prices soaring. Less violent fundamental factors include the anticipated size of the orange crop in the United States and other growing nations, yield, and crop disease.

**The fundamental analyst tries to estimate how much of the commodity will be around in coming months, and how much demand there will be for it.**

**The supply of a commodity comprises imports, current production, and any carryover from previous years. Consumption is the sum of domestic use and exports.**

Fundamental analysis of the financial futures requires a somewhat different approach. In some instances the supply is virtually unlimited. In others there is no tangible asset underlying the futures contract, and settlement is by cash only.

Among the most popular financial futures are those on the three fixed-income securities issued by the U. S. Treasury Department: Treasury bonds, Treasury notes, and Treasury bills. Not far behind is the more recent futures markets in Eurodollars (U. S. dollars on deposit in banks outside the United States). Prices in these markets are tied directly to interest rates. If interest rates rise, the prices of these securities go down. If interest rates fall, the prices of these securities rise. Fundamental analysis, therefore, is directed at projecting the course of interest rates; that involves many complex economic variables, including the demand for loans, interest rates on other instruments such as commercial paper and CDs, the prime rate, the discount rate, prevailing interest rates in other nations, current policies of the Federal Reserve Board, and the general health of the U. S. economy.

Stock index futures were the first futures markets based on an intangible asset. The "delivery unit" underlying the futures contract is the value of the index, not actual shares of stock, and settlement is by cash only. Futures contracts are traded on the four major stock indexes: the S&P 500, the New York Stock Exchange Composite Index, the Major Market Index, and the Value Line Index. Because each index represents a large number of different stocks, fundamental analysis involves not the assessment of individual stocks but the factors that contribute to overall market movement. These include the present state of the business cycle, interest rates, the relative strengths of U. S. and foreign currencies, the amounts of money available for investment, and investor confidence in the U. S. economy.

Demand for foreign currencies is based largely on a nation's shopping habits. If a U. S. retailer imports watches made in Switzerland, he must pay for them with Swiss francs. He buys the Swiss francs with U. S. dollars. This action causes the value of the Swiss franc to rise relative to the U. S. dollar. An American manufacturer who sells his products in England would receive British pounds in payment. He would buy U. S. dollars with them because he can't use pounds to buy materials and pay workers in the United States, and that would have the opposite effect; it would cause the value of the U. S. dollar to decline relative to the pound.

There are other reasons why currencies flow from one nation to another. An unusually high rate of interest or a strongly bullish stock market will attract foreign capital; investors from other nations buy U. S. dollars with their currencies, then use those dollars to buy stocks or bonds in U. S. markets. Tourists buy foreign currencies to spend for hotels, meals, and shopping overseas. When the United States grants economic aid to a foreign nation, the U. S. dollars granted must be converted to that nation's currency before the money can be put to work there. Some developing nations park their cash reserves in one or more foreign currencies.

Note that the examples in the preceding paragraph all relate to demand. The supply of a foreign currency is not a price factor. Except in unusual cases where the government steps in to curtail the movement of its currency in foreign markets, the supply is virtually unlimited.

Commodities whose principal source is overseas present special problems for the fundamental analysts. Sugar, cocoa, coffee, and petroleum are subject to international commodity agreements about price controls and production quotas. Reliable information may be difficult to come by. Nations take steps to protect their own currencies or economies and may not be open and aboveboard about their activities. The briefing sheets in Chapter 16 list some of the public sources of information on foreign commodities that have proven reliable over the years.

## THE IMPORTANCE OF PERSPECTIVE

Suppose you saw in the newspaper that the U. S. trade deficit last year was $160 billion. Is that bullish or bearish for the major foreign currencies? Will it affect interest rates? Could U. S. exports of commodities be curtailed as a result?

If you are long copper futures and read a report that 1.4 million new housing starts are expected next year, what does that mean? Is that a lot of starts? Is the news likely to affect copper prices?

**You have to be able to make comparisons between today's situation and prior situations; to see, for example, where prices were the last time these particular supply and demand conditions prevailed.**

You can't answer fundamental questions like these without more information. You have to be able to make comparisons between today's situation and prior situations; to see, for example, where prices were the last time these particular supply and demand conditions prevailed. Projected housing starts of 1.4 million may be bullish for copper prices if the starts constitute an increase of 20 percent over last year; the same housing report could have a depressing effect on the price of copper tubing and wire if 1.4 million was a surprisingly low number of starts.

It's also important that you evaluate any long-range trends in price, consumption, and usage. This leads to still more questions. Is aluminum wiring replacing copper? What is the projected rate of new family formation next year? What kinds of homes will be built; do they use more or less wire and tubing than the standard detached single-family dwelling?

These are factors that affect copper prices. But you don't own copper. You own copper futures, and there's a subtle difference. It's possible that a fundamental report that looks bullish on its face could turn out to be neutral or even negative for futures prices. The reason would be, of course, that the futures price had already discounted the report; the report was already "in the market." The bulk of traders had expected a sharp increase in projected housing starts and had bought futures contracts in anticipation. The publication of the expected numbers caused no new buying.

## Disappearing Qualifiers

You may have played this game when you were younger. Participants sit in a circle. The one who starts the game writes a simple message down, so it can be later verified, and then relates it verbally to the person sitting next to him. That person repeats it to the next person, and so on, until the it gets back to the one who started it. What comes back is compared to the original written message, and the results are often surprising. What happens invariably is that the qualifiers disappear. What began as "Tom will have almost twenty dollars by next Friday" comes back as "Tom has twenty dollars."

Robert Prechter, the stock market guru, said recently that he was never again going to state a specific number as an ultimate objective for the Dow Jones Industrial Average. He was on record as saying that the Dow would reach the 3500 region some time in the next 2 years, providing certain conditions were met. Readers immediately forgot the conditions, fixating on the number 3500. When stocks collapsed on October 19, 1987, Prechter was inundated with telephone calls and letters asking him where 3500 went.

The same pitfall awaits the fundamental analyst. Many assumptions will have gone into the final conclusion that, say, gold should reach

**An ostensibly bullish or bearish government report will not move prices if traders expected the report and have already bought or sold futures in anticipation.**

$625 an ounce by next spring. But the longer you look at the number "625" the easier it is for you to forget about the "guesstimates" that were made in arriving at that number. The number, viewed alone, implies precision and accuracy.

Some fundamental analysts try to elude this trap by avoiding single numbers in any of their data. If they were analyzing hog prices, for example, they would translate the number of hogs and pigs on farms, stated farrowing intentions, expected pigs per litter, and the resulting price estimate into probable *ranges*. This approach to fundamental analysis has been refined by Jack Schwager, whose book is referenced at the end of this chapter.

## Finding the Information

The data you need for effective fundamental analysis are not easy to find; at least, not all in one place. The U. S. Department of Agriculture (USDA) is a repository of vast amounts of background information on the agricultrual commodities, and much of it is published in periodic reports. The balance is buried in the files. Likewise, the U. S. Bureau of Mines is a mother lode of data on the production and consumption of metals; the Federal Reserve keeps track of a large number of economic indicators and measures that bear on the future course of interest rates; the Department of Commerce has information that would help you determine the health of the U. S. dollar.

There are many journals, newsletters, and charting services that deal with futures price forecasting. Some are purely technical, some are purely fundamental, and some combine both kinds of analysis to arrive at their conclusions. A listing of these periodicals, their contents, and where they may be obtained is presented in *Investment Publications*, which is published by the International Publishing Company, Inc., 625

Michigan Avenue (Suite 1920), Chicago, IL
60611.

There are also private or nongovernment
sources of fundamental data. The most notable
is called *Commodity Year Book*. Published each
year for 50 years by Commodity Research
Bureau in New York City, the Year Book
contains historical charts and tables for more
than 100 commodities, including all of the
major futures markets.

That's all we are going to say about
fundamental analysis here. Individual briefing
sheets in Chapter 16 contain a description of
each commodity, where it is grown or produced,
pertinent fundamental factors, data on the
futures contract, and where you can find out
more about that market.

## Suggested Reading

*Commodity Year Book*, Commodity Research Bureau,
  New York City.

*Modern Commodity Futures Trading*, by Gerald Gold.
  Commodity Research Bureau, New York City, Rev.
  1989.

*The Complete Guide to the Futures Markets*, by Jack
  Schwager. John Wiley & Sons, Inc., New York City,
  1984.

# 10

# Technical Analysis

There are two important differences between fundamental and technical analysis. Fundamental analysis of futures markets is characterized by a great deal of subjective information; it is used to forecast price movement over several weeks or months. The technical analyst deals with only three pieces of data: price, trading volume, and open interest. He evaluates them to form an opinion on the likely direction of prices over the next several days.

*The complete analyst looks at the fundamentals to decide whether a significant price movement is in the cards and employs technical analysis to determine the most propitious time to enter the market.*

As we saw earlier, financial periodicals report four prices for each day's activity in a futures contract: the day's opening price, high, low, and settlement or closing price. (Some newspapers omit the opening price.) Of the four, the closing price is generally considered to be the most

**The complete analyst looks at the fundamentals to decide whether a significant price movement is in the cards, and he employs technical analysis to determine the most propitious time to enter the market.**

meaningful, as it represents the day's final verdict. The opening price is the least significant because it is often distorted by the overnight buildup of market orders.

In the simplest context, a rise in prices reflects growing demand for the futures contract. If the trading volume increases when prices rise, it is a sign that there is interest in the rally—that the price increase is attracting followers. That's a bullish omen. Rising open interest would further strengthen the technical picture, as it would indicate that new buyers are entering the fray.

Obviously, there are several other combinations of these three factors, and each holds a different meaning for the technical analyst. We'll see how they work. But first there are some other things you should know.

## PRICE TREND

A trend is the tendency for prices (or any other value) to move more in one direction than the other. Several years ago, when gasoline supplies were short and prices soared, increasing numbers of light, fuel-efficient automobiles were made. There was a trend toward small cars. If you wanted to place a bet that tomorrow's outside temperature would be higher than today's, you would choose the springtime to do so (in the Northern Hemisphere), because temperatures are trending higher at that time of year. If you have ever sat on an ocean beach and watched the tide come in, you have observed an uptrend. Each wave tends to lap a bit higher on the sand and to recede a bit less.

**A trend is the tendency for prices (or any other value) to move more in one direction than the other.**

An uptrend on a price chart looks very much like an incoming ocean tide. Each peak is higher than the previous peak, and each valley is higher than the previous valley. Figure 3 is a good example. The upward price move began with the extreme low in early July, but the

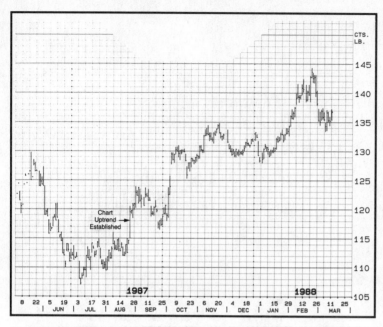

**FIGURE 3.** A chart uptrend is identified by climbing "stairsteps." At least four points are required to establish a new uptrend: a low, a high, a higher low, and a higher high. This uptrend was born on August 25, when daily prices closed above the peak made on August 7. Reprinted with Permission, © 1988 Commodity Perspective, 30 South Wacker Drive, Suite 1820, Chicago, Illinois 60606.

uptrend was not confirmed until prices closed above the previous high in late August. As you can see, the uptrend was still intact in early 1988, some 8 months later.

A downtrend in prices is characterized by lower highs and lower lows, as shown in Figure 4. The lower chart trend was established on September 28, when prices closed below the low set 3 weeks earlier. The lower trend persisted into early March, qualifying it as a major price movement.

When prices meander without any clear direction, as they did in Figure 5, the trend is referred to as sideways or neutral.

**FIGURE 4.** In a chart downtrend the same rules apply, but the stairsteps go lower. Reprinted with Permission, © 1988 Commodity Perspective, 30 South Wacker Drive, Suite 1820, Chicago, Illinois 60606.

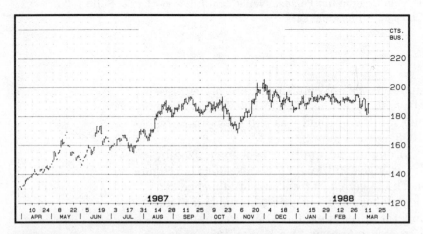

**FIGURE 5.** Extended up or downtrends are not common. Futures prices spend most of the time in trendless price action. Prices in this market, for example, wandered aimlessly for 8 months between $1.60 and $2.00. Reprinted with Permission, © 1988 Commodity Perspective, 30 South Wacker Drive, Suite 1820, Chicago, Illinois 60606.

History has shown that established price trends in futures markets tend to persist. And that, of course, is why they fascinate traders. The existence of a trend enhances the probability that tomorrow's price will be higher or lower than today's, and a trader can use that information to very good advantage.

## TRENDLINES

Technical analysts often draw a straight line through the extreme lows in an established chart uptrend (Figure 6). This is called an up

**FIGURE 6.** An up trendline is drawn across the extreme lows. A minimum of 2 points is required. By January, this trendline had 5 points, making it unusually dependable. Breaking of the trendline, as happened here in early March, is a sign that the trend is losing its force. Reprinted with Permission, © 1988 Commodity Perspective, 30 South Wacker Drive, Suite 1820, Chicago, Illinois 60606.

**FIGURE 7.** A typical down trendline. Reprinted with Permission, © 1988
Commodity Perspective, 30 South Wacker Drive, Suite 1820, Chicago,
Illinois 60606.

*trendline* and is used as a reference. A *down
trendline* is drawn through the extreme highs, as
shown in Figure 7.

Trendlines serve several purposes. One
purpose is for warning. If prices break through a
well-established trendline, it is an indication
that the ongoing trend is losing its force. Figure
6 provides an example. After trending higher for
nearly 7 months, prices suddenly broke down
through the trendline at about $3.15, flashing
the signal that the uptrend had run its course.

A trendline can also be used to enter a
market. In Figure 8, for example, if you were
convinced that the uptrend was well established
and that prices were headed a great deal higher,

the pullback to the trendline in late September would have provided a logical point to take your long position. The probability of short-term adverse (downward) price movement would be minimized, because to do so would require breaking the trendline. And you can place a sell stop order just below the trendline to get you out of market immediately if prices did continue to fall and the trendline was broken.

Breaking of a trendline means the current trend is losing its zip; it does *not* mean that the opposite price trend has begun. Few trends change course abruptly. There is almost always an interim period of trendless activity before any new sustained upward or downward price movement begins.

**FIGURE 8.** A pullback to the trendline can be used to enter or leave a market. In this example, the trendline was pretty well delineated (3 points) by late September. When prices approached the trendline from above, a good technical argument could be made for choosing that site to go long. Reprinted with Permission, © 1988 Commodity Perspective, 30 South Wacker Drive, Suite 1820, Chicago, Illinois 60606.

## SUPPORT AND RESISTANCE

**The price level where a decline may be expected to stop is called a *price support level*.**

**The price level where a rally can be expected to run into trouble is called a *price resistance level*.**

*"Prices met support and closed higher for the day."*

You've probably heard or read a statement something like that. If you didn't know what the word *support* meant, you probably shrugged the comment off as market doubletalk.

*The fact is, prices tend to stop where they have stopped before.*

A rally will tend to fade and prices turn back down again near the point where the previous rally ended. A decline will tend to stop at or near the price where the previous decline stopped.

The price level where a decline may be expected to stop is called a *price support level*. Prices receive support from below. The price level where a rally can be expected to run into trouble is called a *price resistance level*. Sellers there resist any further advances.

The rationale for support and resistance levels is found in human nature. When prices move, three groups of participants are affected. Traders on the right side of the market begin to accrue profits. Traders on the wrong side of the market watch uncomfortably as their paper losses mount. And traders who had intended to be on the right side of the market but who never got around to acting on their beliefs are kicking themselves.

Now what happens if prices return to the point where they started? Traders on the right side of the market consider adding to their positions because the market has demonstrated its ability to move in their direction. Traders on the wrong side of the market, after sweating through a period of paper losses, heave a sigh of relief as they close out their positions with small debits. And the intended, who missed the boat the first time, make sure they won't miss it again.

That's a lot of kinetic energy, and it's all pointing in the same direction.

To take a specific example, suppose copper futures prices had been declining for several weeks. The decline stopped around 83.50 cents per pound, prices milled about for several weeks, and then rallied sharply to 90.00 in what looked like the beginning of a sustained upward move. The longs are smiling, the shorts are looking for an exit, and the bulls in the wings are wondering why they didn't take their long positions last week.

When copper futures prices retreat back to 84.00, all three groups are galvanized into action— the longs to add to their positions, now that the market has demonstrated its bouyancy; the shorts to close out their losing positions; and the intended bulls, who now have an unexpected second chance to get aboard. The buying of these three groups stops the decline near the point where it started, the previous low. Prices have found support at that level.

**Prices tend to stop where they have stopped before.**

Price resistance involves the same psychology but with the picture inverted. Sellers are waiting overhead to roadblock a rally.

Figure 9 provides examples of both of these technical phenomena.

## Other Locations

Price support and resistance are found at locations other than previous highs or lows. When prices move within a narrow range for several weeks, they form what is called a *price congestion area*. This area will provide support when prices approach it from above, and resistance when prices approach it from below. An example is shown in Figure 10.

Somewhat weaker support and resistance are also found at price *gaps*, which are simply areas on the chart where no trading took place.

## Role Changing

An established support level, once broken, will reverse its role and act as resistance the next

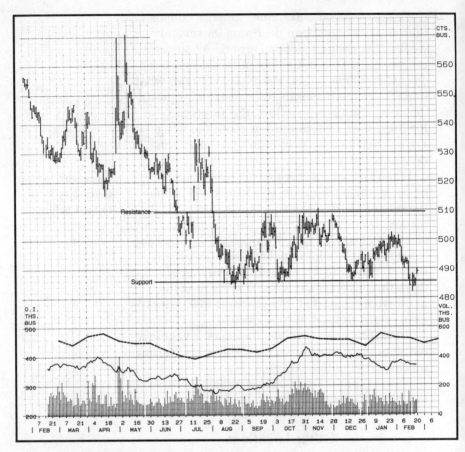

**FIGURE 9.** This daily-action price chart for soybean futures provides examples of both support and resistance. From August to September, the $4.86 level provided support on four occasions, stopping declines and turning price back up. Four times the ensuing rallies ran headlong into resistance at $5.10. Reprinted with Permission, © 1988 Commodity Perspective, 30 South Wacker Drive, Suite 1820, Chicago, Illinois 60606.

time prices approach it from below. A resistance level that has been surpassed will provide support if prices should later fall back to that level. Figures 10 and 11 provide examples of the latter.

## Chart Patterns

A table of commodity prices in the newspaper is a snapshot of price action. A price chart is a

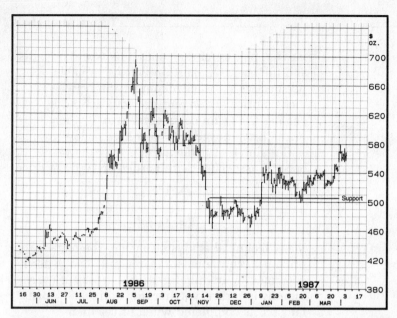

**FIGURE 10.** Congestion areas, where prices have traded in a narrow range for several weeks, can later act as roadblocks. In this example, support at the top of the small 8-week congestion area formed from mid-November to mid-January reversed the decline in February, sending prices back up to new 5-month highs. Reprinted with Permission, © 1988 Commodity Perspective, 30 South Wacker Drive, Suite 1820, Chicago, Illinois 60606.

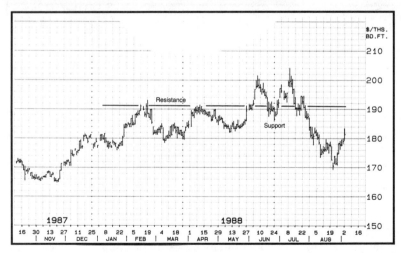

**FIGURE 11.** Support and resistance often swap roles. The $190 level resisted advances in February and April, turning rallies back. The resistance was broken in late May. When prices retraced their steps in late June, the $190 level changed its stripes and acted as support, sending prices to new highs. Reprinted with Permission, © 1988 Commodity Perspective, 30 South Wacker Drive, Suite 1820, Chicago, Illinois 60606.

moving picture of the conflict between the bulls and the bears. A chart provides a valuable perspective. It permits comparison between today's price action and previous action. It enables the technical analyst to spot when prices have moved into new high or low ground.

Certain chart patterns have over the years become associated with particular kinds of price behavior.

## Rectangles

Many technical analysts consider the rectangular price pattern the most meaningful. The pattern is formed by trading for several weeks or even months in a relatively narrow horizontal price range. It is completed when prices then suddenly break out. An extended price move in the direction of the breakout usually follows. An example is shown in Figure 12.

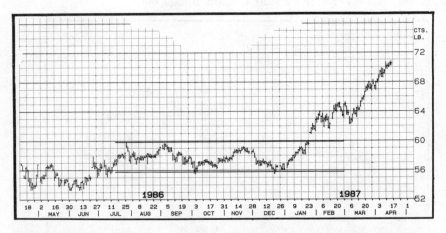

**FIGURE 12.** A rectangular price pattern is formed when overhead resistance and underlying support trap prices in a narrow trading range for several weeks. An extended price move often follows. In this example, futures prices vacillated in a band from about 56 to 60 cents for 7 months. In late January they burst through the top of the rectangle. The subsequent rally carried to 71 cents. Reprinted with Permission, © 1988 Commodity Perspective, 30 South Wacker Drive, Suite 1820, Chicago, Illinois 60606.

This phenomenon makes sense if we look at the rectangle in the same way as we did support and resistance levels. Although it's not depicted on this particular chart, total trading volume during the 7 months while the rectangle was forming was 7 million futures contracts. That means there were 7 million new short positions and 7 million new long positions acquired during the period. Even after allowing for multiple contract positions and traders who were in and out and back in again, the great majority of the traders in this market had a vested interest in the narrow price range.

When prices left that range to the upside, market participants behaved characteristically: longs added to their winning positions; bulls on the sidelines, seeing the breakout, started to buy. Most important, however, were the existing shorts, who represented a large reservoir of potential buying power. As prices moved higher, their losses mounted; gradually they gave up hope and bought futures to cover their short positions, adding more fuel to the rally.

Rectangles may be found at major price turning points. They may also represent price consolidation; that is, sometimes prices will wander around inside a rectangle for several weeks and then resume their previous trend. It is difficult to tell before prices break out of a rectangle just which direction the next move will be, but there may be hints. If prices are historically high when the rectangle forms, the probabilities would favor a downside breakout. The opposite would be true if prices were at 10-year lows.

Anthony Reinach avers that prices tend to leave a rectangle through the boundary where they have spent the *least* time (*The Fastest Game in Town*, Commodity Research Bureau, New York City, 1973). To put it another way, if price action has been concentrated in the bottom half of the rectangle, particularly during the most recent trading activity, the odds favor an exit through the top and vice versa. As it happens, Figure 12 demonstrates that phenomenon also. Of the 30 weeks in the rectangle, prices spent 19 of them below the midline, including the 6 weeks just before the upside breakout.

There are several other chart patterns that technicians recognize, in addition to rectangles. Some patterns contain forecasting power; others are noncommittal. If the subject has caught your interest, you will find them discussed in Appendix A.

## Failed Signals

If prices fail to follow through—if they break out of an established pattern and immediately stall—it is a sign that the breakout was counterfeit and that the most likely course of prices in coming days is *opposite* to the breakout. This doesn't happen very often, but some chartists consider this particular event one of the most important chart signals.

## Point-and-Figure Charts

There is another kind of price chart that technicians use. It is called a point-and-figure chart, and it is more than a record of prices. It comprises a well-defined trading method.

**If a price breakout is immediately followed by stalling price action, the breakout was false, and price movement in the *opposite* direction is more likely.**

The point-and-figure chart is the typically handdrawn and posted daily by the chartist. Figure 13 shows a typical example. Prices are on the left-hand scale, in the spaces between the lines. There is no calendar across the bottom; point-and-figure charts are kept without regard to time. The "X" symbol is used to record rallies and the "O" to record declines. Each time the chartist shifts from one symbol to another, he begins a new column to the right.

The size of each "box" is chosen by the chartist. It is generally some conveniently divisible number. For example, if you were

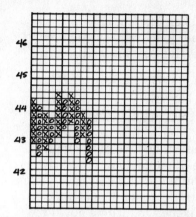

**FIGURE 13.** A typical point-and-figure chart. Prices
are in the spaces rather than on the lines. Xs are used
to record advances, Os to record declines; a new
column to the right is started when the trend reverses.
More than a record of prices, the point-and-figure
chart is a complete trading method.

constructing a point-and-figure chart for hog
futures, you might assign each box the value of
20 points. If a rally were underway and Xs were
being plotted, a new X would be added to the
top of the column with every 20-point gain. If
prices were falling and Os were being plotted, a
new O would be added to the bottom of the
column each time the price fell by another 20
points.

Shifting from Xs to Os (or vice versa) is called
reversal, and the chartist has to decide for
himself how far prices must move against the
prevailing trend before he shifts to the next
column to the right and starts plotting the other
symbol. A "three-box" reversal criteron is
common; that is, if prices would fill three or
more boxes in the direction opposite to the
direction you are presently plotting, you move
one column to the right and shift symbols.

Appendix B presents further information
about these unusual charts, including how to get

a point-and-figure chart started, how to recognize "buy" and "sell" signals, and how to select the most effective box size and reversal criterion.

## MOVING AVERAGES

Moving averages are among the oldest trading tools. The purpose of the moving average is to smooth out short-term ups and downs in prices, to reveal the underlying trend. Use of a moving average has been likened to turning down the treble on your high fidelity sound system, to suppress the higher frequency cycles.

To take an example, assume that the closing prices for copper futures over the past 3 days were 89.50, and 88.70, and 87.25

| Day 1 | 89.50 |
|-------|-------|
| Day 2 | 88.70 |
| Day 3 | 87.25 |
| | 265.45 ÷ 3 = 88.50 |

The total is 265.45. The average price over the 3 days was 265.45 ÷ 3 = 88.50. (Actually it was 88.48, but we rounded.) The next day's close is 86.40. We add that to the bottom of the column and delete the oldest price.

| | ~~89.50~~ |
|-------|-------|
| Day 2 | 88.70 |
| Day 3 | 87.25 |
| Day 4 | 86.40 |
| | 262.35 ÷ 3 = 87.45 |

The new total is 262.35 and the new 3-day average is 87.45. The decline in the closing price caused the moving average to fall. The 3-day average is now moving forward in time; hence its name. The next day's close is 87.40.

~~88.70~~
Day 3     87.25
Day 4     86.40
Day 5     87.40
261.05 ÷ 3 = 87.00

The new total is 261.05 and the new 3-day moving average is 87.00. Here you see an important feature of moving averages demonstrated. The daily closing price went up by 100 points, while the moving average continued to decline. The moving average filtered out the rise in the closing price. It said, in effect, "If I'm going to recognize a gain it will have to be bigger or more sustained than that."

The closing price for copper on the following day was 87.70, another daily gain.

~~87.25~~
Day 4     86.40
Day 5     87.40
Day 6     87.70
261.50 ÷ 3 = 87.15

On this day, the moving average increased from 87.00 to 87.15, finally recognizing that the minor price trend had reversed from down to up.

If prices on Day 6 had gone down instead of up, resuming the previous lower trend, the brief rally would never have shown up in the moving average. This is the smoothing action we mentioned. To demonstrate, substitute a price of 86.65 for 87.70 on the last day.

~~87.25~~
Day 4     86.40
Day 5     87.40
Day 6     86.65 (substitute price)
260.45 ÷ 3 = 86.80

If we substitute a closing price of 86.65 for 87.70 on Day 6, the moving average on Day 6 is 86.80, a decline from its Day 5 value of 87.00; the rally in the closing price on Day 5 is obscured.

Putting all the days together will give you a clearer picture:

| Day | Closing Price | 3-Day Moving Average |
|---|---|---|
| 1 | 89.50 | |
| 2 | 88.70 | |
| 3 | 87.25 | 88.50 |
| 4 | 86.40 | 87.25 |
| 5 | 87.40 | 87.00 |
| 6 | 87.70 | 87.15 |

From Day 1 through Day 4, both the closing prices and the 3-day moving average are going down. On Day 5 an upturn in the closing prices began. However, the moving average continued to decline on Day 5, not turning up until Day 6, a lag of one day.

*This lag is both the cost and the benefit of using a moving average, as it delays a decision about market direction until more data are available.*

## Selecting the Number of Days

Any number of days can be used to build a simple moving average. We used 3 days in our example, but there's no magic to that number. The key is the market where the moving average is to be employed.

The shorter the moving average, the more sensitive it will be to price changes. The longer the moving average, the slower it will be to respond. Early signals from a moving average run the risk of being false; late signals may give up too much of the trend. The technical trader tries to strike the optimum balance between the two.

As we saw, with the 3-day moving average, the lag between the upturn in the price and the upturn in the moving average was only 1 day. That obviously would not provide adequate filtering action in a volatile market. Trading decisions based on turns in the moving average would cause a trader to jump in and out of the market frequently, creating not only frustration but very high commission costs. A longer moving average would reduce these so-called "whipsaws."

By the same token, a long moving average in a very quiet market would not provide very satisfactory results; by the time a new trend showed up in the moving average, the price move could be over. Given these trade-offs, experienced traders generally consider the longer moving averages as more dependable.

Appendix C presents more information about moving averages. It covers linearly weighted moving averages, constructing an exponential moving average, and how moving averages are used in a trading program.

## TRADING VOLUME AND OPEN INTEREST

We briefly mentioned trading volume and open interest in Chapter 2. Trading volume is the number of futures contracts that changed hands during a specific period, usually a day. Open interest is defined as the number of outstanding futures contracts, or those that have not yet been closed out by offsetting futures transactions or delivery of the actual commodity.

To help you understand the nature of open interest and how it changes, let's take an example. Suppose there were a brand-new futures market in bananas, with nobody in it yet. Mr. A, who has been a student of bananas for some time, believes banana prices are headed lower. So he sells short one futures contract. Mr. B holds the opposite opinion; he expects higher banana prices in coming weeks. He buys the futures contract from Mr. A. The buying and selling is done, of course, through their respective brokers.

Those two positions—one long and one short—together comprise one unit of open interest.

Now the banana market starts to attract attention. Mr. C buys a futures contract from Mr. D; open interest increases to 2. Mr. E buys a futures contract from Ms. F; open interest increases to 3.

Mr. G also decides to go long bananas, but something different happens this time. Instead of buying from another new player, Mr. G. buys a futures contract from Mr. B, who was long and has decided that he doesn't want to be in the market any more. Mr. G takes over Mr. B's long position; he replaces Mr. B in the standings, and open interest therefore does not change.

The next buyer and seller to step up are Mr. C and Mr. D, both of whom already hold positions in the market. They close out their positions by reversing their original futures transactions—Mr. C sells and Mr. D buys. The market has now lost two previous players, and open interest decreases by one. (Remember, one long futures contract *and* one short futures contract together comprise one unit of open interest.)

From this sequence you can see that

- Open interest increases when a new long buys from a new short.
- Open interest decreases when an old long sells to an old short.
- Open interest does not change when a new long buys from an old long or a new short sells to an old short, as the new player simply replaces the old player.

## Measuring Trends

Data on trading volume and open interest can be
used to evaluate the status of the current price
trend. The simplest gauge is trading volume.
The axiom is that the volume should "follow"
the trend. If an uptrend is healthy, for example,
trading volume should increase on rallies and
dry up when prices set back temporarily. If
these conditions do not prevail, a shadow of
doubt would be cast on the current trend. The
converse would be true in a bear market.
Trading volume would tend to increase on
declines and fall off when prices staged minor
rallies.

**When price, volume, and open interest rise together, the market is considered technically strong.**

Open interest is a bit more complicated, but it
is also a more valuable diagnostic tool. The
character of open interest and its change in
relation to price changes provide insight into
_why_ the market is moving. For example,
suppose that during the past 2 weeks both
prices and open interest had risen sharply. The
price rise means that aggressive buying is
coming into the market. The rise in open
interest tells you that the buying is coming from
new longs, rather than old shorts who are
closing out their positions. Why? Recall how
open interest changes. If the buying were
coming from departing shorts, open interest
would be flat or going down.

> Thumb rule 1: _When price and open
> interest rise together, the market is
> considered to be technically strong._

A price rise accompanied by flat or falling
open interest is, for the same reason, suspect.
The rally is being sponsored by shorts who are
buying to leave the market and will last only as
long as they last. If no new factor enters the
picture in the meantime, the rally will end
when the last short has bought.

Thumb rule 2: *When prices rise on falling open interest, the market is considered technically weak.*

A price decline that is accompanied by falling open interest also suggests a temporary condition. Sometimes referred to as a "liquidating market," the situation implies that the selling pressure is coming mainly from exiting longs and that it will subside when all the longs have sold out.

Thumb rule 3: *When prices fall on declining open interest, the market is potentially bouyant.*

If prices are falling while open interest is increasing, the presumption is of a legitimate bear market. A lot of selling is going on. The rise in open interest tells us that the selling pressure is coming from aggressive new shorts, who have suddenly been drawn into the market. The lower price trend is therefore on a relatively sound technical footing.

Thumb rule 4: *When prices decline on rising open interest, the market is considered to be technically weak.*

These four rules of thumb may be further distilled into two general observations:

*When price and open interest go up or down together, the current price trend is given a vote of confidence; when prices and open interest diverge, the market may be about to change course.*

We have called these rules of thumb, and indeed they are. They are not hard and fast. They are guidelines, to be applied in concert with other technical indicators to develop a rounded picture of the status of that particular market.

## Contrary Opinion

There are just so many futures traders. They are not easy to count, as FCMs are reluctant to reveal the identity of their customers; but estimates range in the hundred thousands. By comparison, some 30 million investors are said to be involved in the securities markets.

If there be a finite number of futures traders, they can be exhausted. That is to say, it is possible that a particular futures market could literally run out of new players.

To take an example, suppose prices in a certain market have been advancing for several months. Open interest has also been increasing, and now stands at a record high. Given this scenario, it is conceivable that virtually everyone who ever intended to buy one of these futures contracts has already bought. That leaves the market in a precarious balance. The bulls are fully commited, and the bears are watching. Positive news, which helped fuel the rally, now has little or no effect on prices. However, it may take only a scrap of negative sentiment to tip the scale, sending the longs packing and bringing in the short sellers.

An extended advance or decline in futures prices thus may contain the seeds of its own demise.

This philosophy goes under the name of contrary opinion and is based on the observation that markets look most bullish near their tops and most dismal just about the time they are ready to turn up again. Traders who espouse this philosophy attempt to measure the extent to which futures markets have become overloaded to one side or the other and to use these evaluations in making their trading decisions.

## Informed Opinion

There are other ways to consider open interest. Suppose you learned from a reliable source that many of the large speculators in wheat had just moved from the long side of the market to the short side. You could draw conclusions from that. Large speculators are supposed to know what they're doing, and they expect lower prices. Maybe they know something you don't.

Just such changes in market sentiment are gathered from the field and published each month by the Commodity Futures Trading Commission in Washington, DC. The report is called the *Commitments of Traders Report.* It comes out around the 12th of the month and is effective as of the end of the preceding month. The categories reported on are "commercial" (hedgers), "noncommercial" (large speculators) and "nonreportable positions" (small traders). Shown for each category are the number of long positions, short positions, and the changes since the previous report. All major futures markets are covered.

The *Commitments of Traders Report* is available by subscription for $36 per year. To subscribe, write to Communication and Education Section, Commodity Futures Trading Commission, 2033 K Street NW, Washington, DC 20581.

## OTHER TECHNICAL TOOLS

Support and resistance levels, price chart analysis, and moving averages are the most common technical phenomena. Technicians employ other means in their effort to forecast prices. Some analysts take a daily measure of the *rate of change* in the price. This value is referred to a market's *momentum.* Increasing momentum means that price movement is accelerating in the direction of the trend and that the trend is likely to continue. It is a sudden surge in momentum that causes prices to form breakaway gaps, discussed in Appendix

A. A loss of momentum implies that the trend is losing its force and may be about to end.

*Elliott Wave* analysis seems well adapted to longer term price forecasting. Named after a man who lived in the early 1900s, the method finds a major trend complete when it has formed five waves in the main direction. Reactions along the way comprise three waves in a countertrend direction. Mr. Elliott considered the waves as "behavioral tides," found throughout nature.

Investigation has also been made into price *cycles.* Cyclical price activity is most pronounced in the seasonal agricultural commodities, but it is identifiable to some degree in virtually all futures markets.

## CAVEATS

Few traders put all their technical eggs in one basket. Most use more than one indicator. When the indicators disagree violently, the technical trader stays out of the market. When the indicators concur, he can take a position with a degree of confidence. When there are only shades of difference, the trader must decide which technical indicator he trusts most and give it precedence.

An analogy to a weather forecaster is apt. The forecaster doesn't base his prediction on only one aspect. He or she looks at temperature, dew point, wind direction and velocity, cloud cover, and relative humidity before deciding whether or not it's going to rain on your picnic.

The Law of Disappearing Qualifiers also applies to conclusions arrived at through technical analysis. There is as much art as science in identifying support and resistance levels, trends, and price objectives. The technician needs to remind himself from time to time that he is dealing with mathematical probabilities, not certainties.

Not all technical phenomena behave as well as those we have shown in this chapter, which were selected to demonstrate our points. Trendlines occasionally have to be redrawn on the basis of later evidence. Prices sometimes move in fits and starts, apparently trending in one direction for a short time, and then suddenly reversing course. Extended upward or downward price trends are, unfortunately, not common occurrences.

**Technical analysis deals with probabilities, not certainties.**

Technical analysis works best in routine markets, those that are not subject to unusual stress. The best technical forecasts can be overwhelmed by sudden changes in supply or demand. Discovery of a serious crop disease, drought, a surprise announcement of a huge foreign purchase, or an unexpectedly bullish or bearish government report are examples of events that can put technical analysis into abeyance until the news is assimilated and the market affected settles back down again.

# Suggested Reading

*New Commodity Trading Systems and Methods*, by Perry J. Kaufman. John Wiley & Sons, Inc., New York City, 1987.

*Technical Analysis of the Futures Markets*, by John J. Murphy, New York Institute of Finance, New York City, 1986.

*Cyclic Analysis in Futures Trading*, by Jake Bernstein John Wiley & Sons, Inc. New York City, 1988.

# 11

# Hedging Revisited

In Chapter 5 we introduced the rudiments of
hedging. We said that the purpose of hedging is
to reduce the risk of price changes in a cash
commodity, and that a traditional hedge
involves a futures position that is roughly equal
and opposite to the cash position held by the
hedger.

Hedging is not a rote process. Risk exposure
must be evaluated; it may turn out to be
acceptable. The damage that an adverse move in
the cash price would do must be weighed
against the probability of its occurrence. The
price history of the proposed hedge should be
examined. Particularly in financial futures,
prospective hedgers should ensure that their
intended actions do not violate any regulations.

A hedge is not always benign. In all the
examples given up to this point, the hedge was
necessary. Prices subsequently moved against
the hedger's cash position, causing losses on the
cash side and offsetting gains on the futures
side. It is possible for prices to move in the

**Hedging is not a
rote process.**

other direction, creating losses in the hedger's futures position and triggering margin calls. A call for more money is disquieting, even though the "loss" will be recovered when the cash asset is sold. Unless the hedger has made credit arrangements to cover them, a series of margin calls may present a serious cash flow problem.

The hedges we used as examples in Chapter 3 also worked perfectly; that is, the money lost on the cash side and the amount gained on the futures side were identical. That rarely happens in the real world. There are several reasons why the gains and losses in a hedge may not be equal. Most important is the fact that futures prices and cash prices may not change by the same amount because the two prices are subject to different influences. Cash prices respond to the supply and demand for the actual commodity. Futures prices are influenced strongly by traders' expectations.

**Basis is defined as the difference between the cash price and the futures price of a commodity. It can be either a positive or negative value and is best thought of as the cash price minus the futures price.**

What follows is the bond dealer example from Chapter 5, but with a difference. To make it more realistic, we have changed the T-bond futures price in the closing transaction from 94-28 to 94-31.

### Short Hedge in T-Bond Futures

| Cash Market | | Futures Market |
|---|---|---|
| Buy cash bonds at 95-07 | Now | Sell T-bond futures at 95-17 |
| Sell cash bonds at 94-18 | Later | Buy T-bond futures at 94-31 |
| Loss 0-21 | | Gain 0-18 |

Net result = loss of 0-03

Now the hedge does not balance. The dealer lost $21/32$ on his cash bonds while he held them, but the hedge earned back only $18/32$. Three thirty-seconds of the loss taken on the cash side were not offset.

To understand what happened, it is necessary to meet another new concept, that of *basis*. Basis is defined as the difference between the cash price and the futures price of a commodity.

Basis can be either a positive or negative value and is best thought of as the cash price minus the futures price. A change in the basis while the hedge is on is one of the reasons why hedges may not work 100%.

Let's take a look at the basis in the hedge just given.

| Cash Market | | Futures Market | Basis |
|---|---|---|---|
| Buy cash bonds at 95-07 | Now | Sell short T-bond futures at 95-17 | −0-10 |
| Sell cash bonds at 94-18 | Later | Buy T-bond futures at 94-31 | −0-13 |
| Loss 0-21 | | Gain 0-18 | −0-03 |

Net result = loss of 0-03

The basis in the opening transaction was minus 10. In the closing transaction, the basis was minus 13, or ³⁄₃₂ less. It is not a coincidence that the basis change and the loss in the hedge are the same amount, ³⁄₃₂. The change in the basis is what caused the loss.

Potential losses resulting from basis changes cannot be controlled by the hedger. His hedge will protect him against changes in cash prices, but he is always vulnerable to a change in the basis. In this case, the basis fell; that is, it went from minus 10 to minus 13, which is a decrease. If the basis had increased, the hedger would have had the pleasant experience of earning more from his futures position than he lost on the cash bonds.

*When a hedger is short futures* (as the bond dealer was in this example), *any decrease in the basis will cause losses; increases in the basis would create windfall gains. If a hedger is long futures, the situation is reversed: increase in basis causes losses, and a decrease in basis creates gains.*

A hedger is not entirely helpless when it comes to dealing with the basis. In some markets, particularly the agricultural markets,

**When a hedger is short futures, increases in the basis would create windfall gains. If a hedger is long futures, the situation is reversed: a decrease in basis creates gains.**

basis itself has seasonal tendencies, trending higher during certain times of the year and lower during others. A sophisticated hedger will be aware of the trends in the basis and will try to place his hedge during a period when the basis is most likely to move favorably for him.

Here's another example from Chapter 5 with the outcome changed.

### Long Hedge in Corn Futures

| Cash Market | | Futures Market |
|---|---|---|
| Cash corn at $1.85/ bushel | Now | Buy corn futures at $1.96/bushel |
| Buy cash corn at $2.10/ bushel | 3 Months Later | Sell corn futures at $2.25/bushel |
| Loss $.25/bushel | | Gain $.29/bushel |
| | Net result = +$.04 | |

The corn exporter was long futures. The basis on the opening transaction was $1.85 − $1.96 = minus 11. The basis in the closing transaction was $2.10 − $2.25 = minus 15. Recall that when a hedger is long futures, a decrease in the basis creates gains; the basis fell from −11 to −15 while the hedge was in place, providing the hedger with a windfall gain of 4 cents per bushel on his corn sale.

## Solving Hedging Problems

If you are ever called upon to solve hedging problems in a correspondence course or examination, knowledge of the basis provides a way to verify your answers. The rule is:

*If there is a difference between the cash price when the hedge is placed and the effective cash price received by the hedger when the hedge is removed, the basis must have changed by the same amount.*

For an example, let's take another look at the very first hedge we considered:

## Short Hedge in T-Bond Futures

| Cash Market | | Futures Market |
|---|---|---|
| Buy cash bonds at 95-07 | Now | Sell T-bond futures at 95-17 |
| Sell cash bonds at 94-18 | Later | Buy T-bond futures at 94-28 |
| Loss 0-21 | | Gain 0-21 |

Net gain or loss = 0

The bond dealer received 94-18 in the cash market and made 0-21 profit from his short futures position. Those two numbers total to 95-07, the effective price he got for the bonds. That is the same as the cash price for the bonds when he put the hedge on, which means that the basis should not have changed.

To verify, we compare the opening and closing bases. The opening basis was 95-07 minus 95-17 = minus 0-10. The closing basis was 94-18 minus 94-28 = minus 0-10, the same. If the question asks for the dealer's effective price when he sold the bonds, 95-07 is proven the correct answer.

In the more recent example, the bond dealer received an effective price of 94-18 (cash) plus 0-18 (gain in the futures position) = 95-04. That's 0-03 less than the cash price when he placed the hedge, so the basis must have moved 0-03 against him.

Let's check it. The opening basis was 95-07 minus 95-17 = minus 0-10. The closing basis was 94-18 minus 94-31 = minus 0-13. The basis decreased by 0-03. Because the hedger was short futures, the decrease in basis created a loss. The loss and the change in basis are equal, so the answer of an effective price of 95-04 is correct.

**The main reason why a hedge may not provide 100 percent price protection is that cash prices and futures prices do not always change by equal amounts.**

## Other Reasons for an Imperfect Hedge

A change in the basis is not the only reason why a hedge could fail to provide 100 percent protection against cash price changes. Futures contracts are not divisible. A cash position of $470,000 in Treasury notes, for example, cannot be offset exactly, because the T-note futures contract on the Chicago Board of Trade is based on $100,000 par value in T-notes. Five T-note futures contracts ($500,000) would be too much hedge; four futures contracts ($400,000) would leave $70,000 worth of cash T-notes exposed.

When faced with this dilemma, it must be borne in mind that any part of an intended futures hedge that does not have an offsetting cash position is a speculation and carries with it speculative risk. The more conservative business decision in this example would be to underhedge the cash position; that is, to protect as much of it as possible without creating any speculative exposure.

Overhedging a cash position in such circumstances requires a favorable price forecast. In the previous example, overhedging would not even be considered if interest rates are expected to move lower, as the "extra" short futures position would be expected to generate market losses. (Remember: prices of fixed-income financial instruments go up when interest rates go down.) If interest rates are expected to rise while the hedge is on, overhedging could be considered by an experienced trader.

An example will help you understand how an unbalanced hedge works. Assume you are a cattle feeder. It is March, and you have 62 steers out in the feedlot munching corn. They weigh about 800 pounds each now, and you are going to feed them up to about 1000 pounds each. That should take about 7 weeks, at which time you'll market the steers.

The present cash price for fat cattle is 62.50 cents per pound. June cattle futures are trading at 62.90 cents per pound. You want to hedge your cattle. The live cattle futures contract on the Chicago Mercantile Exchange is based on a contract size of 40,000 pounds, or about 40 steers weighing 1000 pounds each. You will have about 62,000 pounds of cattle at market time. Your hedge will have to be unbalanced.

Cattle prices are forecast to ease during the time your hedge will be in place, so you decide to take the risk and overhedge your cash position. You sell short two contracts of June cattle. Your assessment of the market proves to right; when it comes time to market your cattle, prices have declined a little over 1½ cents. The results of your hedge would look something like this (no change in basis):

| _Cash Cattle_ | | | _Futures_ | |
|---|---|---|---|---|
| | 62.50 | March | Sold two June cattle at | 62.90 |
| Sold 62 head at | 60.72 | May | Bought two June cattle at | 61.12 |
| | −1.78 | | | −1.78 |

The cash price and the futures price have changed by the same amount, so it appears at first glance that you received an effective price of (60.72 cash price + 1.78 futures gain =) 62.50 cents a pound for his cattle. However, that's not so, because the underlying assets were different sizes. There were only 62,000 pounds of cash cattle; there were (40,000 × 2 =) 80,000 pounds of cattle futures.

To calculate the price per pound you received for your cattle, you have to figure out your total receipts and divide that number by 62,000 pounds. You were paid $37,646.40 for your cash steers (60.72 cents per pound × 1000 pounds × 62 head). Your short futures hedge of two contracts returned you 1.78 cents per pound times 80,000 pounds, or $1424.00.

The total amount you received for your cash cattle was therefore ($37,646.40 + $1,242.00 =) $39,070.40. That total divided by 62,000 pounds of live cattle equals 63.02 cents per pound.

Because prices moved in a favorable direction (in this case, down) the unbalanced hedge increased the effective price you received for your cattle from 62.50 to 63.02. If prices had instead increased, the unbalanced hedge would have reduced your effective price; you would have lost more on the short futures side than you gained on the cash side.

Another possible reason for an imperfect hedge is a difference between the futures and the cash crop. In some commodities, particularly the agricultural ones, the cash commodity being hedged may not be identical to the commodity underlying the futures contract. The coffee futures contract on the Coffee, Sugar & Cocoa Exchange, for example, is based on Colombian coffee. There are many other varieties. A grower or processor who uses New York futures to hedge another kind of coffee may encounter unexpected gains or losses because the price of his coffee and the price of Colombian coffee diverged.

## Selecting the Delivery Month

In most hedging situations, there will be more than one futures delivery month that could be used for the hedge. The first requirement is that the delivery month be beyond the date when the hedge is to be lifted. Unless you have reason to do so, there's no point in having to close out one expiring futures position and open another to keep your hedge intact.

It is also usually desirable to use the nearest futures contract that meets the first requirement. The closer the futures contract is to maturity, the more responsive it will be to changes in the cash price, and the lower will be the risk of changes in the basis. Nearby futures contracts are also generally more liquid; there is more trading activity in them than in the distant contracts. As a result, your orders to buy or sell will be filled quickly and with minimal impact on the price level.

Experienced hedgers look at other criteria when selecting the futures delivery month they will use. Some delivery months have a history of gaining ground on other delivery months at certain times of the year. One delivery month

may offer a better "opening" basis than another,
setting the stage for a possible planned basis
gain.

## Margins in Hedges

The amount and nature of initial and
maintenance margins required of a hedger
depend on the exchange, the FCM, and the
customer himself. An unknown, thinly
capitalized hedger could be required by the
FCM to post margins greater than exchange
minimums, and in cash. An old, well-heeled
customer of the FCM may be able satisfy both
original and any maintenance requirements with
a letter of credit issued through a local bank.

The point to be made here is that an
established futures hedge may make
considerable further demands on short-term
capital. To take an example, let's assume that
you have a short hedge in soybean futures. The
original margin is $2500, and the maintenance
level is $2000, and you are on a cash basis with
your FCM. You will be called for additional
margin (beyond $2500) if beans go up 10 cents
from your entry level. For every dollar that bean
prices rise, the additional margin required to
maintain your short hedge would be $5000.
That's for one contract of 5000 bushels. If your
hedge is for 50,000 bushels, each dollar gain in
soybean prices would create a margin call for
$50,000. Granted, you get the money back when
you sell your beans at the new higher cash
price. But in the meantime you have to come up
with the necessary short-term financing for the
hedge.

## NONREGULAR HEDGES

There are bona fide hedges that do not fit the
patterns we have been discussing. We don't
want to dwell on these nonstandard hedges, but

we think you should at least be introduced to them. They are cross-hedges, ratio hedges, balance sheet hedging, and on-call transactions.

## Cross-Hedges

If no futures market exists for a certain commodity, it is sometimes possible to use a related futures market for hedging. These are referred to as cross-hedges and are recognized by the Commodity Futures Trading Commission as legitimate. The key is that the two commodities be economically related, so their prices will tend to move up and down together.

**A ratio hedge may be more efficient if the price of the product hedged and the futures price do not have the same volatility.**

A classic example of a cross-hedge is palm oil/soybean oil. Palm oil is one of the major edible oils in the world; it has no futures market. Soybean oil, the most important edible oil, has a very active futures market. The positive correlation between the price movements in the two markets is well above 90 percent. Soybean oil futures can therefore be used effectively to hedge cash positions in palm oil.

Cross-hedging is common in interest rate futures. Commercial paper and CDs can be hedged in T-bill futures. High-quality corporate bonds can be hedged with T-bond futures. The key, once again, is the basis—the relationship between changes in the cash price and changes in the futures price. If history has shown that the two prices tend to move together, a cross-hedge is feasible.

## Ratio Hedges

When you hedge soybean risk in soybean futures, there is little question of how the futures price will respond to a change in the cash price. Cash soybeans and the soybeans underlying the futures contract are identical. Their price volatility is virtually the same. As a consequence, there is no need for the value of

the futures contracts used in the hedge to differ
from the amount of exposure. Or, to put it
another way, a hedge ratio of 1 to 1 is generally
effective: $1 worth of futures for every $1 worth
of cash exposure.

If the price of the product being hedged and
the futures price march to different drummers,
the most efficient hedge may be an unbalanced
hedge. For example, assume that the price
volatility of commercial paper is 1.2 times the
price volatility of T-bills. If T-bill futures are
used to cross-hedge a cash position in
commercial paper, the best combination may not
be 1 to 1; it might be something like 1.2 to 1, or
$1,000,000 worth of T-bill futures for each
$833,333 worth of commercial paper. Then, if
the market value of the more volatile
commercial paper changes by .60, T-bill futures
prices should change by .50, equating the
change in the value in the two holdings (.60 ×
833,333 = .50 × 1,000,000) and enhancing the
probability that losses on the cash side will be
recouped by gains in the futures.

## Balance Sheet Hedging

Earlier we defined a hedge as a futures position
equal and opposite to the cash position held, or
a futures transaction that acts as a temporary
substitute for a later cash transaction. Recent
interpretations by the CFTC have broadened the
concept to include futures positions that, strictly
speaking, have no countervailing cash positions.
The issue arose when fiduciaries—for example,
a pension fund manager—began to use T-bond
futures to lengthen the duration of their
liabilities to match the duration of their assets.

To take a simple example, suppose a pension
fund has assets with an average duration 36
months, whereas its liabilities have an average
duration of only 18 months. The fund is
unprotected against a rise in interest rates
during the 18-month gap. It will continue to

receive returns from its investments at the established interest rate during that period; but if its obligations are indexed and rise with interest rates, the fund could find its operating margin squeezed. To provide some protection against a rise in interest rates, the fund may take a short position in interest rate futures. Then, if interest rates should escalate, the profits on the futures position will offset part of the fund's higher cost of meeting its liabilities.

Unlike a conventional hedge, the pension fund in this example has no cash T-notes on hand during the 6-month period, nor does it have any commitment to sell cash T-notes at some later time.

## On-Call Transactions

Cotton was king in New Orleans at the turn of the century. A practice developed there that capitalized on the fact that a favorable movement in the basis virtually guarantees profits in a fully hedged cash position.

To use an example, suppose a cotton dealer buys 1000 bales of combed cotton from a local grower and stores them in his warehouse. The dealer does not have an immediate buyer for the cotton, so at the same time he sells short two contracts of December cotton futures on the New York Cotton Exchange (each futures contract is 500 bales, each bale is 100 pounds).

At this point, his balance sheet might look something like this:

| Cash | Futures | Basis |
|------|---------|-------|
| Bought 1,000 bales at 61.27 | Sold 2 contracts December cotton at 62.77 | Minus 1.50 |

A week later a buyer phones the cotton dealer. The buyer wants to purchase 1000 bales of cash cotton. During their conversation, the buyer indicates that he believes cotton prices

will soften over the next several days. He asks
the dealer for his best offer.

The dealer reviews his status. He is "long"
the basis (short futures), so every penny that the
basis increases will earn him $1000 in revenue
(1 cent per bale × 100 pounds × 1000 bales).
The dealer would be satisfied with a $1,000
gross profit on the transaction. But he doesn't
tell the buyer that the price for the cash cotton
is 62.27. He tells the buyer that if he buys the
cotton now, he can pay for it at any time he
chooses over the next 10 days at an effective
price of December futures minus .50.

The dealer has forced the basis to move in a
favorable direction. Whether cash cotton prices
go up or down in the interim, the dealer will
earn his $1000 profit. He has also given the
buyer the opportunity to exercise his market
judgment and, if he is correct, to buy the cash
cotton at a better price.

To prove it, we'll continue with our example.
Suppose the buyer were right on the market
forecast; cash cotton fell to 57.44 cents per
pound over the next week, and December
futures kept exact pace by dropping to 58.94. At
that point the buyer elected to pay for the
cotton, giving the dealer the agreed cash price of
50 points "off" December futures, or (58.94 − .50 =)
58.44 cents per pound. The dealer closed out his
short hedge at that time.

Here's how the dealer fared:

| Cash | | Futures | | Basis | |
|---|---|---|---|---|---|
| Bought 1,000 | | Bought 2 contracts | | | |
| bales at | 61.27 | December cotton at | 62.77 | Minus | 1.50 |
| Sold 1,000 | | Bought 2 contracts | | | |
| bales at | 58.44 | December cotton at | 58.94 | Minus | .50 |
| | −2.83 | | +3.83 | | +1.00 |

The dealer received 58.44 cents per pound
from the buyer. He also received 3.83 cents per
pound from his profitable short futures position.

The effective selling price for his cotton was therefore (58.44 + 3.83 =) 62.27 cents per pound. This is 1 cent per pound more than he paid for the cash cotton a week earlier, so he has in fact received his desired gross profit of $1,000 on the transaction. The buyer is also pleased. By waiting a week or so, he saved almost 3 cents a pound on his purchase of cash cotton.

But note this important point in an on-call purchase:

*The buyer is at price risk; the dealer is not.*

If cash cotton prices had risen sharply in the interim, the buyer would have had to pay the higher price; the dealer would still make his $1000 profit. Here are the numbers:

| *Cash* | | *Futures* | | *Basis* | |
|---|---|---|---|---|---|
| Bought 1,000 | | Sold 2 contracts | | | |
| bales at | 61.27 | December cotton at | 62.77 | Minus | 1.50 |
| Sold 1,000 | | Bought 2 contracts | | | |
| bales at | 64.36 | December cotton at | 64.86 | Minus | .50 |
| | +3.09 | | −2.09 | | +1.00 |

The dealer received an effective price of (64.36 − 2.09) = 62.27 cents per pound for his cotton, as before. However, the buyer, because he waited, had to pay a price of 64.36 cents per pound for the cash cotton, which is more than 2 cents a pound higher than the cash price when he first phoned the cotton dealer.

This transaction is referred to an "on-call" transaction. In this case, the payment awaited the buyer's call. The same general approach can be used for transactions based on a seller's call. On-call transactions are not widely used today, although they are still used in the cotton market, and to some extent in the futures markets for sugar and U.S. Treasury bonds.

# Suggested Reading

*Commodity Futures as a Business Management Tool*,
by Henry B. Arthur. Graduate School of Business
Administration, Harvard University, Cambridge, MA,
1971.

*Futures Trading Course*, Futures Industry Association,
Washington, DC, 1987.

# 12

# The Financial Futures

Before financial futures were introduced in the 1970s, futures markets had dealt with consumable commodities like the grains, meats, and metals. These traditional futures markets are similar in many respects and therefore lend themselves well to a general discussion.

Financial futures markets do not fit the same mold. The assets underlying these new futures are not always tangible. The commodities may not be consumed at all but simply change form or ownership. In some cases physical delivery is impracticable, so settlement is by cash only.

Financial futures not only differ from the traditional commodities, they differ among themselves. Financial futures fall into three broad categories. They are

Foreign currency futures

Stock index futures

Interest rate futures

We will look at each category separately, presenting the basic information you need to understand how each market works. Detailed information on individual financial contracts may be found, as for other commodities, in the briefing sheets in Chapter 16.

## FOREIGN CURRENCIES

Exchange rates for the major foreign currencies have fluctuated widely in recent years. But this has not always been the case. From 1944 to 1971, member nations to the Bretton Woods agreement—which included most major world trading partners—pegged their currencies to a specified number of U. S. dollars or given amount of gold (at $35 per ounce). Exchange-rate fluctuations during those years rarely exceeded 2 percent.

This stability was threatened by massive U. S. spending in the late 1960s to support the Vietnam War and fuel expansionary fiscal policies at home. By 1971 the number of dollars in circulation was greater than the total U. S. gold reserves, and President Nixon announced that the U. S. dollar would no longer be convertible into gold. The action removed the basis for parity between currencies. Since 1973 European central banks have allowed their currencies to seek their own levels, and the resulting movement in exchanges rates has been dramatic. It is not unusual for a currency's value to vary as much as 20 percent within a year, and a swing of 25 percent has been recorded in a 3-month period. Such volatility has added a new dimension of risk to international business.

### Using Foreign Currencies

If you are going to buy a product from someone who will accept only a certain foreign currency in payment, you are first going to have to buy that foreign currency. Its exchange rate will have a direct effect on the cost of the product to you.

For example, suppose you ordered a Swiss watch direct from the manufacturer in Zurich. The price is 750 Swiss francs (SF). The following table shows what the watch could cost you in U. S. dollars, depending on the exchange rate for the Swiss franc at the time of your purchase.

| Price of Watch | Exchange Rate | Cross Rate | Cost of Watch in U. S. Money |
|---|---|---|---|
| 750 SF | .55 | 1.818 | (750 × .55) = $412.50 |
| 750 SF | .60 | 1.666 | (750 × .60) = $450.00 |
| 750 SF | .65 | 1.538 | (750 × .65) = $487.50 |
| 750 SF | .70 | 1.428 | (750 × .70) = $525.00 |

The "Exchange Rate" column in the table shows the value of one Swiss franc in U. S. currency, which is the way all foreign currency futures prices are expressed. International banks use a cross-rate, which is the amount of the foreign currency you can buy for one U. S. dollar. The cross-rate is the inverse of the futures price.

(We've taken a liberty with the notation, abbreviating 750 Swiss Francs as 750 SF instead of SF 750, as we think it's easier to read. The notation is uniform throughout the book.)

**Example:** You buy a small cottage on one-half acre in the south of France. The price is 300,000 French francs (FF). The exchange rate at that time is .16, so each franc costs you 16 cents. Your cost for the house is therefore (300,000 FF × .16 =) $48,000.

Six months later you decide it was a bad idea and put the house on the market for 330,000 francs. You are pleasantly surprised when it sells right away, and figure you have recovered nicely from an errant decision. When you go to the bank to convert your draft for French francs into dollars, however, you discover that the exchange rate for the franc has slipped to .14. You receive only 14 cents for each franc, or a total of $46,200 (330,000 FF × .14). A change in the exchange rate turned an apparent profit into a loss.

**Example:** Your U. S. firm makes a product that sells like potato hotcakes in West Germany. You are paid for your product in Deutschemarks. Before you can put that income on your company books, you have to convert the Deutschemarks into U. S. dollars.

Your projected German sales for the first quarter of next year are 2.5 million DM. That includes a profit of 125,000 DM. The Deutschemarks will be wire-transferred from West Germany to your correspondent bank in New York City, where they will be converted into U. S. dollars and placed in your account. The current exchange rate for the DM is .60, so your expected first-quarter receipts are $1.5 million (.60 × 2.5 million DM) and your expected profit is $75,000 (.60 × 125,000 DM).

But something unexpected happens. The value of the Deutschemark begins to decline. The following table shows how your returns would be affected.

| DM Received | Exchange Rate | Effective Receipts |
|-------------|---------------|--------------------|
| 2.5 million | .60 | $1,500,000 |
| 2.5 million | .59 | $1,475,000 |
| 2.5 million | .58 | $1,450,000 |
| 2.5 million | .57 | $1,425,000 |

If the exchange rate falls to .57, your total receipts would $75,000 less than you had anticipated. That was your original expected profit, and it would now be completely erased.

## Futures Markets

It was against the backdrop of freewheeling exchange rates that trading in foreign currency

futures began at the International Monetary
Market in Chicago in 1973. The original list
included nine currencies, some of which you
have already met:

**British pound**

**Japanese yen**

**Swiss franc**

**Deutschemark**

**Canadian dollar**

Dutch guilder

Mexican peso

French franc

Italian lira

Not all these new futures markets have
proved viable. As of this writing, only the ones
shown in boldface are actively traded.

Futures contracts are also actively traded
today on the U. S. Dollar Index, which
represents a basket of the foreign currencies of
10 major world trading partners of the United
States. The index is a weighted average of the
dollar value of those foreign currencies. Its
relationship with the dollar is inverse; that is,
when the value of the foreign currencies rises,
the index declines. Like all index futures, the
U. S. Dollar Index is a broad-based measure. It is
not designed for hedging exchange rate risk in a
single currency. However, it may be used
effectively by international firms or investors
with exchange risks in several different major
foreign currencies. Settlement of U. S. Dollar
Index futures contracts is by cash only.

## Risk

In 1984, CISCO, a futures research firm in
Chicago, surveyed some 200 of the largest
nonfinancial companies in the Chicago area to
inquire (1) whether the company had foreign
exchange risk; (2) if so, whether the risk was

being hedged; and (3) if so, how.[2] Three fourths
of the companies with exchange rate risk
indicated that they hedged their exposure. Most
of the hedgers were conservative in their
approach, aiming to minimize foreign exchange
losses or just break even. Companies with large
foreign exchange exposure were twice as likely
to hedge as smaller companies. Bank forward
contracts were the hedging vehicles most
commonly used.

Forward contracting in foreign currencies is a
natural outgrowth of the relationship between a
multinational bank and its commercial
customer. The customer depends on the bank
for a variety of services and information,
including information on exchange rates. It is
logical step from buying foreign currency for
delivery today to buying the same foreign
currency for delivery at a later time.

As we pointed out in an earlier chapter, the
forward contract offers certain relative
advantages over a futures contract. The forward
contract may be for any amount, of any
currency, for delivery at any time. There is no
explicit cash margin required, although banks
may ask for compensating balances or other
collateral. Futures offer other benefits. Banks
generally consider $1 million as the basic unit
for forward contracting. This may be more
money than a small company needs. The value
of most individual foreign currency futures
contracts falls in the $50,000 to $60,000 range.
Another major benefit of the futures contract is
its flexibility. A futures position can be reduced
or abandoned altogether without incurring
additional transaction costs. Finally, futures may
offer considerably lower transaction costs,
particularly if your business is not located in
one of the major financial centers.

## Hedging

Foreign currency futures are the financial future
that is most like the traditional futures markets.

Settlement of the futures contract can be made either by futures market offset or by physical delivery of the actual foreign currency. Hedging is straightforward; the holder of a foreign currency bank balance would use a short futures hedge to protect against a decline in its exchange rate. An international businessman who would suffer losses if the value of a foreign currency were to rise relative to his own would use a long hedge in the foreign currency future.

An example will make this clearer. Let's say that Barbara Bradford, Inc., an American firm, imports designer buttons from Switzerland. The Bradford company buys in large quantities and resells the buttons to U. S. manufacturers of high-fashion clothes for women. The buttons are priced in Swiss francs when they are ordered. Because many of the buttons are specially made, there is often a considerable lapse of time between order and payment. Ms. Bradford has noticed that on some delayed orders a large part of her expected profit has been lost to changes in the exchange rate.

She has just ordered 125,000 Swiss francs worth of buttons. The exchange rate for the Swiss franc at the time is .70, so she expects the buttons to cost her (125,000 francs × .70 =) $87,500. She has based resale prices to her customers on that cost. To protect herself against an increase in the price of the Swiss franc in the interim, she buys one contract of Swiss franc futures (contract size = 125,000 Swiss francs).

Six weeks later the buttons are received, and Ms. Bradford buys 125,000 Swiss francs in the cash market to pay for them. At the same time she sells her futures position. She notes with satisfaction that the hedge did its job; although the price of the Swiss franc has risen to .7324, her effective exchange rate is still .70 and her effective cost for the buttons is $87,500.

**Settlement of the foreign currency futures contract can be made either by futures market offset or by physical delivery of the actual foreign currency.**

### Long Hedge in Swiss Franc Futures

| Cash Exchange Rate | | | Futures | |
|---|---|---|---|---|
| .7000 | Now | Buys 1 SF at | .7015 | |
| .7324 | 6 weeks later | Sells 1 SF at | .7339 | |
| Opportunity loss = .0324 | | | Gain = | .0324 |

Ms. Bradford actually pays 73.24 cents for each cash Swiss franc she buys; but the gain of 3.24 cents from the long futures position offsets the added cost, reducing her effective price to 70 cents per Swiss franc. If she had not taken the hedge, there would have been no offset, and the francs would have cost her 73.24 cents apiece, or about 5 percent more than she had planned.

Another example, with a bit more to it: your U. S. firm has just acquired a small optics manufacturing company in West Germany. The purchase price is 4 million Deutschemarks in cash. At the time of your negotiations, the exchange rate for the DM is .50. That makes the purchase price $2 million U. S. (4 million DM × 50), which is acceptable to your board of directors. For tax reasons, the seller would like to be paid in four quarterly installments of 1 million DM each. You agree to that. You make the first payment on March 1. The exchange rate for the DM at that time is still .50, so the first installment costs you the expected $500,000.

However, on June 1 the exchange rate for the DM has climbed to .54; that installment therefore costs you (1,000,000 × .54 =) $540,000. On September 1 the exchange rate has risen further to .59; that installment costs you (1,000,000 × .59 =) $590,000. The December 1 installment is $610,000, reflecting an exchange rate of .61 at the time.

In December you total up what you have paid:

| | |
|---|---|
| March 1 payment | $ 500,000 |
| June 1 payment | 540,000 |
| September 1 payment | 590,000 |
| December 1 payment | 610,000 |
| | $2,240,000 |

Your total cost for the company is not $2 million but $2.24 million. The difference of $240,000 is attributable entirely to changes in the exchange rate. Paying 12 percent more than you had expected for the company is an unpleasant surpise for your—and, perhaps, for your board of directors as well.

The most conservative way to control this exchange rate risk is to make a forward contract with your bank calling for the delivery of 1 million DM to you at an agreed rate on each payment date. Futures markets may also be used. In this case, you would want a long hedge in Deutschemark futures. Let's work it out.

The first question is: How many futures contracts are needed? To find the answer, we divide the total amount to be hedged (3 million DM) by the futures contract size (125,000 DM). That equals 24 futures contracts.

The next question is: In which futures delivery month do you place your hedge? You could buy 24 distant contracts and sell them next December after the last quarterly payment was made. But that's not advisable. Basis risk would be greater in the distant contracts. Furthermore, your exchange-rate exposure is not constant during the period. It goes down every time you make a cash payment. The growing number of futures contracts that have no countervailing cash position would be purely speculative. There must be a better way.

You notice that the payment schedule has the same periodicity as the futures market. If you buy eight DM futures contracts in each of the June, September, and December maturity months, your foreign currency risk would be fully hedged; just as important, the size of the hedge would be automatically reduced by the proper amount (1 million DM) each time a cash installment is paid and the matching futures position is closed out.

The easiest way to see the results is to treat the transaction as three separate hedges, each

covering 1 million DM. The first increment
would look something like this:

### Long Hedge in Deutschemark Futures

| *Cash Exchange Rate* | | | *Futures* | |
|---|---|---|---|---|
| .5000 | March | Buy 8 June DM at | .5015 |
| .5400 | June 1 | Sell 8 June DM at | .5415 |
| Opportunity loss = .0400 | | | Gain = .0400 |

Delivery is not taken against the long futures
position; it is closed out with an offsetting
futures market transaction. One million cash
Deutschemarks are bought for your account in
New York and transferred to the account of the
seller in West Germany. You pay the going rate
of 54 cents for each DM. However, barring any
changes in basis (and excluding transaction
costs), the opportunity loss of 400 points on the
cash side is fully offset by the gain of 400 points
in the long futures position. The *effective*
exchange rate is therefore .50, and the cost of
the Deutschemarks to make the June payments
is the expected $500,000 (1 million DM × .50).

Closing out the eight June futures contracts
also reduces the hedge coverage to 2 million DM
(16 contracts × 125,000 DM), which is equal to
the remaining amount to be paid, so the
outstanding cash obligation is not "overhedged."

The next increment is paid on September 1:

| *Cash Exchange Rate* | | | *Futures* | |
|---|---|---|---|---|
| | | | Buy 8 September | |
| .5000 | March | | DM at | .5023 |
| | | | Sell at 8 September | |
| .5900 | September 1 | | DM at | .5923 |
| Opportunity loss = .0900 | | | Gain = .0900 |

Once again, the opportunity loss on the cash
side is offset by the gain on the futures side; the
*effective* exchange rate is still .50, and the cost
of the Deutschemarks to make the September 1
payment is the expected $500,000.

After these transactions the amount owed is 1 million DM, and the remaining hedge comprises eight December futures contracts of 125,000 DM each, so the cash and futures sides are still in balance.

The final installment:

| Cash Exchange Rate | | Futures | |
|---|---|---|---|
| .5000 | March | Buy 8 December DM at | .5034 |
| .6100 | December 1 | Sell 8 December DM at | .6134 |
| Opportunity loss = .1100 | | Gain = | .1100 |

With these transactions, the payments are finished and the futures positions are completely closed out. Even though the exchange rate moved sharply against the buyer (you) in the interim, because of the hedge you paid $2 million U. S. for the West German optics company—no more, no less.

(If the DM had weakened during the period, instead of going up in value, you would still have paid $2 million. Remember what we said earlier: In order to protect against *adverse* movement in the cash price, a futures hedge will also negate any windfall gains that would come from a *favorable* movement in the cash price.)

**In order to protect against *adverse* movement in the cash price, a futures hedge will also negate any windfall gains that would come from a *favorable* movement in the cash price.**

## Short Hedge

The Johnston Company sells personal computers to the British government. It has just received an order for 200 units to be delivered in London in 6 months. The British government has agreed to pay a total of 250,000 British pounds (1250 pounds per unit) on receipt. At the current pound exchange rate of 1.74, that's equal to $2175 U. S. for each computer, and that's an acceptable price to the Johnston people.

The Johnston Company cannot put British pounds on its books. It has to exchange them for U. S. dollars. This places the company at exchange-rate risk. If the value of the British pound were to decline before the computers were shipped and paid for, the effective sales price received by the Johnston Company would be less.

The company decides to hedge the exchange-rate risk. It does so by selling short British pound futures. The amount to be hedged is 250,000 pounds. This is four times the futures contract size of 62,500 pounds, so four futures contracts are sold. Six months later, when the computers are shipped, the pound has fallen to 1.68; however, the Johnston Company still receives an effective price of $2175 per computer.

### Short Hedge in British Pound Futures

| Cash Exchange Rate | | Futures | |
|---|---|---|---|
| $1.74 | Now | Sold at | $1.78 |
| $1.68 | 6 months later | Bought at | $1.72 |
| Opportunity loss = $ .06 | | Gain = | $ .06 |

Each British pound the Johnston Company receives on delivery of the computers can be exchanged in the cash market for $1.68. The 6 cents per pound profit on the short futures position is added to that, making an effective total of $1.74 that the Johnston Company received for each pound. The price in U. S. dollars that the company received for each computer is calculated by multiplying $1.74 times 250,000 pounds and dividing the answer by 200. That equals $2175.

What happens if the value of the British pound goes up? Will the Johnston Company reap a windfall gain? The answer is, "No." The hedge will block any windfall profits because the loss on the short futures position will offset the potential gain in the cash market.

## Short Hedge in British Pound Futures

| Cash Exchange Rate | | | Futures | |
|---|---|---|---|---|
| | $1.74 | Now | Sold at | $1.78 |
| | $1.82 | 6 months later | Bought at | $1.86 |
| Apparent windfall gain = $ .08 | | | Loss = $ .08 | |

The value of the British pound has risen by 8 cents. But so has the futures price. When you add up the gain in the pound and the loss on the short futures position, you find that they offset; the Johnston Company still receives $1.74 for each pound and $2175 for each computer, as it had planned.

If the Johnston Company had not put on the short hedge, they would have had no futures losses. Each pound they received would have bought them $1.82 instead of $1.74, and their effective price for each computer would have been $2,275 ($1.82 × 250,000 ÷ 200). That's $20,000 in additional profits, or a 4½ percent bonus. Does that mean the hedge was a bad idea? Absolutely not. That's hindsight, which is always 20/20 vision. To complain about a hedge after the fact is tantamount to begrudging your term life insurance last year because you didn't die. The hedge did its job. The cash price of $2,175 for each computer was protected.

**Dynamic hedging requires a price forecast, in order that the hedge may be held in abeyance during periods when favorable cash price movement is expected.**

## Dynamic Hedging

The hedging strategies discussed before are static. The hedges are put in place and left there until they are no longer needed. Their goals are to minimize losses or to just break even against exchange-rate movement. Futures allow the hedger to manage risk. This can be demonstrated by modifying the first example.

Let's assume that you pay the first cash installment of 1 million DM on March 1, as before, at a cost of $500,000. However, before making any decisions about how and when to hedge the balance, you ask your economic research staff for a briefing on the Deutschemark. In their judgment, the DM is currently in a downtrend and is expected to move lower over the next few months. They recommend that you leave your short cash position in DM unhedged.

At this point you have to decide whether you are in the business of forecasting foreign currency exchange rates or manufacturing optics. If you defer your hedge, your entire remaining commitment in cash Deutschemarks is exposed to adverse movement in the exchange rate.

To continue with the example, you decide that the foreign-exchange risk is acceptable. You put the hedge on hold and tell your staff to notify you immediately if there are any changes in the situation. On June 1, when the next cash installment of 1 million DM is due, the market estimate is proven correct; the exchange rate has slipped to .46. The June payment therefore costs you only $460,000 (.46 × 1 million DM).

Then, on June 4, three days later, your research people advise you that downward momentum in the DM appears to be subsiding. They expect the West German currency to firm over the near term and recommend that you hedge your remaining exposure of 2 million Deutschemarks in the futures markets. You take their advice and buy eight contracts of September Deutschemark futures and eight contracts of December Deutschemark futures.

It turns out that your research staff were again correct. On September 1, when the next payment falls due, the exchange rate has inched back up to .47. You buy 1 million cash DM and close out the September futures:

| Cash Exchange Rate | | Futures | |
|---|---|---|---|
| .4600 | June 4 | Buy 8 September DM at | .4623 |
| .4700 | September 1 | Sell 8 September DM at | .4723 |
| Opportunity loss = .0100 | | Gain = | .0100 |

Because of the hedge, the cash Deutschemarks cost you the same as they did in June, or (.46 × 1 million DM =) $460,000.

One week later the seller calls you from Munich. He is badly in need of cash and wonders if you would be willing to make the final December payment immediately. In the interest of goodwill, you accommodate him. The exchange rate is still .47 the next day when you buy the cash Deutschemarks and close out your December futures position.

| Cash Exchange Rate | | | Futures | | |
|---|---|---|---|---|---|
| .4600 | June 4 | | Buy 8 December DM at | .4634 |
| .4700 | September 9 | | Sell 8 December DM at | .4734 |
| Opportunity loss = .0100 | | | | Gain = .0100 |

Thanks again to the hedge, the effective exchange rate is still .46, and the final payment also costs you $460,000 (.46 × 1 million DM).

To sum up,

| March 1 payment | $ 500,000 |
|---|---|
| June 1 payment | 460,000 |
| September 1 payment | 460,000 |
| September 9 payment | 460,000 |
| | $1,880,000 |

The total cost of your acquisition is $1,880,000. That's $120,000 less than than you had expected to pay. This windfall gain is attributable to the delay in putting on the hedge while the exchange rate held the promise of moving favorably. Your long futures position provided protection against the subsequent adverse move in the exchange rate and it allowed you the flexibility of closing out your hedge at any time and without penalty by making an offsetting futures market transaction.

The question that remains to be answered is whether this course of action was speculative. Or, more generally, whether it is a speculation to defer any hedge while favorable movement is expected in cash prices. Speculation is usually defined in terms of a futures position that has no cash counterpart. In this case, the situation was reversed. There was no net futures position; the exposure was entirely on the cash side.

Perhaps the question should be asked of one who waited to hedge and wound up sustaining a loss that would have been entirely avoidable.

## Caveat Revisited

We've said it before, and we'll say it again. To keep things simple, we have made a lot of things come out even in the examples above— hedges comprised whole numbers of futures contracts, the basis didn't change, and cash payment dates and futures delivery months coincided. This symmetry is rarely encountered in actual practice.

We also made our futures analysts omniscient. If they had been wrong, and exchange rates had moved adversely while the buyer's exposure was unhedged, there would have been market losses and the overall cost of the acquisition could have been considerably more than the planned $2 million.

## STOCK INDEXES

**Because of the virtual impossibility of delivering one share of each of several hundred stocks, settlement of stock index futures is made by cash only.**

Futures contracts on stock indexes began trading in February 1982 on the Kansas City Board of Trade. The index underlying this ground-breaking new futures contract was the Value Line Composite Index, an unweighted average of the market prices of some 1700 stocks. This was soon followed by futures contracts on the Standard & Poor's (S&P) 500 Stock Index, the New York Stock Exchange Composite Index, and the Major Market Index.

Before the behavior of these new futures could be observed, economists theorized they would spend most of their time at discounts to their underlying cash indexes. After all, stocks pay dividends; stock index futures do not. Gains in stock transactions may be deferred almost indefinitely; gains in futures must be marked to the market on December 31 each year and income taxes paid on any unrealized gains.

In fact, futures prices have been both above and below the prices of the corresponding cash indexes. The key has not been taxes or dividends but traders' expectations. When traders are bullish on the stock market, they buy stock index futures contracts, and futures move to a premium to the cash index. When traders expect lower stock prices, they sell stock index futures in anticipation, forcing futures to a discount to the cash index.

Many other stock index futures contracts have been introduced over the succeeding years, most with only limited acceptance by the investment community. Today, futures are actively traded on four major stock indexes: the S&P 500, the New York Stock Exchange Composite Index, the American Stock Exchange's Major Market Index, and the Value Line Index. Each index represents an average value of the stocks that are included in the index and changes every time the price of any one of the stocks changes. The indexes vary in both their composition and method of calculation. A detailed description of each index may be found in the information sheets in Chapter 16.

**Stock index futures are of little value in hedging a small portfolio because there would be no dependable correlation between the movement of the index and the price movement of the stocks.**

## Using Stock Index Futures

A stock index represents the broad market. Changes in the index reflect price movement in many different stocks. The index can mask the price movement of individual stocks within it. That is, it is possible for a decline in one stock to be offset by a rise in another, and the index not to move at all. Stock index futures are therefore of little value in hedging a small portfolio comprising only a few stocks because there would be no dependable correlation between the movement of the index and the price movement in the stocks. However, stock index futures can act as an effective hedge when used to protect against price changes in a large, diverse portfolio.

## Long Hedge

To take an example, suppose you were a successful private money manager with 50 percent of your assets invested in A-rated common stocks. You know from experience that your $100 million portfolio tracks very closely with the value of the New York Stock Exchange (NYSE) Composite Index. It is now February 1. In May you will receive $5 million in cash from a new client and, in keeping with your asset allocation, you plan to put $2.5 million of it into equities. The problem is, you expect the stock market to rally substantially in the interim and the prices of the issues you intend to buy to be directly affected.

To hedge against this potential opportunity loss, you decide to buy stock index futures. Inasmuch as your portfolio has a high positive correlation with the NYSE Index, you use that futures contract. You choose the June maturity month because it will be more responsive to current economic forces than a more distant futures contract (and will therefore have less risk of basis change) and yet will not expire before you receive the cash.

To calculate how many futures contracts you will need, you first have to determine the value of the futures contract. This is accomplished by multiplying the futures price by $500. Let's say that June NYSE futures are trading at 154.80. Five hundred dollars times 154.80 equals $77,400. That's the present value of one June NYSE futures contract. You divide $77,400 into

$2.5 million, the amount of stock to be hedged, and get 32.3 futures contracts. Because you can't buy three tenths of a futures contract, you settle for 32 contracts, leaving a fraction of your exposure unhedged.

Your forecast proves to be correct. In May, when the $2.5 million in cash is in hand, the stock market is in the middle a broad rally. The NYSE cash index stands at 158.70 and the June futures are 161.30. You set your stock buying program in motion and sell your 32 June NYSE futures contracts. The results would be:

### Long Hedge in NYSE Futures

| *Cash* | | | *Futures* | |
|---|---|---|---|---|
| NYSE Index at | 152.20 | March 1 | Buy 32 June NYSE at | 154.80 |
| NYSE Index at | 158.70 | May | Sell 32 June NYSE at | 161.30 |
| Opportunity loss = | 6.50 | | Gain = | 6.50 |

The cash NYSE Index rose just over 4 percent in the interim. Given that the prices of the stocks you intended to buy moved right along with the index, $2.5 million in cash buys 4 percent less stock in May than it would have in March. However, the hedge gives virtually all of this lost purchasing power back to you in the form of $104,000 in futures profits (6.50 × $500 × 32 contracts).

## Short Hedge

Bill Thompson is the financial trustee for a major eastern university. The endowment fund he controls is $26 million, about half of which is currently invested in high-quality common stocks.

Mr. Thompson does not believe in finessing the stock market. His goal is to buy and hold top-tier securities for long-term appreciation, rather than to make several small trading profits. He is, however, attuned to major market swings, and he has come to the conclusion over the past few weeks that the stock market is due for a sizable correction.

He has several choices: He can sit tight and weather the storm, if any. He could sell a portion of his stocks and put the proceeds temporarily into cash or fixed-income securities. Or he could hedge his holdings with a short position in stock index futures.

Sitting tight does not appeal to him. It leaves him vulnerable to possibly deep interim losses and would look to the world like he either didn't see the setback coming or didn't know what to do about it. Selling off a part of his stock portfolio would be disruptive and create large transaction costs; if he's wrong about the decline, he could be faced with the unsavory situation of having to buy the same stocks back at higher prices.

He knows from his research that the overall value of his stock portfolio tracks very closely with the value of the Standard & Poor's (S&P) 500 Index, so S&P 500 futures would provide an effective hedge. A futures hedge would leave his stock holdings undisturbed. Transaction costs would be limited to nominal futures commissions and the opportunity cost of the margin put up. Further, a sell stop order could be used for the opening transaction, requiring prices to demonstrate a specified degree of weakness before the hedge were triggered.

He decides to hedge. But this still leaves two questions: how many futures contracts will it take, and when should the hedge be put on? The first question is easily answered. The contract size for S&P 500 futures is $500 times the index. With the index at 250.00, for example, the value of one S&P 500 futures contract is ($500 × 250.00 =) $125,000. Stocks comprise half of the $26 million portfolio, or $13 million. Thirteen million dollars divided by $125,000 equals 104; that's the number of S&P 500 futures contracts needed to fully hedge $13 million worth of stocks.

The second question is not as straightforward, as it requires a market judgment. The stop order to initiate the hedge must be placed far enough away so as not to be triggered by random price movements but not so far that serious losses are sustained before the hedge is activated. Technical analysis can be used to good advantage in selecting the price level at which to place the resting sell stop order.

We'll assume that Mr. Thompson places his futures hedge and that his assessment was correct: the broad stock market falls 13 percent over the next 6 weeks. The results of his hedge would be:

### Short Hedge in S&P 500 Futures

| Cash Index | | Futures | |
|---|---|---|---|
| 250.00 | Now | Sold 104 contracts at | 252.44 |
| 217.42 | 6 weeks later | Current price: | 219.86 |
| Loss = 32.58 | | Gain = | 32.58 |

His portfolio, which is represented by the cash index, would have sustained short-term losses of about $1.7 million (32.58 × $500 × 104) during the period if it had not been hedged. Because there was no change in the basis in this example, the short position earned back the same amount, so his unrealized losses are, at the moment, zero. If Mr. Thompson concluded that the decline had run its course and that the prevailing uptrend was about to take hold again, he would close out his short futures position at this point, returning his stock portfolio to an unhedged status.

However, let's assume that that is not the case. New factors have entered the picture during the 6 weeks, causing our money manager to revise his outlook. He no longer considers the setback as a reaction in a bull market but as the first downward step in a new bear market. The assessment calls for him to sell his common stocks and move the money into the fixed-income sector. However, there's no need for him to "dump" his stock, as the hedge will continue to protect his holdings. He sets an orderly selling program in motion. As his portfolio of stocks is reduced, he gradually closes out his futures positions, leaving the hedge as balanced as he can, until all the stocks are sold and the last short futures position has been covered.

What would have happened if Mr. Thompson has misread the market and stock prices had continued to climb after he had placed his short hedge? Like most investment miscalculations, it would have cost him money. However, in this case the losses would be mostly ones of opportunity. He would lose the potential income that the margin money might have earned elsewhere. He would lose the gains from rising stock prices because the loss on the short futures position—as long as he has it—would cancel them out. And, of course, he would be out the brokerage commissions.

## Portfolio Insurance

Portfolio insurance is another name for dynamic asset allocation. It is also known as dynamic hedging, which you met earlier. The idea is straightforward enough. Over the past 10 years, stocks have outperformed all other liquid investment media. The goal of dynamic asset allocation is to keep money in stocks as long as stock prices are going up. When stock prices start to decline, some stocks are sold and the money moved into risk-free media. When the decline has ended and the stock market has turned up again, the stocks are repurchased.

For large portfolios, stock index futures simplify the strategy somewhat by making it unnecessary to sell and rebuy actual shares. If strategy calls for reducing equity exposure by 2 percent, for example, the portfolio manager can sell short an amount of stock index futures equal to 2 percent of the portfolio's value. That is equivalent to converting 2 percent of the portfolio to cash. When the decline subsides, the portfolio manager covers his short position in futures. The portfolio remains undisturbed. Transaction costs are also much less than those incurred in selling and buying actual stock.

However, if the theory of portfolio insurance is simple, the practice is not. There are many complex questions to be answered. The portfolio insurer must decide the minimum performance he will accept from his portfolio. He must determine what percentage of his portfolio is to be hedged and how much of a decline he will accept in portfolio value before he starts selling futures.

The strategy described above assumes that stock prices have an upward bias and that declines will be moderate and soon corrected. That may not be the case. If the market is very volatile, the portfolio insurer may be forced to sell index futures at much lower prices than he expected, receiving, as a result, little or no hedge protection.

Effective portfolio insurance requires very frequent futures transactions. The portfolio insurer must decide on the timing of this reaction to a stock market decline; will he react instantaneously, or will he wait an hour? 2 hours? until tomorrow? A lagged response may lower transactions costs in a sideways trending market, but it could prove deadly if the market collapses in one trading session.

A hedge in stock index futures *options* is an alternative. Taken before the fact, it would preclude some of the foregoing problems. We'll discuss options in Chapter 14.

The book *Portfolio Insurance* listed at the end of this chapter is a newly published compendium of articles written by 27 leading economists and practitioners and is an excellent source for more information on the subject.

## INTEREST RATES

On October 12, 1975, the opening bell rang on a new breed of futures. On that date the Chicago Board of Trade began trading in the first interest rate futures contract—the Ginnie Mae.

Ginnie Mae stands for GNMA, which stands for Government National Mortgage Association, a division of HUD. The asset underlying this new futures contract was a certificate issued by Ginnie Mae. The certificate represented a pool of $100,000 worth of FHA and VA home mortgages. Payment of principal and interest was "passed through" by Ginnie Mae to the bearer of the certificate and was guaranteed by the U. S. government. Later, when the Ginnie Mae futures market was faltering, a cash-settled contract was introduced in an attempt to revive it. It was not successful, and Ginnie Mae futures are no longer traded actively.

Today's interest rate futures markets can be broken down into short-term and long-term interest rates. The short-term markets comprise U. S. Treasury bill futures and Eurodollar futures. The long-term markets are the U. S. Treasury note futures and U. S. Treasury bond futures. In addition, there is a relatively new futures market in municipal bonds that is based on an index.

Before we talk about futures, however, let's take a brief look at the underlying instruments themselves. Bills are the shortest term Treasury securities. They are auctioned every Monday afternoon by the Federal Reserve in 90-day and 180-day maturities. They are the only Treasury security that does not have a coupon; T-bills are sold at a discount and redeemed at par. This price difference represents the effective yield. Treasury bills are widely held, very liquid, and therefore excellent indicators of money market conditions.

Treasury notes have maturities of 1 to 10 years. They are not discounted. Annual yields are stated in the coupons they bear, and payments are made to noteholders every 6 months. Two-year Treasury notes are issued each month; 4-year notes, 5-year notes and longer are sold quarterly. Treasury notes surged in popularity in the late 1970s.

Treasury bonds are the longest term Treasury security, with maturities extending out to 30 years. Like T-notes, they bear coupons and pay interest semiannually. They are the principal source of revenue for funding of the U. S. national debt and stand as international benchmarks for long-term interest rates.

Municipal bonds are coupon-bearing debt obligations of state and local governments and their authorities, issued primarily to finance public works projects. Interest paid to municipal bondholders is generally free of federal income tax and state income tax in the state of issue. The municipal bond market is over the counter and has grown dramatically in recent years.

A Eurodollar is simply a U. S. dollar on deposit in a bank outside the United States. Most are found in the London, England branches of major world banks, where they are the basis for loans of U. S. dollars to European borrowers. The Eurodollar market began in the late 1950s, ostensibly as a way to avoid certain domestic banking regulations and has grown rapidly in size to rival U. S. markets in short-term instruments.

## The Yield Curve

No discussion of fixed-income securities is complete without mention of comparative yields. In the financial markets, yield refers to the rate of return on an investment. If you buy a $1000 par value U. S. Treasury bond with an 8 percent coupon, it will pay you $80 per year in interest. That dollar amount is fixed. But the market price of a Treasury bond is not fixed. It changes with market conditions. If you paid

**A yield curve plots yield against time to maturity for an array of like securities.**

only $900 for the bond, your yield would be 8.1 percent ($80 ÷ $900). That is referred to as the bond's current yield.

There is also something called "yield to maturity." This number takes into consideration that you will receive par value ($1000) for the bond when it matures. If you bought the bond for less than par, its yield to maturity would be slightly higher than its current yield, reflecting the extra cash you will get when the bond matures. By the same token, if you bought the bond at a price above par, its yield to maturity would be less than the current yield.

A shorthand way to express the relationship between the yield to maturity of different securities is to plot them all together on a graph. The plots are then connected to form a "curve." To be certain that it is only yields that are compared, it is necessary that the securities plotted be similar in risk, callability, conversion features, and the like. The idea is to measure yield against time to maturity, and nothing else.

Treasuries make an excellent example. Suppose it is late 1988 and the following conditions pertain:

U. S. TREASURY NOTES AND BONDS

| Maturity Date | Yield to Maturity |
| --- | --- |
| February 1989 | 7.97% |
| June 1990 | 8.69% |
| November 1992 | 8.96% |
| April 1994 | 9.06% |
| August 1997 | 9.28% |
| May 2001 | 9.36% |
| August 2005 | 9.45% |
| September 2009 | 9.73% |
| November 2015 | 9.92% |
| May 2017 | 10.03% |
| February 2018 | 10.17% |

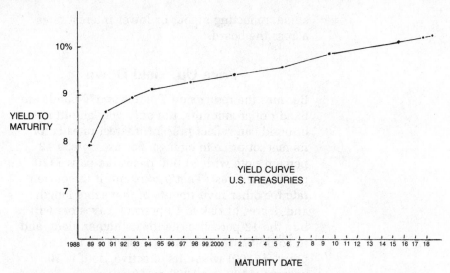

**FIGURE 14.** A yield curve compares securities that differ only in their time to maturity. This example is for U. S. Treasury securities and is based on the maturities and yields shown in the accompanying table. Yields increase as maturities lengthen, so the curve slopes upward to the right. This is referred to as a "normal" yield curve.

A yield curve based on these data is shown in Figure 14. As you can see, short-term yields are lower than the yields farther out. Yields increase as maturities lengthen, so the curve slopes upward to the right. This is referred to as a "normal" yield curve. Investors receive a greater return to compensate them for tying up their money for a longer time. Banks, who generally borrow short-term and lend long-term, find this a healthy economic environment.

When short-term yields are above longer term yields, the yield curve is said to be "inverted." One of the possible causes of an inverted yield curve would be investor expectations that long-term rates are about to fall sharply. Their active buying of long-term paper drives its price up (and yield down).

The entire yield curve structure may also move up or down without changing its shape or

**Prices of fixed-income securities and interest rates are inversely related. When interest rates go up, their prices go down; when interest rates go down, their prices go up.**

angle, reflecting higher or lower interest rates across the board.

## Price Up, Yield Down

Because the returns on T-notes and T-bonds are fixed dollar amounts, the only way an old note or bond can reflect present interest rates is for its market price to change. For example, a 12 percent note with $1,000 par value pays $120 per year interest. That's constant. If the current rate for other investments of that same length and degree of risk is 10 percent, investors will buy the 12 percent note for its higher yield, and in so doing drive its market price up to the point ($1200) where its effective yield is 10 percent ($120 ÷ $1200 = .10).

The process works the same way in the other direction. If a note paying $120 a year is considered by the market to be overpriced (yield too low), investors will sell it and buy something else. Their selling pressure drives the price down. This effectively raises the yield because the $120 per year return does not change.

**$1,000 Par Value Bond with 12% Coupon**

| Ambient Long-Term Interest Rate | Annual Return on Bond | Market Price of Bond* |
|---|---|---|
| 10% | $120 | $1,200 |
| 11% | $120 | $1,091 |
| 12% | $120 | $1,000 (par) |
| 13% | $120 | $ 923 |
| 14% | $120 | $ 857 |

* $120 divided by the interest rate

## FUTURES MARKETS

Interest rate futures markets reflect this inverse relationship. Interest rate futures express the values of the underlying instruments, not the

interest rates themselves. Falling interest rates
mean rising T-bill, T-note, T-bond, and
Eurodollar futures prices. A speculator who is
looking for interest rates to go down buys
interest rate futures. A speculator who is expects
interest rates to rise sells interest rate futures.

## Price Relationships

Interest rate futures prices may be at a discount
or a premium to the prices for cash instruments.
These price relationships do not reflect a
shortage or surplus of the cash commodity, as in
the agricultural futures markets. They reflect the
nature of the yield curve for the underlying cash
asset. If the yield curve of the underlying cash
asset is negative, with yields falling as
maturities become more distant, futures prices
will be at a premium to cash. If the underlying
yield curve is positive (yields rising with
increasing maturities), futures will trade at a
discount to cash.

Arbitrage between the cash and futures
markets keeps these relationships intact. The
rationale is the same as that presented earlier for
grains; arbitrageurs buy the cheaper asset (cash
or futures) and sell the one more dear, forcing
the two prices back into line. As with all futures
contracts, the difference between cash and
futures prices disappears as the futures contract
appraches maturity. However, there are other
considerations, and their complexity puts them
outside the scope of our discussion here.

## Hedging

A hedger who wants to protect against a decline
in interest rates would take a long position in
interest rate futures. For example, suppose a
regional telephone company has just won a
long-standing rate dispute with the state utilities
commission. As a result, the company has been
awarded damages of $5 million in state funds.

The money will be paid in cash and will arrive in about 6 months. The telephone company intends to use the funds to buy a small subsidiary, but that purchase will not take place for about 9 months. The comptroller of the telephone company intends to park the money, when it arrives, in 90-day Treasury bills.

It is now January, and current short-term interest rates are running just under 9 percent. However, the Fed has been loosening money of late. The comptroller fears that short-term rates may slip considerably before his funds arrive and would like to lock in his return now. Cash T-bills are 91.45 and June T-bill futures are trading at 91.25. He buys June T-bills futures. Because the size of the T-bill futures contract is $1 million, he needs five contracts to be fully hedged for 90 days.

On June 1, 6 months later, the comptroller of the telephone company receives a check for $5 million from the state treasurer. He now has two options. He can buy $5 million worth of 90-day T-bills in the cash market and close out his long futures position; or he could take delivery against his long futures position, in which case he will receive (and pay for) $5 million par value worth of cash T-bills with 90 days to maturity. To decide which course to take, the comptroller summarizes the two possible transactions.

If interest rates have fallen, his hedge will have provided protection against the opportunity loss:

### Long Hedge in Treasury Bill Futures

| Cash | | | Futures | |
|---|---|---|---|---|
| T-bills at price of | 91.45 | January | Bought 5 June at | 91.25 |
| Bought 5 at price of | 92.87 | June | Sold 5 June at | 92.87 |
| | +1.42 | | | +1.62 |

If the comptroller closes out his futures position with an offsetting futures transaction and buys the actual T-bills in the cash market, they will cost him 91.25 (92.87 cash less than 1.62 gain in the futures transaction). If he accepts delivery of actual T-bills in settlement of the futures contract, they will also cost him 91.25, the price at which he made his futures contract in January.

If the comptroller's estimate of the situation had been incorrect and interest rates had moved higher in the interim, the hedge results would look something like this:

### Long Hedge in Treasury Bill Futures

| Cash | | | Futures | |
|---|---|---|---|---|
| T-bills at price of | 91.45 | January | Bought 5 June at | 91.25 |
| Bought 5 at price of | 90.50 | June | Sold 5 June at | 90.50 |
| Opportunity gain = | +.95 | | Loss = | −.75 |

It still makes no difference how the comptroller acquires the actual T-bills. If he takes delivery against the futures contract, the T-bills would cost him 91.25; the effective price of T-bills bought in the cash market would be the same: (90.50 cash + .75 futures loss =) 91.25.

In either case, the comptroller has $5 million worth of 90-day cash Treasury bills in June for which he fixed the yield 6 months earlier. These will mature in September, making the cash available for the planned purchase of the small subsidiary telephone company at that time.

## Convergence Cost

As we have said before, the difference between cash and futures prices tends to decrease as the futures contract approaches maturity, and the difference shrinks to very near zero during the delivery period. This convergence of futures and cash prices can create windfall gains or losses for the hedger, depending on the particular situation.

If a short hedge is placed in a normal market (where futures prices are higher than cash), the

**If a short hedge is placed in a normal market (where futures prices are higher than cash), the convergence of futures and cash creates gains for the hedger.**

## CONVERGENCE OF CASH AND FUTURES PRICES

| | SHORT HEDGE | | LONG HEDGE |
|---|---|---|---|

**INVERTED MARKET**

| Cash (Long) | ↓ Loss | Cash (Short) | ↓ Gain |
| Futures (Short) | Loss ↑ | Futures (Long) | Gain ↑ |

**NORMAL MARKET**

| Futures (Short) | ↓ Gain | Futures (Long) | ↓ Loss |
| Cash (Long) | Gain ↑ | Cash (Short) | Loss ↑ |

**FIGURE 15.** Cash and futures prices converge as futures approach maturity and are virtually equal during the delivery period. This convergence changes the basis, creating gains or losses for the hedger, depending on the situation. Long hedgers sustain convergence losses in normal markets and convergence gains in inverted markets. The reverse is true for short hedgers. The effect is so strong, in fact, that short hedges may be inadvisable in a steeply inverted market. The diagram here depicts these effects graphically.

convergence of futures on cash creates gains for the hedger. It doesn't matter whether the (short) futures price goes down or the (long) cash price goes up; both movements create gains. With a long hedge in a normal market, convergence causes losses. These effects are shown graphically in Figure 15.

The situation is reversed in an inverted market. When futures prices are below cash, convergence of cash and futures prices creates gains for a long hedge and losses for a short hedge (see Figure 15).

The two T-bill examples just cited were long hedges in inverted markets, an ideal environment. In both cases the opening basis

was +.20 (91.45 − 91.25), and the closing basis
was zero. The hedger earned a 20-point windfall
gain from the change in basis. That is why the
comptroller paid only 91.25 for his T-bills,
though the cash price for T-bills was 91.45
when the hedge was established.

## Another Example

The financial officer of a small midwestern
college receives a behest from the estate of an
alumnus who has recently died. The gift is in
the form of securities; specifically, $1 millon par
value of long-term U. S. Treasury bonds. The
financial officer's long-range outlook for interest
rates is higher, and he'd rather have the money
in other investment media; however, the
alumnus has specified in his will that the bonds
are not to be sold for 1 year after his death. To
protect the market value of the bonds during
that time, the financial officer hedges by selling
10 T-bond futures contracts on the Chicago
Board of Trade, selecting a maturity month that
is beyond the year waiting period.

The financial officer's forecast turns out to be
correct. One year later, long-term rates have
risen two full percentage points, and the prices
of cash T-bonds have fallen from 94 down into
the low 70s.

The results of the hedge (no basis change):

### Short Hedge in Treasury Bond Futures

| Cash Bonds | | Futures | |
|---|---|---|---|
| 94-22 | Now | Sold 10 contracts at | 93-22 |
| 72-29 | 1 year later | Bought 10 contracts at | 71-29 |
| −21-25 | | | +21-25 |

The 21-25/32 fall in the price of cash bonds
translates to a loss of $212,500 for the $1
million portfolio. If the financial officer had not
hedged the cash T-bonds, they would have lost
more than 20 percent of their value in 1 year. A

performance like that could put him back into the job market.

Is this example realistic? It would not have been 20 years ago, when bond prices moved like turtles. It is now. In 1987–1988, for example, Treasury bond prices lost and then regained 18 full percentage points (576/32) in the space of just 8 months.

## Suggested Reading

*Hedging Foreign Exchange*, by Eric T. Jones and Donald L. Jones. John Wiley & Sons, Inc., New York City, 1987.

*Stock Index Futures*, by Neil S. Weiner. John Wiley & Sons, Inc., New York City, 1984.

*The New Financial Instruments*, by Julian Walmsley. John Wiley & Sons, Inc., New York City, 1988.

*Portfolio Insurance*, edited by Donald L. Luskin. John Wiley & Sons, Inc., New York City, 1988.

# 13

# Money Management for Speculators

It's difficult to say anything provocative about money management. Most advice sounds like little more than common sense. And yet it is not common. Unsuccessful futures trading can almost always be traced back to bad money management. Anyone can be wrong on the markets. To allow a mistaken futures position to wipe out your trading capital is another matter. The philosophy is summed up in an adage that's been around for so long that it can be easily overlooked:

*Cut your losses short, and let your profits run.*

We once knew a speculator who would close out a new position immediately if it ended the day with a loss. He might try again tomorrow, but he would not keep any new position overnight unless it settled that first day with an unrealized profit. This may be a bit extreme, but it epitomizes the philosophy.

**Unsuccessful futures trading can almost always be traced back to bad money management.**

The difficulty with closing out a losing position is that you have to admit to yourself (and to your broker) that you were wrong about the market. The larger the loss, the more egg on your face. You also convert a paper loss into a realized loss. Money that was only in jeopardy before is now irrevocably gone. You can no longer nurture the vain hope that the market will turn around tomorrow and bail you out.

Studies of actual trading performance conducted by the U. S. Department of Agriculture concluded that staying too long with a losing position was one of the major reasons why speculators in the study lost money. Willingness to close out a losing position early was likewise identified as the mark of a successful futures trader.

## Setting Maximum Risk

It seems out of keeping with the computer age, but simply deciding beforehand how much loss you are willing to accept in a trade will substantially increase your chances for success. The maximum acceptable loss can be expressed as an amount of money—say, $500—or as a percentage of original margin. If your unrealized loss reaches that predetermined level, you close out the position.

## Using Stop Orders

The stop order is tailor-made for cutting losses short. It rests at some predetermined point above or below the current price level, waiting to close out the offending position with no further action or decision on your part. You could be on the golf course or vacationing in Europe at the time.

How do you select the price level at which to place the stop order? You can set a maximum acceptable loss, as we discussed just now. Or, you could put technical analysis to work for you. For example, let's say that cotton prices have staged a sustained advance over the past 8 months. You now believe that cotton has topped out and is on the threshold of a sustained decline. You are not in the market.

The contract high in December cotton, which was set 3 weeks ago, is 66.70 cents per pound. Since then, prices have backed off a penny or so. You sell short one contract of December cotton at 65.57 and at the same time place a buy stop just above the old contract high at 66.71. If cotton prices rally to new contract highs, your buy stop will be activated, and you will be out of the market with a loss of about $600 plus commissions. If cotton prices fail to make new highs and the decline you anticipated begins, you will be well positioned.

Another example: You have been long one contract of December gold futures for 4 weeks and have a $2000 profit. To protect it, you intend to close out your long position if gold prices show evidence of weakening. December gold is trading at $462.50 an ounce. You decide, on the basis of technical analysis, that there is good potential support in December gold at 458.00; that if prices break below that level, the market could go much lower. You place a sell stop order at 457.90, which is one "tick" below 458.00.

If weakness sets in and your stop order is hit, it becomes a market order, and your long position is sold out immediately. If gold continues to rally and never touches 457.90, your stop order will never be activated; you would continue to accrue profits. As gold prices climb, you would move your stop order up, each time using technical analysis to help you determine the price level at which to place the stop.

As you may have noticed, the stop order—in addition to cutting losses short—also allows profits to run. Profits are not taken unless the price level stated in the stop order is reached.

**Snuffing out small losses while they are still small is the single most important precept of good futures market money management.**

As long as the market is moving in a favorable direction, the futures position is left open.

A good rule is that a stop-loss order (which is what we have been discussing here) is never moved in the direction of greater losses. In other words:

*A sell stop-loss is never lowered, a buy stop-loss is never raised.*

Raising a buy stop or lowering a sell stop is wrong on two counts. First, it demonstrates reluctance to take the loss, which is a dangerous mind-set. It also cancels what should have been a good argument for placing the stop at its original level.

Snuffing out small losses while they are still small is the single most important precept of good futures market money management. There is no recovery if you hang on stubbornly to a losing position until it has consumed most of the money you have set aside for trading, as you will have no capital left to try again. On the other hand, a series of small losses can be recouped with one good gain.

This is not to say that such stop orders always work without a hitch. Markets can be perverse. Prices have been known to back down, touch off waiting sell stops, and immediately take off on an extended rally. As we have said before, technical analysis deals with probabilities, not certainties.

## OTHER MONEY MANAGEMENT GUIDELINES

Successful futures speculators generally adhere to certain other principles.

### Diversification

If you have a large equity in the futures markets, it is wise not to place it all in one or two commodities. Unlike the stock market, the prices of most commodities move independently. It is possible for the precious metals to be be rallying, the grains to be moving sideways, and the petroleum complex to be in a downtrend—all at the same time. Professional money managers who control large trading accounts will have positions in as many as 10 different futures markets, to take advantage of the fact that a setback in one may be offset by gains in another.

## Have a Plan

When you take a futures position, consider where you are going with it. Decide how much loss you are willing to take, and how much profit you expect to gain. Compare the two. Is the possible profit worth the possible loss? Some traders make a written plan, listing all the factors that bear on a particular trade. Futures positions taken on impulse have a low probability of success.

Even experienced traders can fall into the trap of acting without adequate forethought. A professional floor trader on the Chicago Board of Trade once told this true story to us. He had had a very successful day in the soybean oil pit, where he spends most of his time. He had to pass the silver pit on the way back to his office; it was still active, as it closed later than bean oil. He stopped to say something to a fellow trader there. Before long he was caught up in the buying and selling, and in just a few minutes in that unfamiliar market he lost most of what he had gained that day.

**If the loss of the money you are using to trade would have a significant effect on your life-style, the money does not belong in the futures markets.**

## Keep Your Own Counsel

Don't underestimate yourself. If you have done your homework and made your trading decision, don't let yourself be swayed by random remarks or rumors. There is never any shortage of "expert" opinion on any topic. If conditions really change, of course you'll have to change with them. But be slow to discard the analysis you did.

## Be Open to Divorce

Psychologists have established that most of us are vulnerable to what they call the "endowment effect." In simpler terms, it means that people prefer the status quo even when faced with good arguments for changing it. There's not much you can do about it, except to be aware of the phenomenon when you are deciding whether or not to divorce yourself from a losing futures position.

## How Much Money?

Trading capital should be above and beyond the funds set aside for college, medical emergencies, and retirement. A good rule is: If the loss of the money you are using to trade would have a significant effect on your life-style, the money does not belong in the futures markets.

## Try to Keep Cool

An objective, unemotional approach to the futures markets is easy to maintain—until you take a position. The stakes change when real money is involved. A loss taken on paper is philosophical. A loss taken in your bank account represents a vacation, or a new car, or a paint job for the house that you won't have.

A speculative futures position is a unique stress generator. It makes little difference how you're doing. If you have gains, you are concerned that you will lose them; if you have losses, you are concerned that you will have to take them. The resulting psychological pressure can lead you to cut your profits short and let your losses run, which is the exact opposite of the successful strategy discussed before.

One of the benefits of technical analysis, and one that we haven't mentioned specifically before, is that it provides an objective basis for trading decisions. It supplies a mathematical rationale for picking price objectives. It enables a trader to assign values to market strength or weakness and gives him tangible reasons for selecting one point over another to enter or leave the market. It helps maintain an objective approach.

## Adding to Positions

Never add to a losing position. The fact that the strategy has the name of "averaging down" gives it no credence. You should be closing out the offending position, not increasing it.

Profitable positions may be added to, but care must be taken not to build a top-heavy structure that will collapse at the first small decline. As an example, suppose you bought one contract of June T-bond futures at 92-10. June bonds immediately rose to 93-00. Pleased with your profits, you bought two more contracts at 93-05. The rally continued, and you jubilantly bought four more contracts at 94-12, which is where June bonds are trading now.

The following is a summary of your transactions:

| Purchase | Total Number of Contracts | Average Price |
|----------|---------------------------|---------------|
| Bought 1 at 92-10 | 1 | 92-10 |
| Bought 2 at 93-05 | 3 | 92-28 |
| Bought 4 at 94-12 | 7 | 94-00 |

Because you bought a larger number of contracts at each higher price, the average price of all contracts increased sharply. The average price is now only 12 ticks below the current price; any setback of more than $12/32$ would place your entire position in a loss. You would have called the market right but self-destructed in your trading strategy.

A more prudent way to add to a profitable futures position is to make each successive addition the same or smaller size than the original position. Then the average price will rise more slowly, and you will never find yourself in the situation where a small decline would cancel all your trading profits.

## PROFESSIONAL MONEY MANAGEMENT

People who manage money for others in the futures markets fall into two categories: commodity trading advisors and commodity pool operators.

### Commodity Trading Advisor

A commodity trading advisor (CTA) is defined as anyone who receives pay to counsel others on the advisability of buying and selling futures contracts. The advice can be verbal or written and includes electronic delivery.

CTAs also manage money directly, utilizing the client's power of attorney to order trades for the client's account. In this case, the CTA is required to provide the client, and the client is required to acknowledge in writing, a risk disclosure document. It spells out the financial pitfalls inherent in futures trading, discloses the business backgrounds of the CTA and his principals for the preceding 5 years, describes the trading program the CTA uses, tells how the CTA is to be paid for his services, and presents the CTA's actual past trading performance.

Unless he is also a futures commission merchant, the CTA cannot accept funds directly from a client. The funds must instead be sent to the futures commission merchant through whom the CTA trades, and where the client's account is maintained.

CTAs who manage money directly may charge two kinds of fees. Almost all charge an incentive fee, which is based on performance and typically runs 10 percent to 25 percent of profits above the previous high "watermark." Some CTAs also charge a management fee, which is paid whether or not the account earns a profit. This is generally a fraction of a percentage per month of the funds under management. Most CTAs require a substantial amount of money to open a managed account. Successful and well-known CTAs may have minimum account sizes of $100,000 or more. The client is responsible for all losses incurred by the CTA in trading the client's account.

CTAs must be registered with the National Futures Association, a self-regulatory organization that began operation in 1982. Registration with the National Futures Association does constitute a recommendation of the CTA but signifies only that he has met the Commodity Futures Trading Comission's general requirements concerning experience, education, business affiliations, and financial status.

## Commodity Pool Operator

The commodity pool is the "mutual fund" of the futures markets. Virtually all commodity pools in the United States are organized as limited partnerships, with the commodity pool operator (CPO) acting as the general partner. The public participant in a commodity pool is a limited partner, and as such his financial risk in the enterprise is expressly limited to the capital he initially puts up. The trading advisor for a commodity pool—the one who makes the day-to-day buy and sell decisions based on his market knowledge and experience—is usually a third party chosen by the general partner.

CPOs are required to deliver to each prospective limited partner and receive written acknowledgement of a risk disclosure document. It must fully identify the pool; present the business background of the CPO and each of his principals for the past 5 years; disclose any actual or implied conflicts of interest; and show the pool's actual trading performance for its entire history or the preceding 3 years, whichever is less.

The amount of money needed to participate in a commodity pool varies from pool to pool, but it is generally much less than the minimum amounts required by CTAs. Many commodity pools are sold in units of $1000, with a minimum purchase of as few as two units. Generally, CPOs must be registered with the National Futures Association if they have pools totaling more than $200,000 or any pool with more than 15 participants.

Some commodity pools are huge, controlling millions of dollars in assets. Like any other big business, they have administrative, legal, and accounting expenses, and many pools have front-end sales charges. The risk disclosure document provided by the CPO to prospective participants is required to reveal these expenses on its front page and to state how they are to be defrayed.

A person considering joining a commodity pool should be aware of the trading advisor's track record in the markets. The record should comprise real-time trading, not a hypothetical computer simulation. The performance of commodity pools varies widely. Among the pools (funds) reported on by *Futures* magazine, the best record for the year 1987 was +201.1 percent return on equity. The worst was −37.2 percent, but that does not include pools that were closed out and removed from the list before the end of the year.

Inquiry should be made into the procedure for getting out of the pool. Many pools allow the participants to close out their accounts only on certain predetermined dates; for example, on the last day of each calendar quarter. A prospective participant should also learn the pool's policy for distributing any gains.

The principal advantages of a commodity pool are (1) limited risk and (2) the ability to achieve wide diversification and professional money management for as little as $2000 in equity.

## PROPRIETARY TRADING SYSTEMS

You won't be around the futures markets long before you start to receive unsolicited mail selling books, charting services, market letters, and the like. The highest priced items offered will be trading methods, which can have price tags of $2500 or more.

The trading method will usually have been designed and tested by a private individual, who is now offering it for sale. It is invariably based on technical analysis and may be worked by hand or by computer. Presented in the promotional copy will be a profit/loss record for the advertised method that is very successful.

The first question to ask is whether the trading performance shown in the brochure is real or theoretical. There's a vast difference between trading profits in the real world and a fictitious track record generated by simulated trades using past data.

The simulation process goes something like this: First, some trading rules are devised. They can comprise a few simple criteria or several pages of mathematical formulas. The trading rules are translated into a computer program. This program is fed into a computer along with a bank of historical data containing daily high, low, and closing prices for several futures markets. The computer simulates trading the rules over an extended period in the past. After each run, the results are examined, and the computer program is fine-tuned to optimize the gains and losses. The fine tuning often includes the addition of criteria for increasing the size of

**There's a vast difference between trading profits in the real world and a fictitious track record generated by simulated trades using past data.**

winning positions, as that has a dramatic effect on overall profits.

The final program comprises a full-blown trading method that has worked extremely well in past markets. But that's not the question. No one can trade yesterday's markets. The question is, how well will the trading method work on tomorrow's markets? To protect prospective buyers of proprietary trading methods, advertisers are required by law to include in their promotional copy statements to the effect that

> Unlike an actual performance record, simulated results do not represent actual trading.
>
> Because trades shown have not actually been executed, results may under- or overcompensate for certain market factors; for example, lack of liquidity.
>
> Simulated trading programs in general are designed with the benefit of hindsight.
>
> No representation is being made that any account will or is likely to achieve profits or losses similar to those shown here.

That should be enough said.

# Suggested Reading

*Commodity Market Money Management*, by Fred Gehm. John Wiley & Sons, Inc., New York City, 1983.

*Futures Trading: Concepts and Strategies*, by Robert E. Fink and Robert A. Feduniak, New York Institute of Finance, New York City, 1988.

*The Complete Guide to the Futures Markets*, by Jack Schwager. John Wiley & Sons, Inc., New York City, 1984.

# 14

# Futures Options

Y ou have just been transferred to Washington, DC. You come ahead to house hunt while your wife and children stay with her mother in San Francisco. You find the ideal house. It has just been completed and is standing empty. The price is $225,000. Concerned that the house may be sold to someone else before your wife can see it, you offer the builder $500 for the exclusive privilege of buying the house for $225,000 at any time during the next 10 days. The builder agrees.

You have bought an option on the house. During the next 10 days you may exercise the option and buy the house for the agreed price of $225,000. If you do not exercise the option, it will expire at the end of that time and the builder will keep your $500.

For many years there was an established over-the-counter market in options on common stock in the United States. If you're old enough, you may remember the dealer's advertisements in the newspapers. The stocks on which the options were offered were usually "blue chips" like IBM and AT&T. You bought the option from the dealer, who often represented a third party who owned the stock.

Over-the-counter stock options were not transferable. Unless a special arrangement could be made with a dealer to take it back and resell it, there were only two courses of action open to the option buyer: Exercise it, or let it expire.

An over-the-counter market in options on futures contracts had a short, scandal-plagued life in the early 1970s. Unscrupulous dealers, promising huge possible rewards with low risk, took in millions of dollars in premiums. But they did not hold the underlying futures contracts. They held only the hope that the options they sold would never become profitable to the buyers. The game ended when a sufficient number of option buyers with winning positions went looking for their rewards and found not cashiers' checks but disconnected telephones and no forwarding addresses.

Since 1982, futures options have been traded on futures exchanges, where their financial integrity is warranted by the exchange and an option clearinghouse. The assets underlying these options are futures contracts traded on that same exchange. Exercise of the option results in the transfer of a futures position from the option seller to the option buyer at the striking price.

Exchange traded options, in addition to enhancing investor confidence, added an important third possible course of action for option buyers and sellers. No longer were their choices limited to exercising the option or letting it expire. Like a futures contract, an exchange-traded option position can be offset with an opposing market transaction, and the option buyer or seller is then out of the market. This innovation opened the door to a dramatic increase in futures option activity.

## NUTS AND BOLTS

The option you bought on the house in the preceding example is referred to as a *call*. A call confers the right to *buy* an asset within a certain period of time at an agreed price. (It gives you the privilege of calling the asset to you.) The $225,000 was the option's *exercise price* or *striking price*. The day the option ran out is called its *expiration date*. The $500 you gave the builder is referred to as a *premium*.

There are also options that entitle you to *sell* something to someone else. These are known as *puts*. (They give you the right to put it to the other person.) The definitions of exercise price, expiration date, and premium are the same.

A futures option takes its name from the futures contract underlying it. For example, a call option on December T-bond futures with a striking price of 90-00 would be referred to as

*December T-Bond 90 Call*

Futures contract     Striking price     Kind of option

The name of the futures contract is first. This is followed by the striking price, which is chosen by the exchange and is always a round number (no fractions); and last, the kind of option (put or call).

If you buy a December T-bond 90 call and exercise it, you will receive from the option seller a long position in December T-bond futures at a price of 90-00.

A put option on April hog futures with a striking price of 52.00 cents per pound would be referred to as:

April hogs 52 put

If you bought this option and exercised it, you would receive a short position in April hog futures at a price of 52.00 cents per pound.

**A put option on April hog futures with a striking price of 52.00 cents per pound would be referred to as an April hogs 52 put.**

There are exceptions. There are listed options that mature in months where there is no corresponding futures contract. For example, there are July and August options on Deutschemark futures and December options on world sugar futures; but there are no July or August Deutschemarks nor December sugar. These (and other) options have been added by the exchanges to provide option traders with more choices. The futures contracts underlying these options are those next closest in time. For example, if the holder of a July Deutschemark call option exercises it, he will receive a long position in September Deutschemark futures.

## Actual Prices

We can learn a great deal by examining a typical newspaper price table for a day's trading in futures options. The following is for options on crude oil futures:

### CRUDE OIL (NYMEX); 1,000 Barrels; Dollars per Barrel

| Strike Price | CALLS | | | PUTS | | |
|---|---|---|---|---|---|---|
| | June | July | August | June | July | August |
| 15 | 2.18 | 2.43 | 2.46 | 0.01 | 0.04 | 0.11 |
| 16 | 1.18 | 1.41 | 1.60 | 0.01 | 0.11 | 0.25 |
| 17 | 0.24 | 0.66 | 0.91 | 0.06 | 0.36 | 0.56 |
| 18 | 0.01 | 0.23 | 0.43 | 0.80 | 0.93 | 1.08 |
| 19 | 0.01 | 0.07 | 0.19 | 1.72 | 1.77 | 1.84 |
| 20 | 0.01 | 0.03 | 0.09 | 2.72 | 2.78 | 2.85 |

Est. sales 25,213; Prev. sales 10,898 calls; 13,747 puts
Prev. open interest 106,279 calls; 133,403 puts

The top line identifies the market. The letters *NYMEX* stand for New York Mercantile Exchange, where both crude oil futures and options on crude oil futures are traded. One thousand barrels is the size of the underlying futures contract. The premium for the option is—like the price of the underlying futures

contract—expressed in dollars per barrel.
Volume and open interest data are shown at the
bottom of the table. As you can see, crude oil
futures options are quite active; in fact, they are
second only to T-bond futures options in
liquidity.

The far-left column shows the striking prices
that are currently available for trading. These
striking prices are selected by the exchange, and
new strikes will be added when necessary to
keep with the market. For example, if crude oil
futures prices began to trade in the $20 to $21
per barrel range, the exchange would add
options with strikes of 21 and 22.

The next six columns show call and put
settlement prices (premiums) for the various
maturity months. Calls are available with
maturities of June, July, and August. Puts are
available for the same 3 months. These
maturities coincide with the maturity months of
their underlying futures contracts.

There are always three option maturities
available for trading. In late May, for example,
when the June options mature and are taken off
the board, the exchange will open trading in
September puts and calls.

To translate the premiums you see here into
dollars and cents, you have to do some
arithmetic. The premium is expressed, as we
said before, in dollars per barrel. The premium
of 1.41 for the July 16 call, for example, means
$1.41 per barrel. This number multiplied by the
contract size of 1000 barrels equals $1410.
That's what it would cost you (plus
commissions, of course) to buy the July crude
oil 16 call. That's the amount that would be
deposited into your account if you sold a July
crude oil 16 call.

In most futures options, the premiums are
expressed in the same terms as the underlying
futures markets. Premiums for sugar options are
in cents per pound for 112,000 pounds; so are
sugar futures. Gold option premiums and gold

futures prices are both expressed in dollars per troy ounce. Options on grain futures are all based on 5000 bushels, and their premiums have fractions just like grain futures prices (23¾, for example).

There are three exceptions. They are the options on T-bonds, 10-year T-notes, and Municipal Bond Index futures. In each case the futures price changes in increments of 32nds, whereas option premiums change in increments of 64ths.

## MORE NUTS AND BOLTS

You met some of the special terms that surround options before. We'll go over them again, and then there are a few others you should know.

*Premium.* The market price of an option, paid by the option buyer and received by the option seller.

*Expiration date.* The day on which an option expires. After that date the option is worthless and must be abandoned.

*Exercise (striking) price.* The price at which the futures contract changes hands if the option is exercised.

Because it confers the right to obtain a long position, the value of a call option increases when the price of the underlying futures contract increases. When the call becomes profitable to exercise—that is, when you can make a profit by buying the option, exercising it, and closing out the resulting futures position— the option is said to be *in the money*. A call is in the money, therefore, whenever the underlying futures price is above the option's strike price. As an example, suppose you held a December gold 425 call and December gold futures were trading at 432.70. If you exercised the call you could acquire a long position in

**The premium is the market price of an option, paid by the option buyer and received by the option seller.**

**The exercise or striking price of an option is the price at which the futures contract changes hand if the option is exercised.**

December gold futures at an effective price of $425 per ounce and immediately resell it at $432.70 per ounce in the open market. Your profit would be ($432.70 − $425.00 =) $7.70 per ounce, or a total of $770.00 on the 100-ounce futures contract.

If the price of December gold should fall to 420.00, the call option in the previous example would be referred to as *out of the money*. It would be $5.00 per ounce cheaper to buy the futures contract directly on the exchange (420.00) than to obtain it by exercising the option (425.00).

On the rare occasions when the option's striking price and the price of the underlying futures are the same, the option is said to be *at the money*.

The mechanics of a put are just the opposite. The owner of a put has the right to sell the underlying futures contract at the striking price. Short positions gain in value when prices decline; so, therefore, does a put. A put is in the money when the underlying futures price is *below* the put's striking price because it is then more advantageous to acquire the short position via exercise than through an open futures market sale.

For example, suppose you owned a December T-bond 94 put and December T-bond futures were currently trading at 93-22. You could sell the futures short at 93-22 on the CBOT. But you could in effect sell December T-bond futures short at 94-00—$10/32$ higher—by exercising the put, so the put is in the money. If December T-bonds were to rally up to 94-12, however, it would cost you $12/32$ more to exercise the put than to sell short outright; the put would now be out of the money.

## Option Value

An option has no practical value. You can't live in it or wear it to stay warm on a cold day. An option is worth what someone else will give you

for it. If you had an option to buy a $15,000
sailboat for $5000, you would have no trouble
finding a sailor willing to give you $6000 for the
option, as he could exercise it, buy the boat, and
save himself $4000. You wouldn't find many
willing to give you $10,000 for the option, as it
would offer no advantage at that price.

Like futures prices, option values (premiums)
are established by open bids and offers on the
trading floor of the exchange. If you dissect the
premium, however, you find that it is not
homogeneous but is composed of two different
kinds of value.

To take an example, the July crude oil 16 call
previously mentioned had a premium of 1.41 or
$1.41 per barrel. Although it doesn't show in the
table, the settlement price for July crude oil
futures that day was 17.02, or $17.02 per barrel.
That means the underlying long futures position
in July crude oil could be obtained at the
striking price of $16.00 per barrel and sold at
the market price of $17.02 per barrel, for a profit
of $1.02 per barrel. The call option is in the
money by $1.02. That amount has a name: It's
called the option's *intrinsic value*.

Intrinsic value is the difference between the
option's striking price and the underlying
futures price. An option that is in the money
has intrinsic value. An option that is out of the
money has zero intrinsic value. Intrinsic value
changes when the price of the underlying
futures contract changes. In the preceding
example, if July crude oil futures closed the next
day at 16.84, down .18, the intrinsic value of the
July 16 call would fall to .84. That's also a
decline of .18 (1.02 − .84).

But that's not the whole story. Take another
look at the premium for the July 16 call. It's
1.41. That's greater than the intrinsic value by
(1.41 − 1.02 =) .39. There's something else
going on here. Why would a trader pay more for
an option than it's worth? If you said something
about time, you're right. That .39 is known as

the option's *time value*. It represents what
market participants are willing to pay simply for
the time the option has left to run. Time value is
found by removing the intrinsic value from the
premium. What's left can be nothing else.

Time value reacts not to changes in the
underlying futures price but to the ticking of the
clock. It follows that the more days an option
has until it matures, the greater should be its
time value. We can verify this statement by
using the newspaper price table presented
before. Look at the striking price of 16. For both
calls and puts, the premiums increase as the
options move across the calendar. To prove that
increasing time values are primarily responsible,
we'll separate them out.

### Crude Oil Options

| Option | Premium | Maturity | Futures Price | Intrinsic Value | Time Value |
|--------|---------|----------|---------------|-----------------|------------|
| 16 calls | 1.18 | June | 17.00 | 1.00 | 0.18 |
| | 1.41 | July | 17.02 | 1.02 | 0.39 |
| | 1.60 | August | 17.01 | 1.01 | 0.59 |
| 16 puts | 0.01 | June | 17.00 | 0.00 | 0.01 |
| | 0.11 | July | 17.02 | 0.00 | 0.11 |
| | 0.25 | August | 17.01 | 0.00 | 0.25 |

*Buyers are willing to pay more for options
with longer maturities because they provide
more time for their hopes to be realized. Sellers
demand more for options with longer maturities
because they are at risk for a greater period.*

The preceding breakdown contains other
lessons. All the puts shown are out of the
money, as their exercise price of 16 is well
below their underlying futures prices. Their
intrinsic value is therefore zero. When an option
has zero intrinsic value, it's premium comprises
entirely time value. And this means that if
nothing else changes, the premium will drop to
virtually nothing just before the option expires.

**Buyers are willing
to pay more for
options with longer
maturities because
they provide more
time for their hopes
to be realized.
Sellers demand
more for options
with longer
maturities because
they are at risk of
exercise for a
greater period.**

That's why you sometimes hear an option referred to as a "wasting asset." The June 16 crude oil put provides an example. This out-of-the-money option is very near expiration, and its (all-time-value) premium is only ($.01 × 1000 barrels =) $10.

## Other Influences

We've seen how the time left to maturity affects an option's premium. There are two other major influences on the prices that buyers and sellers are willing to accept: the option's striking price and the volatility of the underlying futures price.

The first is self-evident. If an in-the-money 50 call has a premium of $3, the same call with a striking price of 45 is going to be worth $5 more, as it has an additional $5 of intrinsic value. This effect can be readily seen in the newspaper price table. The expiring June 15 call would cost you 1.00 more than the June 16 call, and that is exactly equal to the difference in their striking prices.

The effect of volatility is not as concrete but is very important. Buyers of options do so in the hope that the underlying futures price will move favorably and the option will increase in value. If the underlying futures price doesn't move, but instead trades quietly in a narrow range, their hopes are dashed. Buyers are therefore willing to pay more for options on high-flying futures, and option sellers likewise insist on receiving more for them.

An extraordinary example of the effect of volatility on option premiums can be drawn from the soybean futures market in early 1988. In April, soybeans traded quietly. Then the specter of drought appeared, and the market erupted. Soybean options should therefore have had much more time value in June than they did in May, before the drought materialized. Here is the actual comparison:

**Soybean Call Options**

| Date | Option | Underlying Futures Price | Premium | Intrinsic Value | Time Value |
|------|--------|------|---------|-----------------|------------|
| May 5 | August | | | | |
| | 675 | 7.08 | 40 | 33 | 7 |
| June 21 | September | | | | |
| | 1025 | 10.36 | 95 | 11 | 84 |

From May 5 to June 21, the time value of a slightly in-the-money soybean call option with 3 months to expiration increased from 7 cents to 84 cents, or 12 times over. The only factor that is significantly different between the two options is the volatility of the underlying futures contract at the time. In May volatility was normal. Six weeks later, soybean futures were swinging wildly between expanded daily price limits.

## STRATEGIES

### Buying Calls

The simplest, most direct use for an option is as a straight bet on the direction of prices over the next several days or weeks. If you believe conditions are right for soybean prices to take off, you could buy a call option on a soybean futures contract. If bean prices escalate, so will the value of your option, which can then be sold at a profit.

Why would a speculator choose an option over an outright long futures position in this situation? The most important reason is limited risk.

*The option buyer's risk is limited to the price he paid for the option. No matter how far prices go against him, the option buyer will never receive a margin call. The worst that can happen is that the option expires worthless and the entire premium is lost.*

**The option buyer's risk is limited to the price he paid for the option. No matter how far prices go against him, the option buyer will never receive a margin call. The worst that can happen is that the option expires worthless and the entire premium is lost.**

Known, limited risk makes a futures option a more conservative investment than an outright long or short futures position. The differences can be readily seen if the two are directly compared:

### Gold: Long Call Option versus Long Futures Position

DECEMBER GOLD FUTURES PRICE = 440.00

DECEMBER GOLD 440 CALL PREMIUM = 9.00

|  | Gold Futures | | Gold 440 Call Option | |
|---|---|---|---|---|
| 1. Gold futures advance to 464.00 | Buy at | 440.00 | Buy at | 9.00 |
| | Sell at | 464.00 | Sell at | 31.00 |
| | | +24.00 | | +22.00 |

When futures prices advanced, gains in the call option virtually kept pace with gains in the futures. The difference in profits was $2.00 per ounce. The reason? The option lost some time value while all this was going on.

The unique advantage of the call option shows in outcome No. 2, where gold prices fell sharply. A long position in futures would have lost 32.00, or $3200. The loss in the option was limited to $900, the premium paid.

|  | | | | |
|---|---|---|---|---|
| 2. Gold futures decline to 408.00 | Buy at | 440.00 | Buy at | 9.00 |
| | Sell at | 408.00 | Expires worthless | |
| | | −32.00 | | −9.00 |

These transactions can be viewed in another light. The margin for the futures position in gold would be in the neighborhood of $3000; the rate of return on investment in the futures position is therefore $2,400 ÷ $3,000 = 80 percent. The premium for the option is $900 ($9.00 per ounce × 100 ounces). The rate of return on the call option is $2,300 ÷ $900 = 255 percent.

Before you rush to the phone to start taking advantage of such dramatic profit possibilities, let's add another possible outcome:

|  | Gold Futures | Gold 440 Call Option |
|---|---|---|
|  | Buy at 440.00 | Buy at   6.00 |
| 3. Gold futures stay | Sell at 440.00 | Expires worthless |
| at 440.00 | 0.00 | −6.00 |

Gold prices don't have to collapse for you to lose your $600 premium. All they have to do is nothing. And if the prospect of limited risk should cause you to become overconfident and buy, say, four of these options, you would have created a situation with more inherent risk than a long futures position. You could lose your entire $2400 without futures prices ever going down one tick.

## In versus Out of the Money

The option bought in the previous example was at the money. Its intrinsic value was (440.00 − 440.00 =) zero. The premium of 6.00 was therefore all time value, which characteristically wasted away as the option approached expiration. It's also possible, of course, to buy options that are well into or out of the money, and each strategy has it own goals and purpose.

The greatest *potential* rates of return are found in out-of-the-money options. A speculator who is convinced that futures prices are on the threshold of a powerful rally would look for likely purchase candidates among calls that currently have no intrinsic value, as they will usually provide the highest percentage return on investment if prices advance.

**Futures prices don't have to change for you to lose your entire premium for an out-of-the-money option. All they have to do is nothing.**

**Example:** It is early May. Crude oil futures prices, which have been in a trading range between 14.00 and 16.00 for the past few months, have started to rally on no particular news. July futures are currently trading at 17.00.

You have reason to believe the advance will continue, and you decide to buy one or more call options. The question now is, which option should you buy?

The following table shows you the options that are available (actual prices).

## CRUDE OIL (NYMEX); 1,000 Barrels; Dollars per Barrel

| Strike Price | CALLS | | | PUTS | | |
|---|---|---|---|---|---|---|
| | June | July | August | June | July | August |
| 15 | 2.18 | 2.43 | 2.46 | 0.01 | 0.04 | 0.11 |
| 16 | 1.18 | 1.41 | 1.60 | 0.01 | 0.11 | 0.25 |
| 17 | 0.24 | 0.66 | 0.97 | 0.06 | 0.36 | 0.56 |
| 18 | 0.01 | 0.23 | 0.43 | 0.80 | 0.93 | 1.08 |
| 19 | 0.01 | 0.07 | 0.19 | 1.72 | 1.77 | 1.84 |
| 20 | 0.01 | 0.03 | 0.09 | 2.72 | 2.78 | 2.85 |

To answer the question about which call option to buy, it is necessary to compare the possible results. The June calls are the cheapest, but they also expire in a matter of days. The August calls allow plenty of time for something to happen, but they are relatively expensive. You decide to compromise on the July calls. For purposes of discussion, we'll choose an upside price target of 19.00 for July crude oil futures.

| Call | Present Premium | Premium if Futures go to 19 | Gain(Loss) | Result as % of Premium Paid |
|---|---|---|---|---|
| July 20 | $ 30 | $ 0 | ($ 30) | −100% |
| July 19 | $ 70 | 0 | ($ 70) | −100% |
| July 18 | $ 230 | $1,000 | 770 | +334% |
| July 17 | $ 660 | $2,000 | $1,340 | +203% |
| July 16 | $1,410 | $3,000 | $1,590 | +112% |
| July 15 | $2,340 | $4,000 | $1,660 | + 71% |

The July 20 and July 19 are currently far out of the money. If the July futures price does not go above 19.00, these two options will expire worthless and your entire investment would be lost.

The July 18 has a spectacular potential percentage return. However, it, too, is out of the money. Its premium of $230 is 100% time value. If July crude oil futures do not move above 18 before the option expires, your entire investment would be lost here, too.

At the other end of the spectrum are the July 15 and July 16 calls. They are already in the money, so virtually every penny gained in July crude oil futures would also be gained in the call premium. If the underlying futures price does not change, the options will still be worth their intrinsic values at expiration; for example, if the futures are still at 17 then, you could in the case of the July 16 retrieve $1,000 of your original $1410 premium by selling the option. You would then be out only the lost time value of $410.

The option you choose for your speculation reflects your market expectations. If you are convinced that the forthcoming rally will be powerful, you might choose an out-of-the-money call. If you believe a more modest rally is due, you might opt for a call that is currently at or in the money. The option you choose also reflects your personal tolerance for risk. The deep-out-of-the-money calls are not for you if the thought of owning them gives you a stomachache.

Reason has to enter into the selection process as well. The possible results shown for the July 18 call, for example, would require a 12% increase in the price of July crude oil futures in the space of about 3 weeks. If you look at a long-term price chart for crude oil futures, you'll see that gains of that magnitude occur only under extraordinary circumstances, such as a threatened OPEC embargo or the establishing of crude oil production quotas among OPEC members.

**Example:** It's mid-December. Last summer, a severe drought in the United States sent soybean prices to new 11-year highs. Since then, prices have come down a great deal, but you believe further declines are in store. Recent reports peg

drought damage as less than originally thought.
Weather in the soybean-growing areas in Brazil
is excellent, and a bumper crop is expected
there. Furthermore, prices have not yet reached
your downside technical chart objective.

Selling soybean futures short entails more
risk than you want to take, as there is still quite
a bit of volatility in the market. If you're wrong
and prices rally, losses could accrue quickly.
You decide to buy put options instead. The
following options are available (actual prices).

**SOYBEANS (CBOT); 5,000 Bushels; Cents per Bushel**

|  | CALLS | | | PUTS | | |
|---|---|---|---|---|---|---|
| Strike Price | January | March | May | January | March | May |
| 725 | 53¼ | 71 | 86 | ⅛ | 7¾ | 18 |
| 750 | 28 | 52 | 68½ | 1 | 14 | 26¾ |
| 775 | 7¾ | 39 | 56 | 1¾ | 24 | 38 |
| 800 | 1¼ | 28 | 47 | 4 | 38 | 51 |
| 825 | ¼ | 19¾ | 38 | 7¾ | 55 | 67 |
| 850 | ⅛ | 14 | 32 | 14 | 73 | 83½ |

March looks like the optimum expiration
month. The January options are too close, and
the May options are pricey; the slightly-in-the-
money May 800 put has a time value of $2050.
March soybean futures are currently trading at
$7.90 a bushel, but you believe they could drop
as low as $7.30 in the next several weeks. On
that basis, let's look at a table of possible
results.

| Put | Present Premium | Premium if Futures Fall to 7.30 | Gain(Loss) | Result as % of Premium Paid |
|---|---|---|---|---|
| March 725 | $ 387.50 | 0 | ($ 387.50) | −100% |
| March 750 | $ 700 | $1,000 | $ 300 | +43% |
| March 775 | $1,200 | $2,250 | $1,050 | +87% |
| March 800 | $1,900 | $3,500 | $1,600 | +89% |
| March 825 | $2,750 | $4,750 | $2,000 | +73% |
| March 850 | $3,650 | $6,000 | $2,350 | +64% |

Given the foregoing scenario, the March 725 put would be out of the money at expiration and would die worthless. The rest of the puts would be in the money at expiration. The one with the best potential return is the March 800.

These conclusions assume, of course, that March soybean futures decline to 7.30 by option expiration. The March 750 and the March 775 puts would also expire worthless and their entire premiums be lost if the underlying futures price did not move below their exercise prices by the time they expire.

Notice the effect of the high price volatility left over from the drought scare. Because premiums are still carrying a lot of time value, possible percentage gains are relatively modest across the board. This kind of analysis also tells you something else that's worth knowing: that the relatively low-risk, in-the-money March 800 has the highest return if the decline you expect materializes.

## Expected Return

Suppose you were offered a local lottery ticket. You have two choices. One is a chance to win $10,000, the other a chance to win $2,000. Each ticket costs $5.00 The ticket seller says to you, "Which one do you want?"

You really don't have enough information to answer that question intelligently. You need to know how many tickets are going to be sold in each category, because that has a direct bearing on your chance of winning.

The same reasoning can be used in evaluating any potential investment. The *expected return* of an investment is its projected return adjusted for the probability that the result will occur. A 20% probability that you will make a $5000 profit has an expected return of $1000 (.20 × $5000 = $1000). A 5% chance at $10,000 has an expected return of only $500 (.05 × $10,000 =

$500). The increase in the prize is more than offset by the decrease in the probabilty of winning.

Strictly speaking, the expected return is the result you would achieve in the long run, if you made the same investment many times. Selecting the alternative with the best expected return does not guarantee that you will win this time, but it does put the odds on your side.

In the preceding two examples, we chose the option expiration month by the seat of our pants. We also selected the target futures price arbitrarily. We made no allowance for the likelihood that our target futures price would be attained. We also did not consider the many other possible combinations of exercise price, expiration month, and futures price; for example, what return we expect if we bought the May 775 put and soybean futures prices fell to $7.20.

We omitted detailed discussion of these considerations in the interest of simplicity. They would be instrumental in any actual options trading program.

## Selling Options

Selling options short is an entirely different matter than buying them. If you sell an option short and do not own the underlying futures position, the sale is considered to be "uncovered." You must post option margin. You are subject to margin calls if prices move against you, and your market risk is virtually unlimited.

**Uncovered short sales of options require margin, can create margin calls, and expose the seller to virtually unlimited market risk.**

To take an example, suppose gold futures are trading at $400.00 an ounce and you sell one uncovered December gold 400 call for a premium of 4.20. You would receive $420. A month later, gold futures are trading at $480.00, and the call you sold is exercised. But you don't own December gold futures, so you have to buy them now.

You pay the current price of $480.00 an ounce for a long position in December gold and immediately deliver it to the call buyer to satisfy the exercise. He pays you $400.00 an ounce, the striking price. The difference is $80.00 an ounce ($480.00 − $400.00), or $8000. From that you can deduct the $420 you received when you sold the call, leaving you with a net loss of $7580.

A loss of almost $8000 would be considered nominal by a trader who was short an S&P 500 put option on the morning of October 18, 1987. In the next 2 days, the nearby December S&P 500 Stock Index futures price fell from 298.00 to 202.00, creating a loss of $48,500 for each uncovered short put. In the aftermath, some FCMs have decided that they will no longer accept orders for the sale of uncovered options from private individual speculators.

## Covered Sale

If you own the underlying futures position—for example, if you sell a silver call short and have a long position in silver futures—the sale is considered to be "covered." You need to margin the futures position, of course; but you do not need to post margin on the short call because you already have the asset (the long futures position) to deliver to the call buyer if the call is exercised. This is considered a more conservative option strategy and amenable to use by nonprofessional traders.

For example, suppose you bought one contract of July silver a month ago for $6.00 an ounce, and it is now trading at $6.45 an ounce. You have a profit of 45 cents an ounce. The contract size is 5000 ounces, so your profit translates to $2250. It appears that silver prices will stabilize at current levels for the next month or so. You consider selling a covered call in the hope that you can pick up the premium while you are waiting for the advance to resume.

Available silver options and their premiums are:

### Silver (COMEX); 5,000 Troy Ounces; Cents per Troy Ounce

| Strike Price | CALLS | | | PUTS | | |
|---|---|---|---|---|---|---|
| | July | September | December | July | September | December |
| 600 | 45.5 | 59.5 | 79.5 | 2.8 | 11.5 | 17.0 |
| 625 | 21.0 | 41.0 | 64.0 | 7.5 | 17.5 | 23.0 |
| 650 | 11.0 | 29.0 | 48.5 | 12.5 | 19.5 | 27.0 |
| 675 | 5.8 | 19.5 | 46.5 | 30.5 | 35.0 | 38.0 |
| 700 | 3.4 | 14.0 | 30.5 | 55.5 | 58.5 | 61.5 |

The July calls with striking prices of 600 and 625 are in the money. If you sell one of them you will receive a big premium, but you also run the risk that the call will exercised and your long position in silver futures will be called away. The July calls with striking prices of 675 and 700 are far out of the money, so there's not much chance they will ever be exercised; but they don't earn you much. For the 675, for example, you would receive 5.8 cents times 5,000 ounces, or $290.

The September calls are richer, but you believe the silver rally will resume before September, and you don't want to be exposed to possible exercise for that long.

The July 650 looks like the best compromise. You would get $550 for it ($.11 × 5000 ounces). If silver prices were to edge higher and the call were exercised, you would receive $6.50 an ounce—the striking price—for your long position in silver futures. But you would also keep the premium, which would make the effective selling price for your long position in silver futures $6.66 an ounce ($6.50 + .11). That's acceptable to you.

If you sell the 650 and it expires unexercised, you would retain the premium of $550 and still have your long futures position. That's the outcome you are hoping for.

## Single Strategy

The acquisition of a futures position and the simultaneous sale of a covered option can be treated as a trading strategy in itself. The goal is to earn most or all of the option premium. The futures position is taken to preclude the risk of being short an uncovered option.

**Long Silver Futures/Short Silver Call**

| *Futures* | | *Option* | |
|---|---|---|---|
| Buy September | | Sell September silver | |
| silver at $6.45 | July 2 | 650 call for | 29.0 cents |
| Sell September | | Buy September silver | |
| silver at $6.45 | August 3 | 650 call for | 4.5 cents |
| 0 | | | +24.5 cents |

The call option you sold was slightly out of the money. The premium is therefore all time value. If the futures price stays flat, as it did in this case, the time value wastes away as the option approaches expiration. Your gain of 24.5 cents per ounce equates to $1225 before transaction costs.

If silver prices decline, your long futures position would begin to generate losses, and you would have decision to make. You received a premium of 29 cents per ounce for the call when you sold it, or $1450. That provides a cushion. If you close out both positions when the loss on the futures and the premium for the option (which you will have to buy back) total $1450, you will come out close to even. Below that level, losses continue to deepen and would be limited only by a silver futures price of zero.

If silver futures advance, your long position will start to earn profits. The call premium will also go up, but it will normally increase at a slower rate because (1) time value is eroding all the while and (2) for reasons we'll explain later, the option and futures prices don't move in lockstep at this level. At futures prices above $6.50, the call will be in the money and subject to exercise. Here's a snapshot of the situation.

**Long Silver Futures/Short Silver Call**

| Futures | | | Option | |
|---|---|---|---|---|
| Buy September | | | Sell September silver 650 | |
| silver at | $6.45 | July 2 | call for | 29.0 cents |
| September | | | September silver 650 | |
| silver at | $6.90 | July 21 | call at | 44.0 cents |
| | +.45 | | | −15.0 cents |

Both positions could be closed out at this point for a gain of 30 cents an ounce. The option is well into the money now, so any further gains in futures will be fully offset by losses on the call. There is still 4 cents of time value left in the call premium; you could hang onto the covered sale in an effort to collect this, but it may not be worth it.

Exercise creates a different outcome.

**Long Silver Futures/Short Silver Call**

| Futures | | | Option | |
|---|---|---|---|---|
| Buy September | | | Sell September silver 650 | |
| silver at | $6.45 | July 2 | call for | 29.0 cents |
| Sold September | | | | |
| silver for | $6.50 | July 22 | Call is exercised | |
| | +$ .05 | | | +29.0 cents |

In this event your gain is 34 cents. You don't have to wait to pick up the last 4 cents of time value. The entire premium is yours immediately upon exercise.

As the preceding scenarios demonstrate, the sale of a covered call is not a neutral strategy. Gains are best when futures prices stay flat or advance. A decline in futures prices begins to eat into potential profits and could lead to involuntary closing of the two positions, or worse. The sale of a covered put against a short futures position would likewise fare better in a moderately bearish environment.

The examples here have been kept simple. There are many other considerations. Although we have omitted commissions to keep matters uncomplicated, they are not negligible,

particularly for the option transactions. Proper
selection of which option to sell should include
a comparison of the expected returns for each
striking price and maturity month. All of the
examples assume that there will be no trading
halts or limit moves that would prevent a trader
from executing the transactions.

## Environment

The preceding examples demonstrate the
environment option traders seek. If buyers want
options on high-flying futures, sellers of options
want the underlying futures market to go to
sleep. Most sellers of options do so for only one
reason: to earn the premium. Risk is least if the
option is simply out of the money when it
expires.

For a full description of the profits and
pitfalls in the sale of covered and uncovered
options, the McMillan book, listed at the end of
this chapter, is especially readable.

## OPTION SPREADS

So far we have talked only about net positions
in options; that is, the buying or selling of calls
or puts. It is also possible to establish spread
positions with options. A call spread comprises
a long position in one call option and a short
position in a different call option. A put spread
comprises a long position in one put option and
a short position in a different put option. In
each spread, the commodity underlying the
options is the same.

> Option spreads cost less than a net position
> because of the premium received for the
> option sold. In return, the spreader accepts
> a cap on the maximum profit he can earn.

The number of possible spreading strategies
with options is legion. Some are very complex.
They have names like "strangle," "condor," and

"butterfly." The two most popular spreads (and, not coincidentally, the two that are perhaps easiest to understand) are (1) a bullish spread constructed of two calls and (2) a bearish spread constructed of two puts. These are the only spreads we will discuss.

## Bullish Call Spread

**In a bullish call spread, the spreader's risk is limited to the cash put up on the opening transaction.**

As you might surmise, a bullish call spread is established when the underlying futures price is expected to advance. The call with the lower striking price (higher premium) is bought, and the call with the higher striking price (lower premium) is sold. The two opening transactions therefore create a debit, requiring that some cash be put up; that cash is the spreader's maximum market risk.

The process is easier to see in an actual example. Let's say that you are mildly bullish on sugar. The time is early May, and the nearby July sugar No. 11 is trading around 8 cents a pound. The following options are available.

### Sugar No. 11 (CSCE); 112,000 Pounds; Cents per Pound

| Strike Price | CALLS | | | PUTS | | |
|---|---|---|---|---|---|---|
| | July | October | December | July | October | December |
| 7.50 | 0.84 | 1.17 | — | 0.06 | 0.21 | — |
| 8.00 | 0.51 | 0.86 | 1.07 | 0.18 | 0.40 | 0.48 |
| 8.50 | 0.26 | 0.61 | — | 0.47 | 0.64 | — |
| 9.00 | 0.14 | 0.45 | 0.66 | 0.82 | 0.99 | 1.07 |
| 9.50 | 0.08 | 0.32 | — | 1.27 | 1.36 | — |
| 10.00 | 0.05 | 0.25 | 0.39 | 1.76 | 1.79 | 1.80 |

You put on a bullish call spread by buying one July sugar 8.00 call and simultaneously selling one July sugar 8.50 call. You pay a premium of .51 (cents per pound) for the July 8.00 call and receive a premium of .26 for the July 8.50 call. Your opening debit is therefore (.51 − .26 =) .25 cents a pound. If you multiply $.0025 times the contract size of 112,000

pounds, you get $280. That is the amount of
cash you have to come up with to put on the
spread (we're ignoring commissions), and that is
also the most you can lose.

Your maximum gain in the spread is the
difference in the two striking prices, which is
.50 cents per pound; .50 times the contract size
of 112,000 pounds equals $560. However, you
would have to deduct the $280 cash you
originally put up, so the most you can net out is
$280.

To get a clearer picture of how it works, let's
track this spread through three possible
outcomes at option expiration: maximum gain,
maximum loss, and somewhere in between.

### Bullish Call Spread

BOUGHT JULY SUGAR 8.00 CALL AT .51

SOLD JULY SUGAR 8.50 CALL AT .26

|  | *July 8.00 Call* | *July 8.50 Call* |
|---|---|---|
| July sugar trading at 8.00 | Bought at    .51 | Sold at    .26 |
| **Outcome No. 1** July sugar climbs to 9.00 | Sold at    1.00 +.49 | Bought at    .50 −.24 |
|  | Net gain = .25 | |

If sugar futures advance, you start to earn
profits. That's why this is called a bullish
spread. If sugar prices go to 9.00, as in this
outcome, you would earn the most you can from
the spread: .25 cents per pound, or $280.00. No
matter how high sugar futures climb, you will
never earn more than $280 because the the two
premiums will go up together, and what you
gain on the long position in the July 8.00 you
will lose on the short position in the July 8.50.

Now let's look at what happens if prices fall.

|  | July 8.00 Call | July 8.50 Call |
|---|---|---|
| July sugar trading at 8.00 | Bought at   .51 | Sold at   .26 |

**Outcome No. 2**

|  | July 8.00 Call | July 8.50 Call |
|---|---|---|
| July sugar falls to 7.90 | Expires worthless | Expires worthless |
|  | −.51 | +.26 |

Net loss = .25

In this case, both options are out of the money and expire worthless. You are left with the debit in your opening transaction. No matter how far sugar prices go down, that is the most you can lose, because the two options will still expire unexercised.

If the sugar market stays flat, results from the spread will be somewhere between the maximum gain and maximum loss:

|  | July 8.00 Call | July 8.50 Call |
|---|---|---|
| July sugar trading at 8.00 | Bought at   .51 | Sold at   .26 |

**Outcome No. 3**

|  | July 8.00 Call | July 8.50 Call |
|---|---|---|
| July sugar is at 8.17 | Sold at   .17 | Expires worthless |
|  | −.34 | +.26 |

Net loss = .08

In this outcome, the 8.50 call is out of the money and expires worthless. The 8.00 call has a bit of intrinsic value left, so part of its original cost can be recovered by selling it. The resulting loss in the spread is .08 cents per pound, or $89.60 ($.0008 × 112,000).

You can glean from the above examples that the break-even point for the spread must be somewhere above 8.17. In fact, it is 8.25, at which point the spreader would just get back the $280 cash he put up when he established the spread:

|  | July 8.00 Call | July 8.50 Call |
|---|---|---|
| July sugar trading at 8.00 | Bought at .51 | Sold at .26 |

**Outcome No. 4**

| July sugar is at 8.25 | Sold at <u>.25</u><br>−.26 | Expires worthless<br>+.26 |
|---|---|---|

Net loss = 0

You can also see that the two striking prices define the playing field. The bullish call spread gains the maximum if futures are anywhere above the higher striking price at option expiration; it loses the maximum if futures prices are anywhere below the lower striking price at option expiration.

There's one other possible outcome: If the call you sold goes into the money, it could be exercised by someone who wants to own a long futures position in July sugar. That would put an end to the spread and generate some unwanted commissions, but it would not force you into the sugar futures market. You could obtain the long futures position you need by exercising the call you bought.

## Bearish Put Spread

It's mid-April. You've been following the cattle market closely, and you expect futures prices to drift lower over the next several weeks. Right now June cattle futures are trading around 71.00 cents per pound. You'd like to take a bearish position but don't want the risk of being outright short. You look into the possibility of a bearish put spread in cattle options.

**Cattle (CME); 40,000 Pounds; Cents per Pound**

| Strike Price | CALLS | | | PUTS | | |
|---|---|---|---|---|---|---|
| | June | August | October | June | August | October |
| 68 | 3.80 | 2.10 | 2.45 | 0.20 | 1.85 | 2.65 |
| 70 | 2.12 | 1.20 | 1.65 | 0.52 | 2.92 | 3.80 |
| 72 | 0.85 | 0.60 | 1.05 | 1.25 | 4.35 | 5.15 |
| 74 | 0.25 | 0.32 | 0.62 | 2.65 | 6.00 | — |
| 76 | 0.05 | 0.15 | 0.37 | 4.45 | — | — |

You put on a bearish put spread by selling the June cattle 70 put and buying the June cattle 72 put. You pay 1.25 (cents per pound) for the June 72 and receive .52 for the June 70, creating an opening debit of .73 (1.25 − .52). That translates to $292.00 ($.0073 × 40,000 pounds); that's what it costs you to put on the spread, and that is the most you can lose in it.

The most you can make in the spread is the difference between the two striking prices (2.00 cents). If you subtract from that what the spread cost you (.73), you get 1.27 cents per pound as the maximum possible gain. That's $508 ($.0127 × 40,000 pounds).

(Notice that the balance between risk and reward is better in this spread than it was in the sugar spread. In sugar we risked $280 to make $280. In the cattle spread we are risking $292 to make $508.)

To get a better idea of how a bearish put spread works, let's once again look at each outcome.

### Bearish Put Spread

BOUGHT JUNE CATTLE 72 PUT FOR 1.25

SOLD JUNE CATTLE 70 PUT FOR .52

| | June 72 Put | | June 70 Put | |
|---|---|---|---|---|
| June cattle trading at 71.00 | Bought at | 1.25 | Sold at | .52 |

**Outcome No. 1**

| | June 72 Put | | June 70 Put | |
|---|---|---|---|---|
| June cattle falls to 69.00 | Sold at | 3.00 | Bought at | 1.00 |
| | | +1.75 | | −.48 |

Net gain = 1.27

The bearish put spread delivers its maximum gain, as you might expect, when the underlying futures prices decline. No matter how far down cattle prices go, the gain in the spread will never exceed 1.27 cents per pound, however, because the growing pluses on the June 72 side will be offset by the growing minuses on the June 70 side.

If cattle prices advance after the bearish put spread is established, losses start to accrue; the loss reaches its maximum when June cattle prices surpass 72, the higher striking price.

### Bearish Put Spread
BOUGHT JUNE CATTLE 72 PUT FOR 1.25
SOLD JUNE CATTLE 70 PUT FOR .52

| | June 72 Put | | June 70 Put | |
|---|---|---|---|---|
| June cattle trading at 71.00 | Bought at | 1.25 | Sold at | .52 |

**Outcome No. 2**

| | June 72 Put | | June 70 Put | |
|---|---|---|---|---|
| June cattle rallies to 73.00 | Expires worthless | | Expires worthless | |
| | | −1.25 | | +.52 |

Net loss = .73

The loss remains at .73 cents per pound ($292.00) no matter how far cattle futures go up because at any level above 72.00 both options will still expire worthless, and the spreader will be left with his original debit.

A June cattle price somewhere between the two striking prices at option expiration will return a modest degree of loss or gain. The break-even point here is a June cattle futures price of 71.27 cents per pound, as shown below.

### Bearish Put Spread
BOUGHT JUNE CATTLE 72 PUT FOR 1.25
SOLD JUNE CATTLE 70 PUT FOR .52

|  | June 72 Put | June 70 Put |
|---|---|---|
| June cattle trading at 71.00 | Bought at 1.25 | Sold at .52 |

**Outcome No.3**

| June cattle is at 71.27 | Sold at .73 | Expires worthless |
|---|---|---|
|  | −.52 | +.52 |

Net gain or loss = 0

The June 72 put is in the money by .73 and thus can be sold to recover some of its original cost. The final result from the June 72 transactions exactly offsets the original cost of the June 70, making the spread a wash. The focal point is 71.27. As the ending June cattle price moves below that level, small gains begin to accrue. Above 71.27, losses begin.

Although we haven't mentioned it before, this spread is technically known as a bearish *vertical* spread; likewise, the one for sugar was a bullish *vertical* spread. The name derives from the fact that the maturity months are the same for both options, so they appear in the same vertical column in a newspaper table.

There are also diagonal spreads, horizontal spreads, and many others. If the subject intrigues you, we repeat that the McMillan book referenced later is an excellent source.

## A Word about Commissions

There are many firms selling options to public customers. They range in size from major FCMs to very small firms who deal only in options. Their commission rates also vary widely. The margin for profit in option spreads is not great. As we stated earlier, the option spreader accepts a limited gain in return for a limited risk. Commission rates that are unusually high may absorb most or all of this potential gain, making the spread transaction futile.

# HEDGING WITH OPTIONS

## Delta

Greek letters are used to identify various aspects of option behavior. There are several, but we will mention only one—delta—because that is the one you hear most often. Delta is a decimal that stands for an option's reaction to a change in the futures price. If the option premium goes up 1 when the futures price goes up 1, the delta is 1.00. If the option goes up .47 when the futures price goes up 1, the option's delta is .47.

*It follows, then, that in-the-money options have high deltas; out-of-the-money options have low deltas.*

Above, when we were talking about out-of-the-money options, we said that one of the problems with buying them is that the underlying futures price has to move a long way before the option's premium reacts very much. Another way of saying that is: The option has a very low delta. By the same token, an option that is deep into the money will have a delta approaching 1; the option premium will change virtually dollar for dollar with changes in the futures price. An option that is at the money will normally have a delta of about .50.

## Option Hedge Example

You have probably deduced that a put option would make a good short hedge. Calls may likewise be used as long hedges. There would never be a margin call. The hedger's risk is limited to the premium paid and is fully known at the outset. Except for a fractional loss in time value as the weeks pass, the option provides the same degree of price protection.

If it is to serve as a hedge, the option's premium must change when the price of the underlying asset changes. In other words, the option must have a high delta (be in the money). If the option premium doesn't change when the price of the underlying asset changes, the hedge offers no protection.

The greatest advantage of an option hedge over a futures hedge occurs when the hedge was, in hindsight, not really needed. For example, let's assume that your company manufactures copper tubing for industrial use. You have enough space to keep 150,000 pounds of copper metal on hand, which is enough for 2 months' production of tubing.

Your chief financial officer tells you that signs point to much higher copper prices in the next 6 months and recommends that you buy copper ahead now. Because you don't have the facilities to store the additional metal, you buy copper futures, thereby—except for changes in the basis—"locking in" today's cash price for the metal you will buy later.

You could have bought call options on copper futures instead. If the options are in the money, their premiums will move virtually in tandem with the price of the underlying futures, and losses on the cash side would be offset by gains in the call premiums.

A numerical comparison will make the differences between the two approaches apparent.

### Long Futures versus Call Option as a Hedge in Copper

| Time | Cash Market | Futures | Calls |
|---|---|---|---|
| May 1 | Copper 62.50 per pound | Buy 10 December copper at 64.30 | Buy 10 December copper 60 at 8.50 |

Following is a comparison of the three possible outcomes from each transaction.

**Outcome No. 1:** *As Expected, Copper Prices Rise*

| Time | Cash Copper | December Futures | December Copper 60 Call |
|---|---|---|---|
| May 1 | 62.50 cents/pound | Buy 10 at 64.30 | Buy 10 at 8.50 |
| Later | 78.80 cents/pound | Sell at 80.60 | Sell at 20.80 |
| | +16.30 | +16.30 | +12.30 |

Cash copper prices went up 16.30 cents per pound. Because there was no change in the basis, futures gained the same amount. The call options did not quite keep pace, because in the interim they lost 4 cents in time value. In retrospect, futures would have provided a better hedge.

**Outcome No. 2:** *Copper Prices Unexpectedly Decline Sharply*

| Time | Cash Copper | December Futures | December Copper 60 Call |
|------|-------------|------------------|-------------------------|
| May 1 | 62.50 cents/pound | Buy 10 at 64.30 | Buy 10 at 8.50 |
| Later | 49.75 cents/pound | Sell at 51.55 | Expire worthless |
| | −12.75 | −12.75 | −8.50 |

Cash copper prices fell from 62.50 to 49.75, a drop of 12.75 cents. Because there was no change in the basis, futures prices also fell 12.75 cents. The loss on the long futures position thus fully offset the lower cash price, negating the potential windfall gain. The option, however, lost only 8.50 cents, as zero was as far down as it could go. Below that, further windfall gains (in the form of lower cash copper prices) were no longer offset.

In this outcome, the effective cost of the cash copper with the futures hedge is 62.50 cents per pound. With the option hedge, the effective cost of the cash copper is the actual cost of the metal (49.75) plus the money lost on the option (8.50 cents) per pound, or a total 58.25 cents per pound. The option was the better hedge by 4.25 cents a pound.

Another relative benefit: Falling prices would have triggered margin calls in the long futures position. There is never a margin call in a long option position.

**Outcome No. 3:** *Copper Prices Don't Change*

| Time | Cash Copper | December Futures | December Copper 60 Call |
|------|-------------|------------------|-------------------------|
| May 1 | 62.50 cents/pound | Buy 10 at 64.30 | Buy 10 at 8.50 |
| Later | 62.50 cents/pound | Sell at 64.30 | Sell at 3.00 |
| | 0 | 0 | −5.50 |

**An option hedge is more effective than a futures hedge when cash prices move sharply in the direction favorable to the hedger.**

If cash copper prices stay flat, you can sell the futures for what you paid and break even. The option, however, would have lost some time value as the weeks passed. If you were able to sell it for only 3.00, say, you would sustain a loss of 5.50 cents per pound (8.50 − 3.00). Futures would be a better hedge in this instance.

There's a *rough* rule in all this:

> *A futures hedge promises to be more effective if cash prices remain unchanged or move in an adverse direction. An option hedge promises to be more effective if cash prices move sharply in a favorable direction.*

Although we have only scratched the surface, this is all we are going to say about hedging with options. For further information on hedging and other strategies for these versatile new trading vehicles, please refer to the following suggested reading list.

# Suggested Reading

*Options as a Strategic Investment*, by Lawrence G. McMillan. New York Institute of Finance, New York City, Rev. 1986.

*Trading Options on Futures*, by John W. Labuszewski and John E. Nyhoff. John Wiley & Sons, Inc., New York City, 1988.

*Trading in Currency Options*, by W.H. Sutton, New York Institute of Finance, New York City, 1988.

# 15

# Rules and Regulations

It would take both hands to pick up the books
of rules and regulations surrounding futures
trading. Most of the regulations are grist for
lawyers. But there are some rules that you
should be aware of, as they could one day
concern your.

## Broker Qualifications

The person most people refer to as their
"commodity broker" is known technically as an
*Associated Person*. He works for a brokerage
firm, takes your phone calls, places your orders,
reports back to you when the order is filled, and
generally handles your trading account. Before
he can conduct public business, he is required
to demonstrate his knowledge of the field by
passing the National Commodity Futures
Examination. He must also be registered with
the Commodity Futures Trading Commission
and be a member of the National Futures

Association, which conducts a check on his background.

## Discretionary Accounts

Some customers give their brokers limited power of attorney to trade the customer's account entirely at the broker's discretion, without obtaining the customer's advance approval for trades. This authority must be given to the broker in writing. By law, a broker must have 2 years experience as a broker before he can accept discretionary authority over a futures or options trading account. He must also obtain the signature of his supervisor on each discretionary trade before sending it to the trading floor for execution.

## Opening an Account

A customer opening a new commodity (or options) account will be asked to fill out and sign several forms. The main purposes of these forms are to inform the customer of the risks associated with futures trading; to determine the customer's net worth and whether he is financially suited to futures trading; and to give the brokerage firm advance authority to transfer the customer's funds within the firm or to close out the customer's positions if necessary to meet a margin call in the customer's futures account.

Of these, the last may need explanation. If you remember from our earlier discussion, original margin to support an open futures position is paid by the customer to the brokerage firm and by the brokerage firm to the clearinghouse. Additional margin is called for when the customer's equity falls below a certain level.

The brokerage firm has to meet its margin calls regardless of whether the customer meets his. The authority to close out positions or transfer funds are emergency measures designed

to protect the brokerage firm from having to
absorb the customer's losses. They are used as
last resorts when the firm has for some reason
been unable to obtain the necessary additional
margin from the customer.

## Errors

Mistakes are unusual, but they do happen. Stop
orders get placed at the wrong levels. An
intended buy order gets entered as an order to
sell. A broker forgets to advise his customer that
an order was filled.

There are two broad principles that govern
mistakes in trading. The first is that the
transaction made between the floor brokers on
the exchange trading floor stands. Any
adjustments will be made elsewhere. The
second is that any loss arising from a broker's
trading mistake is taken by the FCM or the
broker personally; any windfall gains that
might come out of the error belong to the
customer.

We are talking here about relatively minor
adjustments, or course. If the amount involved
is large, it is possible that the customer will get
into the established processes for hearing and
judging grievances. These are discussed in
another paragraph.

## Handling Your Money

Funds held in your name by a brokerage firm
(FCM) are required to be segregated from the
firm's money and separately accounted for. This
segregation is intended to prevent the use of
your money by another customer or the firm
itself. Customer funds held by a brokerage firm
in excess of those needed to fulfill margin
requirements may be invested by the firm in
interest bearing obligations of the United States.
Interest earned on these investments flows to
the brokerage firm.

# Risk Disclosure

When you first open a futures or options account, you will be asked by your broker to read and sign a risk disclosure document. The purpose of the document is to advise you of the risk of loss inherent in futures and options trading and to alert you to the possibility that such trading might not be financially suitable for you. It doesn't mention all the pitfalls, of course, but is just a warning.

# Reports

A great deal of money moves by word of mouth in the futures markets. You give your order to your broker verbally, and he reports its execution back to you the same way. Transactions worth hundreds of thousands of dollars are consumated in the trading pits with the wave of a hand.

Written confirmation of each futures trade is required to be made to you by the following business day. As a practical matter, the notice will not likely arrive in your mailbox until a day or two after that. When you get it, check it over to make sure the numbers are correct. You will aslo receive a monthly statement from the FCM carrying your account. It will show current open positions, net profit or loss from positions closed during the reporting period, and the equity in your account. You should compare these data with your own records also, to make sure that they jibe.

# Reparations

If you believe you have been wronged by a commodity professional and are unable to settle the matter with your broker or his firm, there are two other avenues open to you. The CFTC has a reparations procedure to settle disputes over money damages between private parties. A complaint must be filed with the CFTC within 2 years of the incident causing the complaint. The complaint is heard before an administrative law judge, and his ruling may be appealed by either party. If you receive an award and it is not paid within 30 days, the CFTC can suspend the registration of the commodity professional or prohibit him from trading in all contract markets.

The National Futures Association (NFA) also has grievance procedures. Members of NFA are *required* to submit your claim to arbitration if you request it. Arbitration proceedings are informal and are conducted in a location convenient to both parties; parties may be represented by counsel if they desire. Claims for any amount may be heard, and the ruling of the arbitrator or arbitration panel cannot be appealed.

## Position Limits

There are speculative position limits on most commodities. These limits describe the maximum number of open futures contracts that may be owned or controlled by one person at one time. Bona fide hedges are exempt from speculative limits. The CFTC sets the limits on several of the agricultural markets; the exchanges themselves set the limits on the rest. The limits are quite large. In soybeans, for example, the speculative position limit for all delivery months combined is 12 million bushels.

An FCM must advise the CFTC when one of its speculative accounts exceeds the limit and must continue to advise the CFTC daily until the customer's position falls back below the limit.

## Floor Brokers

A floor broker cannot execute a trade for his own account while he holds the same trade for a customer's account. This prevents him from taking a small position ahead of a large order that he knows will move the market favorably.

Unless you consent, a floor broker cannot fill your order by selling to you *from* his own account or buying from you *for* his own account.

He cannot prearrange trades to avoid making them by open outcry, except under special circumstances approved by the CFTC and the exchange.

A floor broker is not permitted to disclose orders that he holds. This stops him from tipping off other floor brokers, who could benefit by buying or selling ahead of a large order and later splitting the gains with the broker who had held the order.

## Guarantees

It is against the law for a commodity professional to say that he can guarantee you against loss in any commodity transaction. Except for joint accounts, pools, or partnerships where your written permission is given, it is also illegal for him to share in either the profits or losses from your futures transactions.

## Attorneys

Commodity law is highly specialized. Today, more and more law firms are establishing separate departments to deal with this rapidly growing field. Law firms that are members of the Futures Industry Association would be presumed to have an interest. Information on these firms may be obtained directly by calling or writing the Futures Industry Association at 1825 Eye Street NW (Suite 1040), Washington, DC 20006. Telephone: 202-466-5460.

## Taxes

You should seek professional tax advice if you are going to be involved with futures or options, as the rules are ever changing. However, the following general guidelines apply.

As was mentioned earlier in the book, futures contracts outstanding at the end of the year are marked to the market, and income taxes are paid on unrealized gains net of unrealized losses. The effect is as if each futures contract were sold for fair market value on the last business day. The resulting gains or losses are considered 40 percent short-term capital gain and 60 percent long-term capital gain, although there is presently no difference in the tax rates for long- and short-term capital gains. All capital gains are taxed as ordinary income.

Hedges are exempt from the mark-to-market rule. A hedge is defined as a normal business transaction intended to reduce the risk of change in the cash price of property or the risk of changes in interest rates or foreign currency exchange rates.

Most gains or losses from hedging transactions are ordinary. Hedges to protect inventory, receivables, or other assets in the normal course of business—for example, a miller hedging in wheat futures—create ordinary income or loss. However, it is possible in unusual circumstances for a hedge to create capital gains or losses. A possible example would be a foreign currency futures hedge taken to protect an investment in an overseas subsidiary.

# 16

# Contracts in Brief

This chapter presents basic information on the major futures markets. The markets are presented alphabetically by commodity group; for examples, currencies, foods and fibers, grains, and so on. Within each group the individual markets are described. Included are technical data on the futures contract itself; information about where the actual commodity is produced, who uses it, and what causes its price to change and a listing of sources for current supply and demand information.

The following abbreviations are used to identify the major exchange on which each futures contract is traded:

CBOT—Chicago Board of Trade
COMEX—Commodity Exchange, Incoporated
CME—Chicago Mercantile Exchange
CSCE—Coffee, Sugar & Cocoa Exchange

FINEX—Financial Instrument Exchange, a
    division of the New York Cotton
    Exchange
IMM—International Monetary Market
IOM—Index and Option Market of the
    Chicago Mercantile Exchange
KCBT—Kansas City Board of Trade
MGE—Minneapolis Grain Exchange
NYCE—New York Cotton Exchange
NYFE—New York Futures Exchange
NYMEX—New York Mercantile Exchange

Put and call options are available on all
futures contracts except where indicated.

## CURRENCIES

Futures contracts are actively traded on the
British pound, Deutschemark, Japanese yen,
Swiss franc, and Canadian dollar. All are traded
on the International Monetary Market, a division
of the Chicago Mercantile Exchange.
Minicontracts in the first four currencies are also
traded on the MidAmerica Commodity Exchange
in Chicago.

Factors affecting the prices of foreign
currencies on world markets include relative
rates of inflation between nations, balance of
trade, interest rates, government intervention,
and economic growth rate.

A high inflation rate creates distrust of a
currency. A nation experiencing severe price
inflation will eventually suffer a weakening of
its currency in relation to that of its world
neighbors. If a nation is buying more than it
sells, it has an "unfavorable" balance of trade.
Capital is flowing out. As a result, the demand
for its currency diminishes relative to the
currencies of its customers, and that causes its
value to decline.

Prices for a foreign currency also reflect comparative interest rates. If a nation's interest rates are high, foreigners will invest their money there. This creates demand for the currency and will cause its value to rise relative to the currencies of nations where lower interest rates attract fewer foreign investors. A country undergoing robust economic growth likewise attracts foreign investment.

Most government actions today are taken in the name of stabilizing foreign currency relationships. This does not rule out the possibility that they may one day exercise their greater powers to impose quotas, tariffs, embargos, or take other actions that would have a significant and immediate effect on foreign currency values.

There is also some seasonality to the demand for some foreign currencies, caused by the ebb and flow of tourist activity and imports or exports of hard goods.

### Where to Find More Information

Foreign currency prices are affected in some measure by almost every economic happening. Broad sources of information on the relationship between the U. S. dollar and foreign currencies would include the U. S. Department of the Treasury and the U. S. Department of Commerce in Washington, DC.

In addition, there are three informative periodicals in the field: *The Economist* (527 Madison Avenue, New York, NY 10022); *Financial Times of London* (75 Rockefeller Plaza, New York, NY 10019); and *Euromoney* (14 Finbury Circus, London EC2, England).

For the European currencies, a book that would be helpful is *The Eurocurrency Market Handbook*, by Eugene Sarver. It is published by the New York Institute of Finance in New York City.

## Commodity: **British Pound**

Delivery months: March, June,
  September, December
Price in dollars and cents per British
  pound
Minimum tick: $.0002 = $12.50

Exchange: IMM
Contract size: 62,500 pounds

Great Britain is a major trading country and an international center for finance and business. London is the heart of the Eurodollar market. The Bank of England is the central bank and is responsible for issuing banknotes and managing the national debt. For the past 7 years, Great Britain has imported more than it sells; the gap has grown even wider in 1985 and 1986. The pound has been allowed to float in value since June 1972. Futures prices have ranged widely, from just over $1.00 to $2.60.

## Commodity: **Canadian Dollar**

Delivery months: March, June,
  September, December
Price in dollars and cents per
  Canadian dollar
Minimum tick: $.0001 = $10.00

Exchange: IMM
Contract size: $100,000 (Can)

Canada is one of the world's leading trading nations. A major exporter of agricultural products, it is also the leader (in terms of value) in seafood exports. The nation is rich in minerals, leading all others in the production of zinc and nickel. The net flow of capital between Canada and the United States has been southerly. In the 1980s, Canadian-owned investments in the United States increased 68 percent; U. S. investments in Canada during the same period rose only 30 percent.

    The Canadian dollar fell from a premium to a discount to the U. S. dollar in the 1970s and was as low as 69 cents (U. S.) in early 1986.

### Commodity: **Deutschemark**
Delivery months: March, June,
September, December
Price in cents per Deutschemark    Exchange: IMM
Minimum tick: $.0001 = $12.50    Contract size: 125,000 marks

The Federal Republic of Germany is western
Europe's leading economic power. Its currency,
the Deutschemark, is issued by the Deutsche
Bundesbank (German Federal Bank), which is
also responsible for its stability on world
markets. The West German economy is
dominated by industry, and foreign trade plays
an important role. Deutschemark futures prices
on the IMM have ranged from a low 28 cents to
a high of 64 cents since trading began in 1972.

### Commodity: **Japanese Yen**
Delivery months: March, June,
September, December
Price in cents per yen                        Exchange: IMM
Minimum tick: $.000001 = $12.50       Contract size: 12,500,000 yen

Japan's economy achieved a very high growth
rate in the years after World War II. It currently
ranks second in the world (after the United
States) in industrial production. Some 70
percent of the nation is forested, and it is self-
sufficient only in rice. Industry therefore
depends heavily on import of raw materials for
production of motor vehicles, steel, machinery,
chemicals, and electrical equipment.
    The yen has been in the world financial
spotlight in the 1980s because of Japan's huge
trade surplus and the yen's resulting strength
against other major currencies.

### Commodity: **Swiss Franc**
Delivery months: March, June,
September, December
Price in cents per Swiss franc    Exchange: IMM
Minimum tick: $.0001 = $12.50    Contract size: 125,000 francs

Switzerland's well-ordered economy reflects an extended period of peace. With no important natural resources except water power, the Swiss economy is based on diversified industry and commerce and depends heavily on foreign labor from neighboring countries. Its perennial deficit in its foreign trade account is more than offset by surpluses in banking, insurance, and tourism.

Futures prices for the Swiss franc have ranged from 35 cents to 80 cents (U. S.) over the past 5 years, with the high set in late 1987.

## FOODS AND FIBERS

Included in the category of foods and fibers are cocoa, coffee, sugar, cotton, and orange juice. Futures contracts in the first three are traded on the Coffee, Sugar & Cocoa Exchange. Cotton and orange juice futures are traded on the New York Cotton Exchange. Both exchanges are in New York City.

Commodity: **Cocoa**
Delivery months: March, May, July,
   September, December
Price in dollars per ton                 Exchange: CSCE
Minimum tick: $1.00 = $10.00     Contract size: 10 tons

Cocoa production is centered in Africa, where the leading producer is the Ivory Coast. Cocoa is also grown in Brazil, Ghana, and Nigeria. About 75 percent of the world crop comes to harvest in the 5-month period from October to March. A second, smaller harvest occurs in the May–July period. The principal use of cocoa is the making of confections. The United States is the leading consumer. West Germany is second; more recently, the USSR has become a growing importer of cocoa.

Cocoa futures have traded in a broad range. Since 1965, prices have been as low as $500 per ton and as high as $5400 a ton; the latter was an

extraordinary peak reached in 1977. The
International Cocoa Agreement (ICA), formed in
1980, attempted unsuccessfully to control prices
by buying or selling buffer stocks. The ICA is
not a price factor today but could regain minor
importance.

Seasonal influences cause prices to set highs
in summer and again in late fall. Prices are
usually lowest in the first quarter. Real or
rumored changes in supply caused by such
incidents as price fixing, crop disease, hot, dry
summer growing weather, or shipping
disruptions have the most direct effect on price
levels. However, the rugged terrain in which
cocoa is grown and the fact that it is produced
almost exclusively in developing nations make
communications difficult. Information about the
size of the crop, its welfare, and the level of
stockpiles is hard to get and not always reliable.

One measure of consumption is the grinding
of the processed cocoa beans to cocoa powder,
which is widely reported. Over the longer term,
changes in disposable income also affect the
price of cocoa, as manufacturers generally
respond to lower chocolate consumption by
reducing the amount of chocolate in their
confections.

### Where to Find More Information

Gill & Duffus Ltd., a private British firm (130
John Street, 20th floor, New York, NY 10038)
provides a widely followed weekly report that
presents worldwide cocoa supply/demand data.
The Coffee, Sugar & Cococa Exchange (4 World
Trade Center, New York, NY 10038; telephone:
212-938-2800) is an excellent source for both
current and background information. Foreign
Agriculture, published monthly by the U. S.
Department of Agriculture (USDA) does on
occasion carry data on cocoa yield and crop
sizes that are released by the producing
countries themselves. For information, contact

Office of Information, USDA, Washington, DC
20250 (telephone: 202-447-7451).


Commodity: **Coffee**

Delivery months: March, May, July,
  September, December

Price in dollars and cents per pound    Exchange: CSCE

Minimum tick: 1/100 cent = $3.75    Contract size: 37,500 pounds


Although many nations grow coffee, Brazil and
Colombia are the most important producers.
Brazil's main coffee harvesting season is April to
September; Colombia's is October to March. The
United States is the world's largest single
importer of the breakfast beverage, followed
closely by Europe. The most popular are the
mild coffees from Colombia, and they also
usually top the price list. Robusta coffee from
the Ivory Coast has been growing in importance
in recent years, reflecting its use for instant
coffees.

Coffee is a weather market. Winter in Latin
America coincides with summer in the Northern
hemisphere, and the threat of tree-damaging
frost in June and July has been known to send
futures prices rocketing upward. Drought has
also played a part. Since 1975, futures prices
have ranged from 45 cents a pound to $3.40 a
pound, a swing of some 755 percent.

Other factors influencing coffee prices are the
quantities of green coffee on hand, labor unrest
in exporting countries that leaves coffee sitting
on the dock, overt steps taken by the
governments of producing countries to control
coffee production and prices, and insect damage
to the growing crop.

On a longer term basis, consumer preferences
are also important. Although coffee consumption
has a reputation of staying high in spite of sharp
price increases from time to time, there has been
a long-term trend toward less coffee drinking in
the United States in recent years.

*Where to Find More Information*

USDA publishes several souces of current
information on coffee. They include *Foreign
Agricultural Trade of the U.S.A.*, put out by the
Economic Research Service, plus *Foreign
Agriculture*, and the *Foreign Agriculture
Circular*. These reports may be obtained from
the Foreign Agricultural Service, USDA,
Washington, DC 20250. Other good information
sources are the literature and annual report of
New York Coffee, Sugar & Cocoa Exchange, 4
World Trade Center, New York, NY 10048.

Commodity: **Cotton**

Delivery months: March, May, July,
  October, December

Price in cents per pound                  Exchange: NYCE

Minimum tick: ⅟₁₀₀ cent = $5.00       Contract size: 50,000 pounds =
                                          100 bales

Cotton is grown in several countries, including
China, India, Brazil, Pakistan, Egypt, Turkey, the
United States, and the USSR. The United States
and the USSR are the world's leading producers.
Growing areas in the United States are, in order
of importance, Texas, California, Mississippi,
Arizona, and Arkansas. Planting starts as early
as February, although the bulk of the U. S.
cotton crop is planted in April. Harvesting is
done mainly in October and November.

The United States is the largest cotton
consumer in the world. About half of the cotton
consumed in the United States is used to make
apparel. The rest finds its way into sheets,
pillowcases, towels, and other industrial and
household uses. Cotton exports from the United
States are a major factor in world markets and
are highest in the first quarter. Consumption by
cotton mills peaks in the fall as the new crop
arrives, then tapers off toward spring.

Over the past 30 years, cotton futures price
have ranged from a low of 30 cents a pound to a

high of just under a dollar a pound. On a
seasonal basis, spot prices for combed and
cleaned cotton are usually highest in the spring.
Nonseasonal factors would include the level of
government stockpiles, the government loan
level for cotton, and actions taken by foreign
cotton producers to control prices or supplies.
However, the overwhelming price determinants
are the price of U. S. cotton relative to the prices
of foreign cotton and synthetic fibers; and
consumer preferences, such as the recent
popularity of all-cotton denim clothing.

### Where to Find More Information

USDA publishes a weekly *Cotton Market Review*
and the *Cotton & Wool Situation*. USDA cotton
production estimates are released monthly,
starting in July and continuing until the crop is
harvested in the fall. For information on the cost
and availability of these reports, contact Office
of Information, USDA, Washington, DC 20250
(telephone: 202-447-7451) and request a copy of
the pamphlet, "How to Get Information from the
U. S. Department of Agriculture."

Other sources comprise the *Weekly Trade
Report* of the New York Cotton Exchange and
monthly data published by the U. S. Census
Bureau on cotton consumption and mill
margins.

Commodity: **Orange Juice (Frozen Concentrated)** (no options traded)
Delivery months: January, March,
   May, July, September, November
Price in cents per pound          Exchange: NYCE
Minimum tick: ⁵⁄₁₀₀ cent = $7.50      Contract size: 15,000 pounds

Florida is the home of citrus in the United
States, and more than 75 percent of its orange
crop is processed into frozen concentrated
orange juice (FCOJ). The most important harvest
periods are the month of January and the period

from mid-April to mid-June; the latter is when the Valencia oranges, prized for their flavor, are gathered.

FCOJ is the quintessential weather market. Temperatures below 28°F damage the oranges; three degrees less, and the trees also start to suffer. Since 1900 there have been some 35 major "cold spells" (26°F for 2 to 3 hours) in the Florida Orange Belt. Most freezes have occurred in December and January, but they have come as early as November and as late as March. Damage has ranged from a slight loss of fruit to the destruction of a large number of trees. Even the threat of a cold spell in growing regions can start FCOJ futures prices climbing.

Reports on the amount of FCOJ produced and shipments to food stores are released to the print and wire services each week by the Florida Citrus Processors Association (P.O. Box 780, Winter Haven, FL 33880) and are the most important short-term price factors. Other influences include government buying of orange juice for distribution in school lunch programs; the amount of imported fruit, mainly from Brazil, which has grown in importance in recent years; the level of stocks in the hands of processors; and the popularity of other soft drinks and breakfast beverage substitutes.

FCOJ futures price have at times also reacted sharply to the first official estimate of the current Florida orange crop, which is issued by USDA in October.

### Where to Find More Information

USDA provides two sources of information: reports of estimated orange production and juice yield, which are issued monthly from October through July (except November); and the Fruit Situation Report, issued several times a year, which covers both whole oranges and FCOJ. For information on the cost and availability of these reports, contact Office of Information, USDA, Washington, DC 20250.

The Florida Crop and Livestock Reporting
Service (1222 Woodward Street, Orlando, FL
32803) sends out weekly reports containing
weather and crop news and also publishes an
informative yearly called *Citrus Summary.*

## Commodity; **Sugar**

Delivery months: March, July,
  October

Price in cents per pound        Exchange: CSCE

Minimum tick: $\frac{1}{100}$ cent = $11.20     Contract size: 112,000 pounds

Many countries produce sugar. Sugar cane,
grown mainly in tropical regions, is a perennial.
Sugar beets, which produce an identical
sweetener, thrive in more varied climes and
need to be replanted each year. Cane is the
predominant source.

Brazil, Cuba, India, and the USSR are the
leading producers of sugar, accounting for more
than 30 percent of total world output. Major
importers of sugar are the United States, Japan,
the USSR, Italy, People's Republic of China, and
the United Kingdom. In the United States,
purchases for home use account for 25 percent
of consumption. Bottlers of soft drinks, bakeries,
and candy makers take the rest.

Factors affecting sugar prices include weather
in growing regions, stockpiles of sugar on hand,
and government actions taken to prop up prices.
An International Sugar Agreement (ISA) was
concluded between some of the producing
nations in 1978, in an attempt to control sugar
prices with quotas and stockpiling measures. It
has been ineffectual, in part because the
European Community (EC), a large producer of
sugar, refused to join in the agreement.

Demand for sugar has grown consistently
over the years, reflecting a growing world
population and increasing standards of living in
developing nations. Whether this increase in
demand will continue depends in large part on

the extent of use of artificial sweeteners in soft drinks and confections.

The Coffee, Sugar & Cocoa Exchange lists two futures contracts: sugar No. 11, which is world sugar and trades actively; and sugar No. 12, which is based on the price-regulated domestic sugar market and seldom has much of a following. Only about 10 to 15 percent of the sugar produced enters the "free" world market, so relatively small changes in the supply of sugar can have a sharp impact on world sugar prices.

### Where to Find More Information

USDA publications that contain information about sugar are *Foreign Agriculture*, a monthly magazine; the *Sugar & Sweetener Situation* report; and the Foreign Agriculture Circular, *Sugar, Molasses and Honey*. For information on the cost and availability of these materials, contact Office of Information, USDA, Washington, DC 20250 (telephone: 202-447-7451) and request a copy of the pamphlet "How to Get Information from the U. S. Department of Agriculture."

The preeminent private statistical organization is F. O. Licht, a German firm that publishes widely followed data on world sugar production and consumption. Their address is F. O. Licht International Sugar Report, P.O. Box 1220 (D-2418), Ratzburg, F. R. Germany.

## GRAINS

Active grain futures markets include corn, wheat, and oats. Though classed as oilseeds, soybeans and their by-products (soybean oil and soybean meal) are also generally included in this group. Grain futures are traded on the Chicago Board of Trade, the Kansas City Board of Trade, and the Minneapolis Grain Exchange.

They are also traded on the Winnipeg (Canada) Commodity Exchange, and minicontracts are traded in the United States on the MidAmerica Commodity Exchange in Chicago. We will limit our discussion to the full-size contracts on the first three exchanges.

Commodity: **Corn**

Delivery months: March, May, July, September, December

Price in dollars and cents per bushel        Exchange: CBOT

Minimum tick: ¼ cent = $12.50                Contract size: 5,000 bushels

The United States is the world's largest corn producer. The leading states are Illinois and Iowa. Some corn is also grown in Indiana, Minnesota, and Nebraska. Corn is a summer crop, planted in the spring and harvested in the fall. Major consumers of the yellow grain are livestock, with hogs, cattle, and poultry accounting for almost 90 percent of the disappearance. The United States is also the world's largest exporter of corn, sending about 25 percent of each year's crop overseas.

Like most field crops, corn has a seasonal price pattern. Lows are set at harvest, when supplies weigh relatively heavy on the market. Prices tend to advance from these levels to a high in the spring, just before the new crop is planted.

Other factors influencing corn prices are the price and availability of substitute livestock feeds, which include soybean meal, milo, and wheat; the loan level and other government provisions for price or yield control; and the size of the corn crop in Argentina, Brazil, and other exporting nations. The principal price-making factor, however, is the number of poultry and livestock that comprise the market for corn.

An irregular but very potent price-making factor is weather, as was observed in the price

behavior of the 1988 crop. In fact, it has been
said that the fate of the corn crop in the United
States depends on whether it rains in the Corn
Belt in June and July.

### Where to Find More Information

The USDA is the best single source of supply
and demand information. Publications include
the weekly *Feed Market News* and the quarterly
*Feed Situation* and *Stocks in All Positions*.
Demand for corn can also be inferred from
USDA *Hogs and Pigs* reports, *Cattle on Feed*
reports, and *Livestock and Meat Situation*
reports, all of which show the current projected
numbers of corn consumers. *Feedstuffs*, a
weekly publication, provides timely information
on factors affecting feed demand.

For information on the cost and availability of
USDA reports, contact Office of Information,
USDA, Washington, DC 20250 (telephone: 202-
447-7451) and request a copy of the pamphlet
"How to Get Information from the U. S.
Department of Agriculture."

Commodity: **Wheat**

Delivery months: March, May, July,
   September, December
Price in cents per bushel      Exchange: CBOT
Minimum tick: ¼ cent = $12.50    Contract size: 5,000 bushels

Commodity: **Wheat**

Delivery months: March, May, July,
   September, December
Price in cents per bushel      Exchange: KCBT
Minimum tick: ¼ cent = $12.50    Contract size: 5,000 bushels

Commodity: **Wheat** (no options traded)

Delivery months: March, May, July,
   September, December
Price in cents per bushel      Exchange: MGE
Minimum tick: ¼ cent = $12.50    Contract size: 5,000 bushels

The most important wheat producing country in the world is USSR. The United States is second, followed at a distance by China, India, Canada, and France. Wheat production in the United States in centered in the Great Plains. The major producers are Kansas, Oklahoma, Nebraska, and Colorado.

Most wheat is winter wheat, planted in the fall and harvested in June and July. That which is planted in the spring and harvested in the fall is referred to as spring wheat.

There are three relatively active futures contracts. The most liquid is the contract on the Chicago Board of Trade; it is based on No. 2 soft red winter wheat, which is milled for making crackers, cookies, cakes, and pastries. Second in activity is the Kansas City contract; it calls for delivery of hard red winter wheat, which comprises our major wheat export. Hard red spring wheat is traded on the Minneapolis Grain Exchange; it is a high-protein grain and is often mixed with lower protein soft wheats. Despite the disparity in their growing periods and end uses, prices in the three wheat markets do not tend to diverge greatly.

Virtually all wheat that is not exported goes into foods. It takes about 2½ bushels of wheat to produce 100 pounds of flour. However, on the rare occasions when wheat and corn prices are about the same, wheat has also been used as food for livestock and poultry.

Exports play an important role in wheat prices. The United States is the world's largest exporter, selling about half of its annual crop overseas. Major world importers of wheat include Brazil, China, Japan, Korea, and The Netherlands. The levels of wheat production in other nations also have an effect on our prices. Wheat grown in the Southern Hemisphere reaches world markets a half year later than U. S. wheat.

### Where to Find More Information

The best single source of supply and demand
information is the USDA. Their *Wheat Situation
Report*, released five times a year, presents
foreign crop news, wheat stock levels, prices,
and projects quarterly disappearance. *Stocks in
All Positions* is a quarterly publication that
shows wheat on hand and disappearance during
that quarter. There is also a weekly USDA
publication, *Grain Market News*, that provides
information on cash sales, wheat and flour
exports, grain impoundings, exports by port and
destination, and receipts and shipments of
wheat.

The Foreign Agriculture Service, a part of the
USDA, publishes a *Weekly U. S. Export Sales
Report* that covers transactions of 100,000 tons
or more. *Milling and Baking News* is a
commercial trade publication that contains data
and commentary on the current situation in
wheat from crop growing conditions to flour
prices.

For information on the cost and availability of
USDA reports, contact Office of Information,
USDA, Washington, DC 20250 (telephone: 202-
447-7451) and request a copy of the pamphlet
"How to Get Information from the U. S.
Department of Agriculture."

### Commodity: **Oats**

Delivery months: March, May, July,
   September, December
Price in dollars and cents per
   bushel                   Exchange: CBOT
Minimum tick: ¼ cent = $12.50    Contract size: 5,000 bushels

Oats are grown in Minnesota, the Dakotas, Iowa,
and Wisconsin. The crop is planted in the
spring and harvested in late July/early August.
The United States grows about one quarter of

the world's oats and consumes virtually all of it domestically.

The principal use for oats is livestock feed. Only a fraction finds its way into oatmeal for human consumption. Farmers who grow oats keep two thirds or more of their production to feed their own animals.

Oat prices have ranged between $1.00 and $2.00 per bushel for most of the time over the past 15 years. Prices respond to a number of influences. There is an ongoing decline in the amount of acreage being planted to oats, which will eventually cause higher prices. Drought or crop disease that threatens supply can send prices sharply higher, as was seen in the dry summer of 1988; oats rocketed to just under $4.00 a bushel, the highest price ever registered.

Other supply aspects include the cost and availability of other animal feeds, especially corn. A bushel of oats weighs about half as much as a bushel of corn; if feeding values be the same, a bushel of oats should theoretically cost about half as much as a bushel of corn. In fact, oat prices generally run about 10 percent to 15 percent below corn prices, by weight.

On the demand side, the numbers of poultry and livestock are the overriding consideration.

### Where to Find More Information

The best single source of supply and demand information is the USDA. Publications include *Feed Market News* and *National Grain Stocks Summary*, both issued weekly. The regular USDA *Feed Situation* report also shows commercial stock levels and movement of oats.

For information on the cost and availability of USDA reports, contact Office of Information, USDA, Washington, DC 20250 (telephone: 202-447-7451) and request a copy of the pamphlet "How to Get Information from the U. S. Department of Agriculture."

Commodity: **Soybeans**

Delivery months: January, March,
  May, July, August, September,
  November

Price in cents per bushel        Exchange: CBOT
Minimum tick: ¼ cent = $12.50     Contract size: 5,000 bushels

The United States is the world's leading
producer of soybeans, followed by Brazil and
the People's Republic of China. Soybeans vie
with corn as the most important cash crop in
the United States. They are grown in Illinois,
Iowa, Indiana, Ohio, Missouri, and Minnesota—
the Corn Belt. Soybeans are planted between
mid-April and June, but they may be put in the
ground somewhat later without harmful effects
and are often used as an alternate crop when
weather prevents the planting of corn or cotton.
The soybean harvest is usually complete by
October.

Although they are often grouped with grains
for discussion, beans are an oilseed. They are
grown for their yield of soybean oil and soybean
meal. A 60-pound bushel of soybeans will
produce 47 pounds of meal, which is the
driving market, and 11 pounds of oil. About two
thirds of the U. S. crop is crushed at home. The
balance is exported out of the Great Lakes and
Gulf ports, bound primarily for Japan and
Western Europe.

There is a seasonal tendency for cash soybean
prices to rise from a low around harvest time to
a peak the following spring. The supply of
competing soybeans, such as those from Brazil,
also affects U. S. soybean prices in world
markets. Even the prices of corn and cotton
have an indirect effect because corn and cotton
compete with soybeans for growing space.
However, the most significant factor for soybean
prices is the crush margin, or the difference
between the cost of the beans and the prices of
their end products. If the prices for soybean

meal and soybean oil are relatively high, crushers will bid for beans and drive bean prices up.

### Where to Find More Information

The progress of the soybean crop is closely followed. The USDA *Preliminary Planting Survey* (January) and *Planting Intentions* (mid-April) provide the first clues to production prospects. In July, the final figure for planted acreage is released, and monthly production estimates are provided from July to December. The weekly USDA *Export Sales Report* contains information on soybean export commitments and sales. The USDA *Fats and Oils Situation* report presents statistics and projections of supply and demand for the entire soybean complex. For information on the cost and availability of these reports, contact Office of Information, USDA, Washington, DC 20250 (telephone: 202-447-7451) and request a copy of the pamphlet "How to Get Information from the U. S. Department of Agriculture."

Data on soybean crushing, stocks, and disappearance are also provided monthly by the U. S. Census Bureau. The National Soybean Processors Association (1255 23rd Street NW, Washington, DC 20037; telephone: 202-452-8040) publishes a yearbook of trading rules relating the purchase and sale of soybeans, plus weekly and monthly statistical reports. Information on the cost and availability of these materials may be obtained by contacting the association directly.

Commodity: **Soybean Meal**

Delivery months: January, March, May,
  July, August, September, October,
  December

Price in dollars per ton

Minimum tick: 10 cents = $10.00

Exchange: CBOT

Contract size: 100 tons

Soybeans are crushed to obtain their oil and
meal. Of the two, meal is considered the more
valuable by-product; its price is also more
volatile, because it cannot be stored for long.

Soybean meal is rich in protein (40 percent to
45 percent) and is a major ingredient in high-
quality feed for hogs, cattle, and poultry in the
United States. Meal in the United States is
produced in some 100 processing plants. Eighty
percent of the meal is consumed domestically;
the remaining 20 percent is exported, mainly to
Western Europe, Canada, and Japan. The most
important competitors for soybean meal in the
world market are fish meal and peanut meal.
The former comes primarily from Peru, the latter
from India.

There is some seasonality to meal prices,
which tend to be lowest in the fall and to peak
out in the winter when demand is heaviest.

The supply of soybean meal is determined by
the amount of crushing, and that is a function of
the crush margin, or the profitability of crushing
beans. If beans are relatively inexpensive,
crushers will continue to operate, and meal
prices will fall. The total annual supply of
soybean meal from 1978–1979 to 1986–1987
has ranged from 23.2 million tons to 27.1
million tons.[3]

Demand for meal depends on the price and
availability of competing products, the level of
stocks on hand, the rate of disappearance, and
most important, on the number of high-protein-
feed-consuming animals in the United States
and other nations around the world.

### Where to Find More Information

The supply of soybean meal depends largely on
the supply of soybeans. The USDA *Preliminary
Planting Survey* (January) and *Planting
Intentions* (mid-April) provide the first clues to
soybean production prospects. In July, the final
figure for planted acreage is released, and

monthly production estimates are provided from
July to December. The weekly USDA *Export
Sales Report* contains information on soybean
export commitments and sales. The USDA *Fats
and Oils Situation* report presents statistics and
projections of supply and demand for the entire
soybean complex. For information on the cost
and availability of these reports, contact Office
of Information, USDA, Washington, DC 20250
(telephone: 202-447-7451) and request a copy of
the pamphlet "How to Get Information from the
U. S. Department of Agriculture."

Data on soybean crushing, stocks, and
disappearance are also provided monthly by the
U. S. Census Bureau. The National Soybean
Processors Association (1255 23rd Street NW,
Washington, DC 20037; telephone: 202-452-
8040) publishes a yearbook of trading rules
relating the purchase and sale of soybean meal,
plus weekly and monthly statistical reports.
Information on the cost and availability of these
materials may be obtained by contacting the
association directly.

### Commodity: **Soybean Oil**

Delivery months: January, March,
  May, July, August, September,
  October, December

Price in cents per pound                    Exchange: CBOT
Minimum tick: $\frac{1}{100}$ cent = $6.00     Contract size: 60,000 pounds

The United States is the major world producer
of soybean oil and accounts for 90 percent of all
soybean oil exports. One 60-pound bushel of
soybeans gives up 11 pounds of this golden
liquid, the single most important vegetable oil in
world trade. Virtually all of the soybean oil
produced is consumed by the food industry,
where its major uses are in shortening, salad
dressings, cooking oils, and margarine.

The long-range supply of soybean oil is
dependent on the size of the soybean crop plus

any carryover from previous seasons. The new supply can be estimated by assuming that a normal 60 percent of the new crop will be crushed. Unlike soybean meal, soybean oil stores well. The average annual supply of soybean oil during the 9 years from 1978–1979 to 1986–1987 was 12.4 million pounds.[3] Of that amount, about 80 percent went for domestic use and 20 percent for exports.

Because other fats and oils can be used in place of soybean oil in many products, the prices of substitutes are especially important. Lard, cottonseed oil, and butter prices all have an effect on domestic soybean oil demand. On a broader scale, soybean oil also competes with palm oil, coconut oil, rapeseed oil, groundnut oil, and sunflower seed oil. The most important of these are the first two. Palm oil, from Malaysia and Indonesia, is used in shortening. Coconut oil comes from the Philippines and is used primarily in candy and bakery goods.

### Where to Find More Information

The USDA *Preliminary Planting Survey* (January) and *Planting Intentions* (mid-April) provide the first clues to soybean production prospects. In July, the final figure for planted acreage is released, and monthly production estimates are provided from July to December. The weekly USDA *Export Sales Report* contains information on soybean export commitments and sales. The USDA *Fats and Oils Situation* report presents statistics and projections of supply and demand for the entire soybean complex. For information on the cost and availability of these reports, contact Office of Information, USDA, Washington, DC 20250 (telephone: 202-447-7451) and request a copy of the pamphlet "How to Get Information from the U. S. Department of Agriculture."

Data on soybean crushing, stocks, and disappearance are also provided monthly by the

U. S. Census Bureau. The National Soybean
Processors Association (1255 23rd Street NW,
Washington, DC 20037; telephone: 202-452-
8040) publishes a yearbook of trading rules
relating the purchase and sale of soybean oil,
plus weekly and monthly statistical reports.
Information on the cost and availability of these
materials may be obtained by contacting the
association directly.

## INDEXES

Indexes comprise a relatively new category of
futures market. The asset underlying the futures
contract is not a tangible commodity but the
value of the index. Settlement is only by transfer
of cash at the maturity of the futures contract.

Active futures markets currently exist in four
stock indexes, a futures price index, a dollar
index, and a municipal bond index.

Commodity: **CRB Index** (no options traded)
Delivery months: March, May, July,
  September, December
Price in index points and hundredths    Exchange: NYFE
Minimum tick: .05 = $25.00    Contract size: $500 × Index

The CRB (Commodity Research Bureau) Futures
Price Index was first devised in 1957 and has
been modified over the years to reflect changes
in the futures markets. The index today reflects
the price activity in 21 different nonfinancial
futures markets and is considered a broad
measure of market sentiment and price trends.
CRB Index futures can be used to speculate on
aggregrate moves in a number of commodities;
and as an inflation hedge, by buying CRB Index
futures and selling NYSE Index futures.

The underlying CRB Index is calculated in
two steps: First, prices in each individual
futures market are averaged arithmetically; then

these 21 values are averaged geometrically to
arrive at the current index value. The base year
for the Index itself is 1967, which is set equal to
100. An index of 263.25, for example, would
mean that the average commodity price as
measured by the index is 2.63 times greater than
it was in 1967.

CRB Index futures began trading on the NYFE
in early 1986 and have ranged from about
200.00 to 275.00. The last trading day is for the
futures contract the third Friday of the maturity
month, and settlement is by cash only.

The futures markets underlying the index are
also broken down into eight subindexes; these
include grains, livestock and meats, precious
metals, industrials, oilseeds, imported softs,
energy, and miscellaneous. There are no futures
contracts on the subindexes.

### Where to Find More Information

Like all indexes, the CRB Index reflects the
balance of price changes among its constituent
commodities. These include cattle, cocoa, coffee,
copper, corn, cotton, crude oil, gold, heating oil,
hogs, lumber, oats, orange juice, platinum, pork
bellies, silver, soybeans, soybean meal, soybean
oil, sugar No. 11, and wheat. Financial,
currency, and index futures are not included;
this makes the index a relatively accurate
indicator of the cost of living.

CRB Index futures are relatively new, and
little has been written about them *per se*. The
best source for information is the New York
Futures Exchange, whose administrative offices
are at 20 Broad Street, New York, NY 10005.

Commodity: **Major Market Index** (no options traded)
Delivery months: March, June,
   September, December
Price in index points and
   hundredths                            Exchange: CBOT
Minimum tick: .05 = $12.50      Contract size: $250 × index value

The Major Market Index (MMI) comprises 20
blue-chip stocks traded on the New York Stock
Exchange. A broad section of heavily capitalized
industry is represented, including drugs,
chemicals, computers, oil and gas,
pharmaceuticals, merchandising, and consumer
products. The index is calculated by adding up
the prices of the individual stocks and dividing
by a number that changes from time to time to
allow for dividends and stock splits. No
allowance is made for the number of shares of
stock each company has outstanding.

The underlying MMI cash index was devised
by the American Stock Exchange in 1986. Since
that time, the cash index has ranged between
about 330.00 and 540.00, although futures fell
below this range briefly during the panic selling
on October 19, 1987.

Seventeen of the stocks in the MMI are also
in the Dow Jones Industrial Index, making the
MMI an excellent surrogate for the Dow Jones.
The futures contract size is determined by
multiplying $250 times the futures price.
Delivery is by cash only.

Factors affecting the value of the MMI are
those that impact the prices of its component
stocks. A real or anticipated downturn in
business activity depresses stock prices on a
broad front. Changes in interest rates also affect
the stock market but in conflicting ways. The
prospect of lower interest rates promises gains
in the fixed-income sector, yet low interest rates
also make money more affordable for use in
business expansion. Inflation seems to be
generally regarded as a nemesis by the stock
markets. Singular events can also play a role. As

of this writing, the indexes have still not recovered from the crash of October 1987.

### Where to Find More Information

The Chicago Board of Trade (Literature Services Department, LaSalle at Jackson, Chicago, IL 60604) publishes a series of trading strategy brochures utilizing MMI futures. The exchange also publishes a Home Study Course entitled *Stock Index Futures*. A more general introductory book that would be helpful is *How the Stock Market Works*, edited by John M. Dalton and published by the New York Institute of Finance in New York City.

### Commodity: **Municipal Bond Index**

Delivery months: March, June,
   September, December
Price in percentage points and
   32nds
Minimum tick: $\frac{1}{32}$ = $31.25

Exchange: CBOT
Contract size: $1,000 × Index value

The municipal bond futures contract is based on *The Bond Buyer*™ index of 40 actively traded general obligation and revenue bonds. Each bond in the index is priced daily by five brokers, and the results are used to update the index. During the settlement month of a munibond futures contract, the index is updated twice each day.

The constituency of the index is reviewed twice a month, at which time bonds may be added or deleted; however, their number remains 40. To be included, bonds must meet high standards.

Municipal bond prices respond to real or anticipated changes in long-term interest rates, to legislation affecting the tax treatment of their yields, and to investor demand. Prices are expressed in percentage points and 32nds of a percentage point. A price of 94-24, for example, stands for 94 percent of par plus 24/32 of 1

percent of par, or $94,000 plus $750 = $94,750.
Municipal bonds have not been exempt from the
extreme volatility of interest rates in recent
years. Since they began trading in mid-1985,
munibond index futures have ranged in price
from 82-00 to just above 103-00.

Because of their tax status, municipal bonds
trade at premiums to bonds of similar quality
whose interest payments are not tax-free.
Settlement is by cash only. As with other
coupon futures, a conversion factor is used to
standardize the bonds to an 8 percent yield.

### Where to Find More Information

The home exchange is an excellent source for
both current and background information on
Municipal Bond Index futures. Write to Chicago
Board of Trade, Marketing Department, LaSalle
at Jackson, Chicago, IL 60604. *Monetary Trends*
and *National Economic Trends* are publications
of the Federal Reserve Bank of St. Louis, MO.
Information on the health of business in the
United States may be found in two publications
of the U. S. Department of Commerce Bank,
Washington, DC. They are the *Survey of Current
Business* and *Business Conditions Digest*.

Two books that would be helpful are *Fed
Watching and Interest Rate Projections*, by
David M. Jones, and *Yield Curve Analysis*, by
Livingston Douglas. Both are published by the
New York Institute of Finance in New York City.

Commodity: **New York Stock Exchange Composite Index**
Delivery months: March, June,
   September, December
Price in index points and hundredths
Minimum tick: .05 index points =       Exchange: NYFE
   $25.00                Contract size: $500 × Index

The New York Stock Exchange (NYSE)
Composite Index includes all of the more than
1500 stocks traded on the NYSE. To calculate

the index, the price of each stock is first
weighted according to its capitalization (current
stock price times the number of shares
outstanding). The arithmetic average of these
weighted prices is compared to a base value of
50, which represents the average value of all the
stocks on the NYSE as of December 31, 1965. A
current NYSE index value of 200.00, for
example, would mean that the average value of
the stocks listed on the NYSE is four times their
average value at the end of 1965. The index is
recalculated from scratch each day, so the
previous day's index has no effect.

Factors affecting the value of the NYSE Index
are those that impact stock prices. A real or
anticipated downturn in business activity
depresses stock prices on a broad front. Changes
in interest rates also affect the stock market but
in conflicting ways. The prospect of lower
interest rates promises gains in the fixed-income
sector, yet low interest rates also make money
more affordable for use in business expansion.
Inflation seems to be generally regarded as a
nemesis by the stock markets. Singular events
can also play a role. As of this writing, the
indexes still have not recovered from the crash
of October 1987. Since NYSE futures began
trading in May 1982, their values have ranged
from a low of 58.00 to a high of about 190.00.

Though their compositions appear to be quite
different at first glance, the NYSE and the
Standard & Poor's (S&P) 500 virtually duplicate
each other in their responses to stock market
price movement.

### Where to Find More Information

The New York Futures Exchange (administrative
offices: 20 Broad Street, New York, NY 10005)
publishes background information as well as
current data on NYSE Index futures. An
introductory book that would be helpful is *How
the Stock Market Works*, edited by John M.

Dalton and published by the New York Institute of Finance in New York City.

Commodity: **Standard & Poor's 500 Stock Index**
Delivery months: March, June,
    September, December
Price in index points and hundredths
Minimum tick: .05 index points =          Exchange: IOM
    $25.00                                Contract size: $500 × Index

The Standard & Poor's (S&P) 500 Stock Index, as its name implies, is made up of 500 listed and over-the-counter stocks. Four hundred of the stocks are those of industrial companies; the remainder comprise 40 financials, 40 utilities, and 20 transportation issues.

The S&P 500 Index is not a simple arithmetic average. The price of each stock in the index is first weighted according to the total number of shares outstanding. For example, a stock with a price of $20 and 10 million shares outstanding would have twice the impact of a stock with a price of $20 and only 5 million shares outstanding.

The base for the S&P 500 Index is the average value of those 500 stocks during the 1941–1943 period, and that has been set at $10. An index price of 272.00, for example, would mean that the average market value of the basket of stocks is 27.2 times greater than it was then.

Factors affecting the value of the S&P 500 Index are those that impact stock prices. A real or anticipated downturn in business activity depresses stock prices on a broad front. Changes in interest rates also affect the stock market, but in conflicting ways. The prospect of lower interest rates promises gains in the fixed-income sector, yet low interest rates also make money more affordable for use in business expansion. Inflation seems to be generally regarded as a nemesis by the stock markets. Singular events can also play a role. As of this writing, the

indexes still have not recovered from the crash
of October 1987.

Though their compositions appear to be quite
different at first glance, the Standard & Poor's
(S&P) 500 and the NYSE Composite Index
virtually duplicate each other in their responses
to stock market price movement.

### Where to Find More Information

The Index & Option Market of the Chicago
Mercantile Exchange publishes background
information as well as current data on S&P
Index futures. An introductory book that would
be helpful is *How the Stock Market Works*,
edited by John M. Dalton and published by the
New York Institute of Finance in New York City.

Commodity: **U.S. Dollar Index**

Delivery months: March,
   June, September,
   December
Price in index points and
   hundredths
Minimum tick: .01 =          Exchange: FINEX
   $5.00                     Contract size: $500 × U. S. Dollar Index

The U. S. Dollar Index represents a basket of
foreign currencies of 10 major U. S. world
trading partners. When the value of their
currencies goes up, the U. S. dollar Index goes
down and vice versa. Each currency is weighted
in the Index according to that country's share of
world trade.

The base of the Index is the value of the
dollar against the 10 foreign currencies in March
1973 and is set equal to 100. The current index
represents the percentage change in value of the
U. S. dollar since that time. For example, an
index of 198.72 means that the U. S. dollar has
appreciated 98.72 percent against the group of
currencies since March 1973.

The Index is published by Reuters and is
updated every 30 seconds. Countries whose
currencies are represented are West Germany,
Japan, France, United Kingdom, Canada, Italy,
The Netherlands, Belgium, Sweden, and
Switzerland. Settlement is by cash only.
Potential users of U. S. Dollar Index futures
include any business or investor whose costs or
assets are exposed to multiple foreign exchange
rate risk.

### Where to Find More Information

U. S. Dollar Index futures are relatively new,
and little has been written about them. The
exchange publishes several pieces of literature,
which may be ordered directly. The address is
Financial Instrument Exchange, 4 World Trade
Center, New York, NY 10048.

Inasmuch as the index is the obverse side of
the foreign currency values, information on the
currencies themselves is germane. Broad sources
of information on the relationship between the
U. S. dollar and these 10 currencies would
include the U. S. Department of the Treasury
and the U. S. Department of Commerce in
Washington, DC.

In addition, there are three informative
periodicals in the field: *The Economist* (527
Madison Avenue, New York, NY 10022);
*Financial Times of London* (75 Rockefeller
Plaza, New York, NY 10019); and *Euromoney*
(14 Finbury Circus, London EC2, England).

A book that would be helpful is *The
Eurocurrency Market Handbook*, by Eugene
Sarver. It is published by the New York Institute
of Finance, New York City.

Commodity: **Value Line Average Stock Index** (no options traded)
Delivery months: March, June,
   September, December
Price in index points and hundredths    Exchange: KCBT
Minimum tick: .05 = $25.00    Contract size: $500 × Index

The Value Line Average (VLA) is built from the
1700 or so stocks that are covered in the *Value
Line Investment Survey.* About 88 percent of the
stocks in the VLA are also traded on the New
York Stock Exchange; 1 percent is traded on the
American Stock Exchange; 10 percent are traded
over the counter, and the remaining 1 percent
on regional exchanges.

Each stock receives equal weight in the
calculation of the VLA. No allowance is made
for capitalization. A 3-percent change in the
price of General Motors stock would have the
the same effect on the VLA as a 3-percent
change in the price of Gibson Greetings stock.
As a consequence, the Value Line Average tends
to be more sensitive than the other major stock
indexes to fluctuations in lower priced stocks
and the stocks of smaller companies.

The VLA is also computed differently. The
percentage change of each stock in the index is
calculated. The geometric mean of these changes
is added to yesterday's Index to obtain today's
index. The index is set to a base of 100, which
represents the value of the VLA on June 30,
1961. A current Index of 250.10, for example,
would mean that the index is worth 2.50 times
its base value.

Factors affecting the value of the Value Line
Average Index are those that impact stock prices.
A real or anticipated downturn in business
activity depresses stock prices on a broad front.
Changes in interest rates also affect the stock
market but in conflicting ways. The prospect of
lower interest rates promises gains in the fixed-
income sector, yet low interest rates also make
money more affordable for use in business
expansion. Inflation seems to be generally

regarded as a nemesis by the stock markets.
Singular events can also play a role. As of this
writing, the indexes still have not recovered
from the crash of October 1987.

### Where to Find More Information

The Kansas City Board of Trade publishes
background information as well as current data
on Value Line Average Index futures. Their
address is 4800 Main Street, Kansas City, MO
64112. Telephone: 816-753-7500. A recently
released introductory book that would be
helpful is *How the Stock Market Works*, edited
by John M. Dalton and published by the New
York Institute of Finance in New York City.

## INTEREST RATES

Futures contracts are traded on all three
Treasury securities: bonds, notes, and bills.
There is also a very liquid futures market in
Eurodollars.

Eurodollar and T-bill futures, which represent
short-term interest rates, are traded on the IMM.
T-bond and 5- and 10-year T-note futures,
representative of long-term rates, are traded on
the Chicago Board of Trade. Five-year T-note
futures are also actively traded on the Financial
Instrument Exchange, a division of the New
York Cotton Exchange. In addition, there are
minicontracts of T-note and T-bill futures on the
MidAmerica Commodity Exchange in Chicago.

### Where to Find More Information

The home exchanges are very good sources for
both current and background information on
these highly active futures contracts. The
address of the International Monetary Market is
30 South Wacker Drive, Chicago, IL 60606. The
address of the the Chicago Board of Trade is

LaSalle at Jackson, Chicago IL 60604. FINEX is
at 4 World Trade Center, New York, NY 10048.

The Federal Reserve Bank of St. Louis, MO,
publishes *Monetary Trends* and *National
Economic Trends*. Information on the health of
business in the United States may be found in
two publications of the U. S. Department of
Commerce Bank, Washington, DC. They are the
*Survey of Current Business* and *Business
Conditions Digest*.

A biweekly newsletter focusing on Federal
Reserve policy and Treasury financing is
published by Goldsmith-Nagam, Inc., 1545 New
York Avenue NE, Washington, DC 20002. Called
*ROG/Bond and Money Letter*, it is available by
subscription for $275 per year. *Fedwatch*, a
weekly newsletter published by MMS
International (275 Shoreline Drive, Redwood
City, CA 94065) covers Federal Reserve policy,
monetary aggregates, economic indicators, and
Treasury auctions.

Two books that would be helpful are *Fed
Watching and Interest Rate Projections*, by
David M. Jones, and *Yield Curve Analysis*, by
Livinston Douglas. Both are published by the
New York Institute of Finance in New York City.

Commodity: **Eurodollar**

Delivery months: March, June, September,
December

Price in percent of par (100%)  Exchange: IMM
Minimum tick: .01% = $25.00  Contract size: $1 million

A Eurodollar is a U. S. dollar on deposit outside
of the United States. Most Eurodollars reside in
the London branches of major world banks.
They are the basis for dollar loans made by
European banks to commercial borrowers. There
are also fixed-income securities denominated in
Eurodollars.

Eurodollars are part of what is known as the
"money market." Their price reflects short-term

interest rates in Europe; specifically, the 3-month London Interbank Offered Rate (LIBOR). The factors that affect short-term interest rates are many. They include actions taken by central banks to raise or lower the money supply, interest rates in other nations, balance of trade, the present level of demand for short-term loans, the availability of other sources for money, interest rates on other instruments such as CDs and Treasury bills, and general economic conditions.

The Eurodollar futures contract was introduced in December 1981 and has grown rapidly. Futures prices have ranged from 83 percent to just above 94 percent, representing short-term interest rates from 17 percent to just below 6 percent. The asset underlying the futures contract is a 90-day Eurodollar time deposit of $1 million. Settlement is by cash only.

The 3-month Eurodollar/T-bill futures spread is popular. Called a TED spread, it increases when interest rates rise, while the spread effect reduces downside risk.

## Commodity: **Treasury Bills (90-day)**

Delivery months: March, June, September, December
Price = 100% minus Treasury bill yield
Minimum tick: .01% (1 basis point) =           Exchange: IMM
$25.00                                          Contract size: $1 million

Cash Treasury bills (T-bills) with maturities of 3, 6, and 12 months are auctioned at regular intervals by the federal government. They are bought at a discount and redeemed at par, the difference representing the yield. The asset underlying the T-bill futures contract is a 90-day T-bill.

Prices of cash T-bills are quoted in *basis points*, with each point equal to $\frac{1}{100}$ of 1 percentage point, or .01 percent. T-bill futures prices are expressed in terms of an index that is equal to 100 minus the T-bill's annual yield. For example, a T-bill with an annual yield of 7.50 percent would be quoted on the IMM at 92.50.

T-bills are the bellwether of the "money market." The supply of new T-bills depends on the government's need for funds. Prices in the secondary (dealer) market reflect the demand for short-term investments by business and private investors. From a larger perspective, T-bill prices also respond to changes in midrange and long-term interest rates.

Forecasting the course of interest rates is complex. Some of the domestic factors to be taken into consideration include demand by business for funds to construct new plants, carry inventory, or retire debt; government spending for public works, social welfare, and military personnel and hardware; changes in income tax; operations by the Federal Reserve Board to control inflation; changes in the money supply; and the level of consumer personal income, debts, and savings.

Interest rates are also affected by interest rates in other nations, balance of trade, the availability of other sources for money, interest rates on other short-term instruments such as CDs and commercial paper, and general economic conditions.

### Commodity: **Treasury Bonds**

Delivery months: March, June, September,
   December

| | |
|---|---|
| Price in percent and $\frac{1}{32}$% of par | Exchange: CBOT |
| Minimum tick: $\frac{1}{32}$ = $31.25 | Contract size: $100,000 |

U. S. Treasury bonds are sold through the Federal Reserve to domestic and foreign investors to meet long-term obligations of the federal government. Like Treasury notes, T-bonds are coupon-bearing; they pay a fixed dollar amount of interest semiannually. T-bond maturities are from 10 to 30 years. They are marketed in two time frames. Bonds that mature in 20 years are sold at regular quarterly auctions. Bonds that mature in 30 years are not sold at regular intervals but are marketed about every 3 years. The secondary (dealer) market for T-bonds is extremely broad and liquid.

U. S. Treasury bonds are the international flagship for long-term interest rates, and their cash and futures prices reflect the smallest change in the interest rate picture. Some of the domestic factors to be taken into consideration when forecasting the course of interest rates are demand by business for funds to construct new plants, carry inventory, or retire debt; government spending for public works, social welfare, and military personnel and hardware; changes in income tax; operations by the Federal Reserve Board to control inflation; changes in the money supply; and the level of consumer personal income, debts, and savings.

Interest rates in the United States are also affected by interest rates in other nations, our balance of trade, the availability of other sources for money, interest rates on other short-term instruments such a CDs and commercial paper, and general economic conditions.

### Commodity: **Treasury Notes (10-year)**

Delivery months: March, June, September,
  December

| | |
|---|---|
| Price in percentage and $\frac{1}{32}$% of par | Exchange: CBOT |
| Minimum tick: $\frac{1}{32}$ = $31.25 | Contract size: $100,000 |

### Commodity: **Treasury Notes (5-year)** (no options traded)

Delivery months: March, June, September,
  December

| | |
|---|---|
| Price in percentage and $\frac{1}{32}$% of par | Exchange: CBOT |
| Minimum tick: $\frac{1}{2}$ of $\frac{1}{32}$ = $15.625 | Contract size: $100,000 |

Commodity: **Treasury Notes (5-year)**

Delivery months: March, June, September,
   December

Price in percentage and $\frac{1}{32}$% of par        Exchange: FINEX

Minimum tick: $\frac{1}{2}$ of $\frac{1}{32}$ = $15.625      Contract size: $100,000

Treasury notes are midrange on the yield curve, maturing in from 1 to 10 years. They are sold to public investors by the Federal Reserve to fund ongoing government operations and refinance the national debt. Two-year notes are auctioned monthly. Notes maturing in 4 or 5 years or longer are sold quarterly. There is also an active secondary (dealer) market.

As shown above, there are three active T-note futures contracts. They differ in the maturity of their underlying cash instruments, their pricing, and where they are traded. The delivery vehicle for the 10-year futures contract is a T-note that matures in $6\frac{1}{2}$ to 10 years; the minimum futures price change is $\frac{1}{32}$. The delivery vehicle for the two 5-year futures contracts is any of the four most recently issued 5-year Treasury notes, and the minimum futures price change is $\frac{1}{2}$ of $\frac{1}{32}$, or $\frac{1}{64}$.

Domestic factors to be taken into consideration when forecasting interest rates are demand by business for funds to construct new plants, carry inventory, or retire debt; government spending for public works, social welfare, and military personnel and hardware; changes in income tax; operations by the Federal Reserve Board to control inflation; change in the money supply; and the level of consumer personal income, debts, and savings.

Interest rates in the U. S. are also affected by interest rates in other nations, our balance of trade, the availability of other sources for money, interest rates on other short-term instruments such as CDs and commercial paper, and general economic conditions.

# MEATS

Futures contracts are traded on live cattle,
feeder cattle, live hogs, and frozen pork bellies.
The Chicago Mercantile Exchange is the home of
all of these futures contracts and has published
a wealth of information on them over the years.
The address of the exchange is 30 South Wacker
Drive, Chicago, IL 60606.

Current information on the supply of and
demand for these commodities is provided both
by private research sources and the U. S.
Department of Agriculture. Pertinent
publications for each market are listed at the
end of each briefing sheet.

## Commodity: **Cattle (Live)**

Delivery months: February, April,
June, August, October, December
Price in cents per pound                Exchange: CME
Minimum tick: 2½ cents = $10.00       Contract size: 40,000 pounds

Cattle raised for beef comprise the largest single
segment of American agriculture. Fresh beef
cannot be stored; prices will adjust to sell all the
beef that is in the supply pipeline. In the past
30 years, cattle futures prices have ranged from
a low 25 cents to a high of 80 cents a pound.

Cattle are fed on grass or corn. They are
placed on feed at a weight of about 700 pounds
and marketed some 8 to 10 weeks later at
weights of 1000 to 1200 pounds. Most fed cattle
come from the feed grain areas of the Midwest.
More calves are born in the spring than any
other time of the year, so most yearlings are put
on feed in the fall. Cattle prices tend to be
seasonally lowest at this time and highest in
early spring.

Cattle prices are affected by several factors.
These include the weather during the feeding
season, the condition of range and pasture land,

government buying programs, and the prices of competitive meats like chicken and pork. From a larger perspective, consumer preferences also play a significant role. Average per capita consumption of beef has been declining in recent years.

Cattle have an irregular long-term price/ production cycle of about 8 years, in which the numbers of animals available for slaughter respond to changes in the prices of cattle and feed, rising gradually when cattle prices remain relatively high and falling when cattle prices are low.

### Where to Find More Information

USDA is the primary source of current information on the supply and demand situation in cattle. USDA publications include weekly, monthly, and quarterly releases. The weekly reports contain summaries of market news. There are monthly reports on the placement of cattle on feed, numbers on feed by weight group, and marketing of cattle in the major feeding states. USDA also publishes a comprehensive quarterly *Cattle on Feed* report; and in February and July, the USDA *Livestock Inventory Report* shows, among other data, the number of potential feedlot cattle available.

Other USDA titles include *Livestock and Meat Situation Report*, *Feed Situation Report*, *Livestock, Meat and Wool*, and *Livestock Slaughter and Meat Production*.

For information on the cost and availability of these reports, contact Office of Information, USDA, Washington, DC 20250 (telephone: 202-447-7451) and request a copy of the pamphlet "How to Get Information from the U. S. Department of Agriculture."

Commodity: **Feeder Cattle**

Delivery months: January, March,
   April, May, August, September,
   October, November

Price in cents per pound

Minimum tick: 2½ cents = $11.00

Exchange: CME

Contract size: 44,000 pounds

Feeder cattle are yearling steers. They comprise the input for cattle feeders, who fatten them up and sell them for beef. Feeder cattle futures have been traded since 1971; their prices have ranged widely, from 25 cents to 90 cents a pound. The futures contract is cash settled.

Cattle are fed on grass or corn. They are placed on feed at a weight of about 700 pounds and marketed some 8 to 10 weeks later at weights of 1000 to 1200 pounds. More calves are born in the spring than any other time of the year, so most yearlings are put on feed in the fall. Cattle prices tend to be seasonally lowest at this time and highest in early spring.

The demand for feeder cattle reflects prices for finished cattle. Finished cattle prices are affected by several factors. These include the weather during the feeding season, the condition of range and pasture land, government buying programs, and the prices of competitive meats like chicken and pork. From a larger perspective, consumer preferences also play a significant role. Average per capita consumption of beef has been declining in recent years.

Cattle have an irregular long-term price/ production cycle of about 8 years, in which the numbers of animals available for slaughter respond to changes in the prices of cattle and feed, rising gradually when cattle prices remain relatively high and falling when cattle prices are low.

### Where to Find More Information

USDA is the primary source for information on the supply and demand situation in cattle. USDA publications include weekly, monthly,

and quarterly releases. The weekly reports
contain summaries of market news. There are
monthly reports on the placement of cattle on
feed, numbers on feed by weight group, and
marketing of cattle in the major feeding states.
USDA also publishes a comprehensive quarterly
*Cattle on Feed* report; and in February and July,
the USDA *Livestock Inventory Report* shows,
among other data, the number of potential
feedlot cattle available.

Other USDA titles include *Livestock and Meat
Situation Report, Feed Situation Report,
Livestock, Meat and Wool,* and *Livestock
Slaughter and Meat Production.*

For information on the cost and availability of
these reports, contact Office of Information,
USDA, Washington, DC 20250 (telephone: 202-
447-7451) and request a copy of the pamphlet
"How to Get Information from the U. S.
Department of Agriculture."

## Commodity: **Hogs (Live)**

Delivery months: February, April,
  June, July, August, October,
  December

Price in cents per pound

Minimum tick: 2½ cents = $7.50

Exchange: CME

Contract size: 30,000 pounds

Most hogs are raised where their food is grown:
in the Corn Belt. Iowa is the leading hog
producer by a large margin. Other hog-
producing states are Illinois, Minnesota, Ohio,
and Wisconsin.

Although the pattern has been modified
recently by confined hog raising, sows tend to
farrow (give birth) in the spring and the fall. The
time from farrowing to a market weight of 220
pounds is about 6 months. Slaughter of mature
animals is lowest in midsummer, and prices
tend to firm them. Demand also peaks during
the summer barbecue season. Prices are
seasonally lowest in the November–December
period, when slaughter is at its highest.

One factor that affects the supply of hogs is the hog/corn ratio, which is the number of bushels of corn it would take to buy 100 pounds of live hog. When corn prices are high relative to hog prices (the ratio is low), hog production is discouraged. A high ratio (cheap corn, high-priced hogs) acts as a spur to hog production.

There is also a long-term "cycle" to hog production, as producers respond to the ups and down in hog prices: High hog prices lead to increased production; this pushes hog prices down, and that causes production to slow, which pushes prices back up again. In the past, the hog cycle has had an average length of about 4 years.

Demand for hogs reflects consumer demand for pork products, which include bacon, ham, roasts, chops, and frankfurters. This demand, in turn, reflects pork prices, the prices of other red meats, consumers' levels of disposable income, and dietary preferences.

### Where to Find More Information

The quarterly USDA *Hogs and Pigs* report is a comprehensive source of information. The March and September reports cover 14 states representing about 85 percent of hog production; the June and December reports cover all 50 states. The report shows hogs on farms by weight category and farmers' stated farrowing intentions, from which forthcoming supplies may be estimated. Other pertinent USDA publications include *Livestock and Meat Situation*, *Livestock Slaughter and Meat Production*, and *Feed Situation*. For information on the cost and availability of these reports, contact Office of Information, USDA, Washington, DC 20250 (telephone: 202-447-7451) and request a copy of the pamphlet "How to Get Information from the U. S. Department of Agriculture."

The monthly newsletter *Pork Pro* contains supply/demand information and data on trends

in hog production, sales, and prices. It is
published by Oster Communications, 219
Parkade, Cedar Falls, IA 50613.

Commodity: **Pork Bellies, Frozen**

Delivery months: February, March,
   May, July, August

Price in cents per pound                    Exchange: CME

Minimum tick: 2½ cents = $9.50          Contract size: 38,000 pounds

A pork belly is uncured bacon. One hog yields
two pork bellies of from 12 to 14 pounds each.
Pork bellies tend to accumulate in freezers from
October to April, reflecting both low demand
and high hog slaughter during the period. Net
movement of frozen bellies is out of storage
during the summer months.

   Demand for bacon does not change much
when the price of bacon changes. As a
consequence, the principal price-making factor
for pork bellies is their supply, and a relatively
small change in supply can have a great effect
on price. The forthcoming supply of fresh pork
bellies can be approximated by projecting hog
farrowings forward for 6 months and
multiplying the resulting number of hogs by 26
pounds. This number would be added to known
supplies of bellies on hand to derive the total
projected supply for any particular period.
Longer term, the supply of pork bellies depends
on the number of hogs that are slaughtered. This
brings the hog/corn ratio and the hog cycle into
the equation.

   Although bellies are not seasonal in the sense
of the grains, February bellies are considered
"new crop," and bellies in storage before
November 1 cannot be delivered against the next
year's February futures contract.

### Where to Find More Information

The USDA's monthly *Cold Storage Report* gives
the frozen belly inventory. USDA also publishes

information on the bacon slice, which reflects demand for the end product.

The quarterly USDA *Hogs and Pigs* report is a comprehensive source of information. The March and September reports cover 14 states representing about 85 percent of hog production; the June and December reports cover all 50 states. The report shows hogs on farms by weight category and farmers' stated farrowing intentions. Other pertinent USDA publications include *Livestock and Meat Situation, Livestock Slaughter and Meat Production,* and *Feed Situation.* For information on the cost and availability of these reports, contact Office of Information, USDA, Washington, DC 20250 (telephone: 202-447-7451) and request a copy of the pamphlet "How to Get Informaton from the U. S. Department of Agriculture."

The monthly newsletter *Pork Pro* contains supply/demand information and data on trends in hog production, sales, and prices. It is published by Oster Communications, 219 Parkade, Cedar Falls, IA 50613.

# METALS

Metals futures markets comprise copper, gold, platinum, and silver. The last three are generally looked on as precious metals, whereas copper is considered to be an industrial metal.

The principal futures markets for copper, gold, and silver are on the Commodity Exchange Inc. (COMEX) in New York City. Platinum futures are traded on the New York Mercantile Exchange. Smaller size contracts of gold and silver are traded on the MidAmerica Commodity Exchange in Chicago.

### Where to Find More Information

The U. S. Bureau of Mines in Washington, DC periodically releases information based on the level of metal imports, secondary recovery in the United States, and stocks of the metal held by importers, dealers, and fabricators of this country. They also publish the *Minerals Yearbook* and the *Mineral Industry Surveys*. The American Bureau of Metal Statistics publishes a monthly report that contains information on worldwide prices, production, deliveries, and stocks. General information on metals supply and demand may also be found in the *Statistical Abstract of the U. S.*, which may be obtained from the Superintendent of Documents, Government Printing Office, Washington, DC 20402.

Magazines devoted to the subject include *Engineering and Mining Journal* (McGraw-Hill, New York, NY), *Iron Age* (Chilton, Radnor, PA), and *Modern Metals* (Chicago, IL).

## Commodity: **Copper**

Delivery months: January, March,
   May, July, September, December
Price in dollars and cents per pound    Exchange: COMEX
Minimum tick: $\frac{1}{100}$ cent = $2.50    Contract size: 25,000 pounds

Most of the world supply of copper is produced in the United States. Other leading world producers are Zambia, Chile, Canada, Zaire, and Peru. Mine production in the United States is centered in Arizona. The United States is also the world's largest consumer of copper, accounting for about 25 percent of total world usage. CIPEC, a trade organization comprising major world producers, accounts for about 70 percent of international trade in copper.

Copper is an excellent conductor of heat and electricity and virtually does not oxidize. Its principal uses are in electric and electronic equipment, building construction, and engines. However, it is found in almost every product in an industrialized nation.

Because of its international nature, copper prices are directly affected by supply-reducing strikes or political unrest in foreign producing countries. Foreign exchange rates influence the effective price of copper to an importing nation. Other price factors include government embargos, production curtailments because of water shortage or other environmental considerations, overt efforts by CIPEC to control prices, and the amount of stockpiled copper, particularly at the London Metal Exchange (LME), which is a major world repository.

From a longer perspective, copper prices also reflect changes in the level of economic activity in consuming countries, and the prospect of another metal (aluminum) or a man-made material substituting for it in some uses.

### Commodity: **Gold**

Delivery months: February, April,
June, August, October, December
Price in dollars and cents per troy
ounce                                    Exchange: COMEX
Minimum tick: 10 cents = $10.00          Contract size: 100 troy ounces

Traditional supply/demand analysis of gold is difficult because of the psychological factors involved. Gold is a charismatic metal. It was once thought to have magical powers. It is considered a hedge against inflation and a safe haven for wealth when paper currencies fall into disrepute.

The largest producer of gold is South Africa, which accounts for some 65 percent of annual world production. The USSR is the next largest, with about 15 percent. Gold is also generated by the melting down of scrap. This secondary supply is more difficult to gauge than gold refined from ore, but about one quarter of annual supplies are estimated to be derived from this source.

As an industrial metal, gold also has unique properties. It does not rust or corrode. It is an excellent conductor of heat and electricity and is the most malleable of all metals. It finds it

way into a variety of products, including
jewelry, electrical and electronic components,
dentistry, coins, and medals and medallions. Of
these, jewelry is the most significant, taking
about 70 percent of the available supply in
recent years.

The demand for gold has several facets. An
important one is the demand for jewelry, which
in turn, reflects the level of world discretionary
spending power. The prospect for lower interest
rates may cause gold buying, in anticipation of
business expansion and a general increase in
economic welfare. Sales of gold by central banks
to raise foreign exchange would put pressure on
gold prices. An increase in gold production
would also have a depressing effect. Changes in
inflation pressures, as measured by popular
indexes, may cause investor demand for gold to
rise or fall.

The Gold Institute (1026 16th Street NW,
Suite 101, Washington, DC 20036) publishes a
bimonthly newsletter as well as several reports
on gold mining, fabrication, and usage. A 28-
minute videotape is also available. Information
on these may be obtained by contacting the
institute directly.

A book that would be helpful is *Gold
Investment*, by Eugene J. Sherman. It published
by the New York Institute of Finance in New
York City.

Commodity: **Platinum** (no options traded)
Delivery months: January, April, July,
  October
Price in dollars per troy ounce          Exchange: NYME
Minimum tick: 10 cents = $.50          Contract size: 50 troy ounces

Production of platinum is dominated by South
Africa, which accounted for 92 percent of the
free world supply in 1986. South Africa ores are
as much as 10 times richer than anywhere else
in the world. Canada, a distant second, produces

platinum only as a by-product to its nickel and copper mining operations.

Demand for platinum is three-pronged: in jewelry, as a catalyst in the refining of crude petroleum, and for use in automotive catalytic converters. About 70 percent of the annual free-world production of platinum goes into emission control devices on gasoline driven cars and light trucks in the United States. Changes in this aspect of demand would derive from relaxed Environmental Protection Agency (EPA) emission standards, the discovery of a substitute for platinum in catalytic converters, or increasing concern with automotive air pollution in Japan and Western Europe.

The largest consumer of platinum for jewelry is Japan, where for centuries the metal has been preferred by women over gold for necklaces and wedding and engagement rings. However, gold has been making inroads into the Japanese jewelry market in recent years. Platinum's role in the petroleum cracking process is as a catalyst for certain necessary chemical reactions.

Like gold, the metal also is used by investors as a store of value, and its price has from time to time been higher than the price of gold. Platinum prices are also more volatile than gold prices, for two reasons: the platinum futures market's relatively small size and low liquidity, and the fact that aboveground holdings of investment platinum in the form of bars and wafers are small.

Commodity: **Silver**

Delivery months: January, March, May,
  July, September, December
Price in cents per troy ounce                Exchange: COMEX
Minimum tick: $\frac{1}{10}$ cent = $5.00          Contract size: 5,000 ounces

Silver comes from three sources: Primary production comes from the refining of newly mined ore and consistently falls short of world silver demand. Secondary production fills the gap; it comprises silver that is recovered from melted art objects and flatware, used photographic film, and scrap electrical connectors. The third source is world silver stocks, held in such repositories as COMEX, the London Metal Exchange (LME), and government coffers.

Mexico is the world's largest producer of silver, followed by Peru, Canada, Australia, and the United States. From 1982 to 1986, the average total free-world annual silver supply was about 410 million ounces.

Demand for silver arises from several sectors of the economy. Silver is an excellent conductor of heat and electricity, is resistant to corrosion, and has beauty. Its most consistent use is in photographic film and solutions, which take 120 million ounces annually. Electronic components in the free world consume another 60 to 80 million ounces each year, and this amount is likely to rise with the increasing industrialization of the Western World. Silver is the favorite metal of European jewelry makers. The demand for silver in jewelry is more responsive to changes in the metal's price. For example, jewelry demand is estimated to have fallen more than 50 percent during the silver bull market of 1979–1980.

Other uses for the white metal are dentistry, the making of storage batteries, and as a hedge against inflation or currency unrest, like gold.

The Silver Institute (1026 16th Street NW, Suite 101, Washington, DC 20036) publishes a bimonthly newsletter as well as several written reports on silver mining, fabrication, and usage. A 28-minute videotape is also available. Information on these may be obtained by contacting the Silver Institute directly.

## PETROLEUM

In terms of value of the physical product, petroleum is the largest business in the world.

Petroleum futures markets were introduced in the mid-1970s, in response to the sudden price volatility caused by Organization of Petroleum Exporting Countries' (OPEC) oil embargoes in 1973 and 1974. Crude oil is the basis for all petroleum products. Once pumped to the surface, water and gas are removed, and the crude is graded for density and sulphur content. It is then transported to refining centers.

Futures are traded on crude oil; they are also traded on heating oil No. 2 and unleaded gasoline, two of the most important derivatives of crude oil.

### Where to Find More Information

The New York Mercantile Exchange publishes an excellent quarterly magazine called *Energy in the News*. It contains current articles on pricing and production of petroleum, futures trading, and industry background. For further information, contact the marketing department of the exchange at 4 World Trade Center, New York, NY 10048 (telephone: 212-938-2213).

A monthly newsletter published by the American Petroleum Institute provides analysis of recent developments in the production, imports, refining, and inventories of petroleum and petroleum products. The address of the Institute is 1120 L Street NW, Washington, DC 20005.

A source for background information is the *International Petroleum Encyclopedia*, published by the Penn-Well Publishing Company, Tulsa, OK. There are several periodicals in the field. *Oil and Gas Journal* is also published by Penn-Well. *Platts' Oilgram* is put out by McGraw-Hill, 1221 Avenue of the Americas, New York, NY 10020. The Department of Energy (National Energy Information Center, EI231, Washington, DC 20585) publishes the *Monthly Energy Review*, *Monthly Petroleum Statement*, and *Weekly*

_Petroleum Status Report_ and can tell you about
their cost and availability.

Commodity: Crude Oil

Delivery months: 18 consecutive
    months
Price in dollars and cents per barrel      Exchange: NYMEX
Minimum tick: 1 cent = $10.00      Contract size: 1,000 barrels

Demand for crude oil derives mainly from
refineries, which "crack" it into several different
by-products. The most important of these are
motor gasoline, heating oil, jet fuel (kerosene),
diesel oil, and propane. In fact, the first three
account for some 80 percent of all refinery
output in the United States.

Because its demand is derived, price factors
for crude oil are really those of its by-products.
A series of cold winters, a significant increase in
automobile use, or a new fuel-saving widebody
airplane would all influence crude oil prices in
the long run. The most visible short-term price
factors are OPEC efforts to reduce production
and thereby raise prices.

Cash crude oil transactions may take place at
several locations around the world. In the
United States, a large volume of crude oil
trading occurs in Cushing, Oklahoma, and St.
James, Louisiana.

Commodity: Gasoline (unleaded) (no options traded)

Delivery months: 15 consecutive
    months
Price in dollars and cents per gallon      Exchange: NYMEX
Minimum tick: $\frac{1}{100}$ cent = $4.20      Contract size: 42,000 gallons

Gasoline's principal use is as fuel for private
automobiles, and its nature varies from one
section of the country to another and from one
season to another, to reflect driving conditions.
The strongest seasonal demand is during the

summer months. Prior to 1974, refiners added tetraethyl lead to their gasoline to improve octane ratings. Virtually no leaded gasoline is produced in the United States today.

The popularity of automobile travel is a major factor in the demand for gasoline. Retail gasoline prices are slow to respond to changes in its production costs. Likewise, gasoline demand is relatively inelastic; that is, even hefty increases in prices at the pump don't seem to have much effect on automobile use.

Gasoline futures are part of the "crack" spread, whereby a refiner buys crude oil futures, sells gasoline futures, and thus establishes in advance his profit margin for that part of the refining process.

## Commodity: **Heating Oil No. 2**

Delivery months: 18 consecutive
  months

Price in dollars and cents per gallon         Exchange: NYMEX

Minimum tick: 1/100 cent = $4.20         Contract size: 42,000 gallons

The principal use of heating oil is in furnaces to warm residential and commercial buildings. Ninety percent of heating oil supplies come from domestic refinery production; the remainder comes from imports and inventory.

There is a strong seasonal tendency in cash prices for heating oil. Stored supplies tend to build up in the fall and are depleted during the winter heating season. Prices tend to firm with the arrival of frost. Increases or declines in the price of the source—crude oil—also eventually pass through to the price of heating oil.

Demand for heating oil is relatively constant, although consumers will lower their thermostats when prices are extremely high. Persistent high petroleum prices encourage the development and use of alternate heating means, such as electricity or natural gas.

The heating oil futures contract on the New York Mercantile Exchange calls for delivery in

New York harbor. Since futures began trading in
late 1978, prices have ranged from a high of
$1.05 a gallon to a low of 30 cents a gallon.
Heating oil futures are part of the "crack"
spread, whereby a refiner buys crude oil futures,
sells heating oil futures, and thus establishes in
advance his profit margin for that part of the
refining process.

# WOOD

There is only one wood futures contract actively
traded today. It is lumber and is traded on the
Chicago Mercantile Exchange. For some years
there was also a futures market in plywood, but
it has fallen to a lack of trading activity.

Commodity: **Lumber**

Delivery months: September,
   November, January, March, May

Price in dollars and cents per
   1,000 board feet

Minimum tick: 10 cents per 1,000       Exchange: CME
   board feet = $15.00                 Contract size: 150,000 board feet

Most of the lumber produced in the United
States comes from the Pacific Northwest.
Douglas fir is the leading wood and is grown
primarily in Oregon, Washington, and northern
California.

The bulk of the lumber produced goes into
the construction of new residential homes, so
the actual and anticipated level of housing starts
are important influences on prices. There is also
a seasonal price movement; sawmills tend to
acquire a large inventory of logs at the end of
the warm-weather cutting season, and cash
lumber prices tend to hit annual lows then.
Prices are usually highest in the spring, as the
building season gets under way. Prices are also
affected by the level of logging and mill
operation, and any strikes, fires, drought, or

heavy precipitation that would slow operations will reduce supply and have a positive effect on prices.

In addition to the level of housing starts, demand for lumber is also indirectly influenced by interest rates, the availability of mortgage credit, and weather during the building season.

### Where to Find More Information

The U. S. Department of Commerce makes monthly reports on housing starts and building permits. These reports are widely published and are followed closely by lumber interests. There is also a large amount of trade literature available. The WWPA organization, 1500 Yeon Building, Portland, OR 97204, publishes *Western Lumber Facts, Lumber Price Trends,* and a *Statistical Yearbook.* The Forest Service of the USDA publishes *Lumber Production & Mill Stocks*; it is sold through the Government Printing Office, Division of Public Documents, Washington, DC 20402. *Random Lengths* is a monthly publication of Random Lengths Publications, Inc., Box 867, Eugene, OR. *Crow's Weekly Letter* is put out by C.C. Crow Publications, Inc., Terminal Sales Building, Portland, OR 97205.

# Appendix A

## More Chart Patterns
## and What They Mean

### Triangles

Triangles come in more than one variety. The
*symmetrical* triangle looks like the equilateral
triangle you probably first met in freshman
math, with all three sides and all three angles
equal. It has some of the qualities of a rectangle.
The difference is that the top and bottom sides
of the pattern are not parallel but converge to a
point at the right.

   If the rectangle signifies a standoff between
the bulls and the bears, the triangle represents a
pitched battle between them. With each rally,
the sellers step in at a lower point to turn prices
back. Each decline is met with buying at a
higher level. The battle is over when one side
finally prevails and prices break out of the
triangle. Figure 16 shows an example.

   When a symmetrical triangle interrupts a
swift price move, it often marks the middle of

**FIGURE 16.** The symmetrical triangle is formed by two minor trendlines, one upward and the one downward. Prices are typically "squeezed" toward the apex before breaking out. In this example, the market fell sharply during the month of October, then began an 11-week triangular consolidation pattern. The pattern was completed on January 15 when prices fell through the bottom of the triangle and the downtrend resumed. Reprinted with Permission, © 1988 Commodity Perspective, 30 South Wacker Drive, Suite 1820, Chicago, Illinois 60606.

that move. That is, the travel of prices beyond the triangle will be about equal to the travel of prices before the triangle. Referring to Figure 16, the steep decline began at about 637 and carried to 485, a distance of 637 − 485 = 152. A chart technician would project that same distance downward from the point where prices broke

out of the triangle (500) and arrive at a tentative
price objective of 500 − 152 = 348.

There are two other kinds of triangles, and
each contains a built-in indication of where
prices are likely to go next. They are both right
triangles. They are called *ascending* and
*descending* triangles.

An ascending triangle has the flat side on the
top, as in Figure 17. The rising line at the

**FIGURE 17.** An ascending triangle indicates that the bulls are becoming
increasingly aggressive, as they are stopping declines at successively higher
levels; the sellers, on the other hand, are just holding their own. The pattern
therefore holds the promise of an upside breakout, as in this example.
Reprinted with Permission, © 1988 Commodity Perspective, 30 South
Wacker Drive, Suite 1820, Chicago, Illinois 60606.

bottom of the triangle indicates that buyers are becoming increasingly aggressive, as they are stopping each decline at a successively higher level. Sellers are not stepping up their activities; rallies meet resistance and are turned back at about the same price each time. The pattern holds the promise that the confrontation will be won by the more aggressive bulls, when overhead resistance is finally overpowered. This was the case in Figure 17.

Figure 18 shows a descending triangle pattern. Here the bears are becoming increasingly aggressive, as rallies are turned

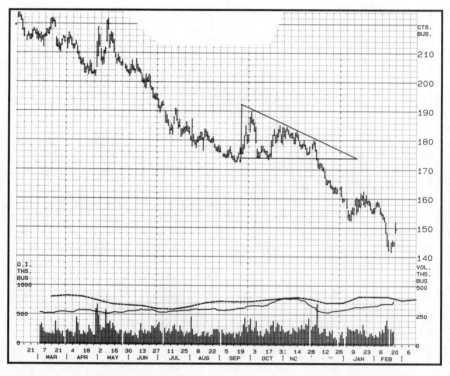

**FIGURE 18.** In a descending traingle, the sellers have the upper hand. They step in to meet each rally at a successively lower price level, while the buyers hold the same line. In this example of price consolidation, the sellers finally overwhelmed the bulls, and prices resumed their lower trend. Reprinted with Permission, © 1988 Commodity Perspective, 30 South Wacker Drive, Suite 1820, Chicago, Illinois 60606.

back at a lower price each time. When the reservoir of buying power at $1.74 was tapped out, prices fell through the floor of the triangle and resumed their lower course.

Triangles may mark either price reversal points or areas of price consolidation. As with rectangles, there are clues. A descending triangle at the end of a long upward price move would carry the presumption of a reversal pattern. An ascending triangle in an extended bear market would have a good probability of marking the bottom. A symmetrical triangle in the same position would be less conclusive because it does not carry any implication of subsequent price movement. A symmetrical triangle that formed relatively early in a move could be a short-term turning point or simply a pause before continuing.

## Double Tops and Bottoms

A double top occurs when an ongoing rally fails in an attempt to make a new high. The pattern is a harbinger of change. It symbolizes diminished buying power. After pushing prices to a succession of new peaks, the bulls have suddenly lost some of their strength. If, in the ensuing decline, prices should close below the intervening low, it would indicate that not only are the bulls getting weaker, but the bears are getting stronger. It is at that point that the topping pattern is considered complete.

A double bottom is the same pattern, inverted. After pushing prices relentlessly down to a series of new lows, the bears are unable to do it again. Prices stop instead at about the same level as the immediately previous decline. From that point they rally. When the intervening high is surpassed, the bottoming pattern is confirmed and a new uptrend begun. Double bottom patterns are not seen as often as double tops.

Figure 19 provides an example of a double top.

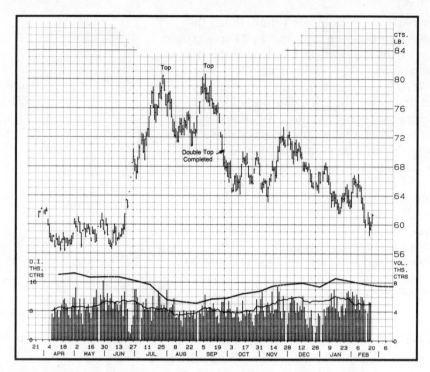

**FIGURE 19.** Failure to reach a new high creates a double top. Prices rallied strongly from 56 cents to 81 cents in June and July. The attempt in September to surpass 81 cents failed. When prices closed below the 71-cent level, the low between the two peaks, the double top was completed, and a fresh lower trend established. The 81-cent level marked the high in that market for the next two years. Reprinted with Permission, © 1988 Commodity Perspective, 30 South Wacker Drive, Suite 1820, Chicago, Illinois 60606.

## Expanding Tops and Bottoms

An expanding top marks a major turning point. The price pattern looks like an unstable boat in rough water. Each new high is higher, and each new low is lower, until the market finally capsizes. There are generally five clearly visible turning points, starting with the first high. The pattern is considered completed when prices close below the low of the day on which the last high was made. On occasion there will be a

sixth and seventh point before prices finally
turn downward.

Figure 20 shows an example of an expanding
top.

In an expanding bottom, the pattern is
inverted. Expanding bottoms are rare.

## Gaps

A gap is a price range on the chart where no
trading took place. If tomorrow's low price is
higher than today's high price, the two price
ranges will not overlap; white space would be
left on the chart, and an upside gap would be

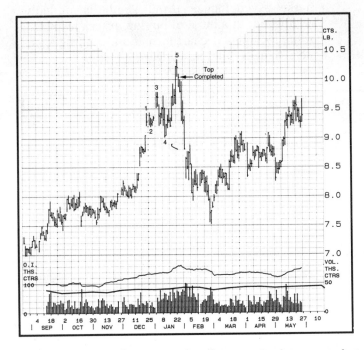

**FIGURE 20.** Expanding tops generally comprise five waves, but a sixth and
seventh wave may occur before prices reverse course. The top is completed
when prices close below the low of the day on which the high was
registered; that was on July 26, at a price near 10 cents. Reprinted with
Permission, © 1988 Commodity Perspective, 30 South Wacker Drive, Suite
1820, Chicago, Illinois 60606.

formed. If today's high price is lower than yesterday's low, a downside price gap would be created.

Gaps are formed on the opening of trading. They are caused by the overnight buildup of orders in the pit and are not unusual. However, most of them are "closed" later in the day, as subsequent trading activity eventually moves through the empty price range, and the gap never appears on the chart.

Gaps that are not closed symbolize powerful market forces. Look at Figure 21. For 7 months, prices traded quietly in a narrow range between 56 cents and 60 cents. The market was in equilibrium. Neither the bulls nor the bears predominated. On January 26, a major change in market psychology occurred. The bulls suddenly stampeded. In a burst of buying, prices leapt out of the rectangular chart formation, creating a gap more than 100 points wide.

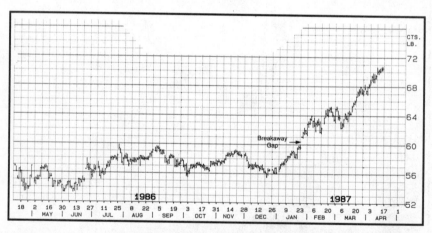

**FIGURE 21.** After trading in a narrow range for 7 months, prices suddenly leaped out of the rectangular chart formation. The result was a space more than 100 points wide where no trading took place. This "breakaway" gap was caused by a strong surge in bullish momentum. If the gap remains open (no trading in that range) for the next few days (as happened here), it portends an extended price move. Reprinted with Permission, © 1988 Commodity Perspective, 30 South Wacker Drive, Suite 1820, Chicago, Illinois 60606.

What caused the abrupt change in market psychology? It could have been any one of a number of factors: a report that showed far fewer cattle on feed than expected; news of the outbreak of bovine disease in the United States or overseas. Whatever the cause, the continued advance during the next several days removed the buying activity from the category of a market aberration, providing technical evidence that a new upward price trend had begun.

Figure 21 demonstrates another aspect of gaps. It is not unusual for prices to gap when leaving an established price pattern. It is as if they need the extra inertia to break clear, like a rocket leaving earth's gravity. Gaps found in such locations have a special name; they are called *breakaway* gaps.

Price gaps work the same way in the other direction. In Figure 22, the wide price gap formed on June 29 signaled a sudden increase in selling pressure. The ensuing decline carried prices all the way back down to the February lows. There's another price gap in Figure 22, formed on June 13. It has two special qualities. It is the widest gap on the chart, and it is found at the end of a long rally. These two properties qualify it as an *exhaustion* gap, signaling the end of the ongoing higher price trend.

Gaps may also be found at the midpoints of extended price moves. Called *measuring* gaps, they are not as common nor considered as reliable as the breakaway gap and exhaustion gap. Figure 23 shows an example of a measuring gap that kept its promise. The decline began at a price of 28 and carried all the way to 10. The large downside price gap formed at the end of January marked almost the exact midpoint of the long bear market.

Some other incidental intelligence: For a gap to be significant, its presence must be unusual; charts of thinly traded markets are full of gaps that mean nothing. The gap should also be unusually wide. The price action immediately

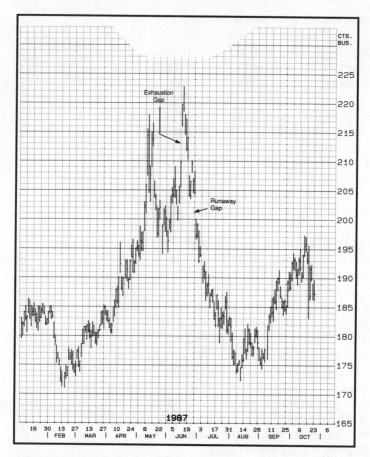

**FIGURE 22.** There are two meaningful price gaps on this chart. The wide upside price gap on June 13 signaled "exhaustion" of the steep advance. The second, a 5-cent downside gap 2 weeks later, indicated a sudden increase in selling pressure and a "runaway" decline. Reprinted with Permission, © 1988 Commodity Perspective, 30 South Wacker Drive, Suite 1820, Chicago, Illinois 60606.

following the gap is also important. If the gap is closed in the next day or two, it's a sign that the buyers or sellers who created the gap may not have sufficient numbers to keep the price move going, and the gap's significance would be reduced. As we mentioned earlier, gaps may also provide support and resistance; but their performance in this regard is erratic.

## Island Reversals

Among the annals of price chart patterns, island reversals may well be the most dependable. Unfortunately, they are quite rare. The island is formed by a pair of price gaps. Prices gap to new highs or lows, trade in that area for a day or two, them immediately gap sharply in the other direction. The day or two of intervening

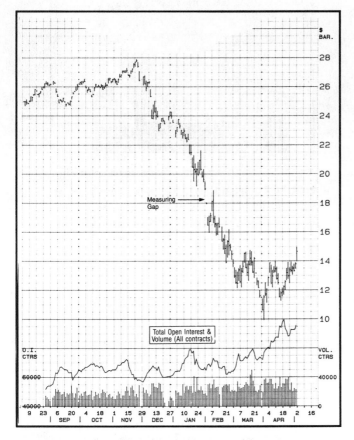

**FIGURE 23.** The downside gap that formed in early February turned out to be of the "measuring" kind. That is, it occurred almost exactly in the middle of the long downward price spiral. Reprinted with Permission, © 1988 Commodity Perspective, 30 South Wacker Drive, Suite 1820, Chicago, Illinois 60606.

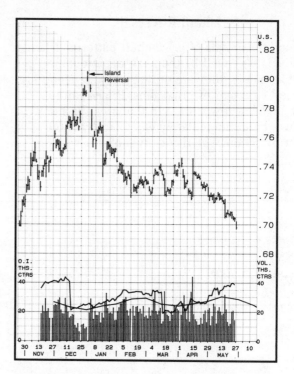

**FIGURE 24.** Island reversals are among the most trustworthy of chart patterns. This 1-day island reversal on December 31 stands like a flag on a mountain top, marking a peak that, as of this writing, has not been scaled again. Reprinted with Permission, © 1988 Commodity Perspective, 30 South Wacker Drive, Suite 1820, Chicago, Illinois 60606.

price action is left floating in white space, an island that marks a market turning point.

Figure 24 shows a 1-day island reversal that marked a summit in that Swiss franc futures. The stage was set on December 31, with an upside (exhaustion) gap. The next day prices gapped downward, and the island was formed.

Strictly speaking, a legitimate island reversal is completely disconnected from the mainland of trading activity. As in Figure 24, there should be open water all around it.

# Appendix B

## More about Point-and-Figure Charts

To give you a better idea of how a point-and-figure chart works, let's build an actual point-and-figure chart from scratch. We'll use T-bill futures, a box size of 10 points, a three-box reversal, and the following prices:

| Day | High | Low | Close |
|-----|------|-----|-------|
| 1 | 91.20 | 90.96 | 91.00 |
| 2 | 91.55 | 91.10 | 91.30 |
| 3 | 92.02 | 91.78 | 91.95 |
| 4 | 91.95 | 91.72 | 91.87 |
| 5 | 91.63 | 90.92 | 91.41 |
| 6 | 91.23 | 91.02 | 91.03 |
| 7 | 91.18 | 90.92 | 91.05 |
| 8 | 91.63 | 91.22 | 91.47 |
| 9 | 91.44 | 90.84 | 91.12 |
| 10 | 90.84 | 90.65 | 90.71 |

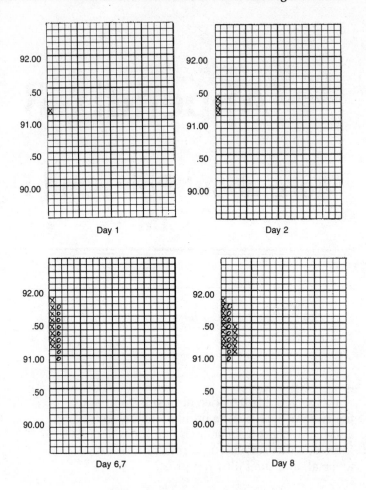

Day 1          Day 2

Day 6,7         Day 8

We'll begin our chart with Day 1. Looking back over the price action of the previous few weeks, we see that an advance is under way; so we'll start by plotting Xs. We put an X in the 91.20 box, the high on Day 1 (see Figure 25).

After the close the next day (Day 2) we update our chart, using that day's low and high prices. The first thing we look for is a possible reversal. There was none. The low on Day 2 was 91.10. That's only one box below yesterday's high of 91.20. According to the rules we set up ourselves for this chart, the daily low must be at least three full boxes below the most recent high

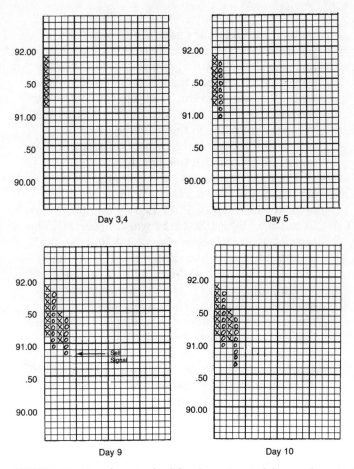

**FIGURE 25.** Ten days in the life of a point-and-figure chart. Prices are in the table on p. 275. The arrow on Day 9 marks a point-and-figure "sell" signal— when the present O column drops one space below the immediately previous column of Os.

before it is considered a reversal. We then check to see if there was a new high. There was, at 91.55. Staying in the same column, we put an X in the 91.30 box and an X in the 91.40 box. We do not put an X in the 91.50 box because it was not completely "filled"; that is, prices did not completely traverse the 91.50 box but stopped in the middle of the box at 91.55.

The rally continues. After the close on Day 3 we again update our chart. We look first for a possible reversal. Again, there was none. We next check the day's high price. It was 92.02, a new peak. To record the advance, we add five Xs to the chart—in the 91.50 box, the 91.60 box, the 91.70 box, the 91.80 box, and the 91.90 box. We make no mark in the 92.00 box because prices did not reach the upper boundary of that box at 92.10; they stopped at 92.02.

The next day (Day 4), the high and low prices are 91.95 and 91.72. We check for a possible reversal. The low of 91.72 is only one box below 91.90, the highest X. There was no reversal. The high of 91.95 is below yesterday's high, so no X is added to the column. As a result, *nothing* is added to the point-and-figure chart this day.

The following day (Day 5), the high and low are 91.63 and 90.92. The low of 90.92 is nine boxes below our highest X at 92.00. That more than meets our three-box criterion for a price reversal. We move one column to the right and, starting with the 91.80 box, we add Os down to and including the 91.00 box. We don't put an O in the 90.90 box, because the decline stopped at 90.92; approaching it from the top, prices didn't completely "fill" the 90.90 box.

Our point-and-figure chart has just recorded a change in the price trend from up to down.

On Days 6 and 7, the lower trend continued. However, no entry was made on either day because there was no new low. On Day 8, the high price was 91.63. That exceeds our three-box reversal criterion, so we move one column to the right and put Xs in the 91.10 box, 91.20 box, 91.30 box, 91.40 box, and 91.50 box. For an X in the 91.60 box, prices would have had to reach 91.70 or beyond; the rally stopped at 91.63, so we leave the 91.60 box empty.

Prices turn down again on Day 9, creating a reversal to the downside and causing Os to be placed in the boxes for 91.40, 91.30, 91.20, 91.10, 91.00 and 90.90. The decline continues

on Day 10, when the 90.80 and 90.70 boxes
receive Os.

We would continue to plot Os in this column
until we observe a daily high that is at least
three full boxes above the lowest O. That would
be an indication that the trend had reversed
back to the upside; we would move to the next
column to the right and start to plot Xs.

## Adjusting Values

Because you select the box size and reversal
criterion yourself, it is possible for you to "fine-
tune" the point-and-figure chart. The smaller the
box size, the more sensitive the chart is to price
changes. The smaller the reversal criterion, the
greater the number of trend changes that will be
signaled. For volatile markets, you would use
relatively large box sizes and reversal criteria, so
the chart would ignore jittery short-term price
fluctuations. In a quieter market you would use
smaller values, to pick up the more subtle price
movements.

The key is to strike a happy medium. What
you want your point-and-figure chart to do is to
send you a signal when the underlying price
trend has changed but ignore as much as
possible the minor price changes that do not
affect the present trend. Selecting the values to
be used in a point-and-figure chart is as much
art as science and is accomplished mainly by
trial and error.

## Trading Signals

Point-and-figure charts have another attribute
not found in bar charts: Point-and-figure charts
can give "buy" and "sell" signals. A simple
point-and-figure sell signal occurs when the
column of Os currently being plotted falls below
the immediately preceding column of Os, as
shown on Day 9 in Figure 25. A buy signal is
given when an ongoing column of Xs tops by at
least one box the immediately preceding column

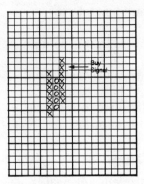

**FIGURE 26.** A point-and-figure "buy" signal occurs when a column of Xs rises one box above the immediately previous column of Xs, as in this chart excerpt.

of Xs, as in Figure 26. Point-and-figure chartists recognize and use several other price patterns in making their trading decisions, but most are a variation on these simple buy and sell signals.

## Optimizing

Technical analysts use computers to reconstruct past market activity and test trading theories. The underlying assumption is that a trading system that worked well in the past will work well in the future. Some analysts sell their findings in the form of proprietary trading methods, providing specific point-and-figure box sizes and reversal criteria that have worked well in a certain markets over recent months. The process is called "optimizing" because it seeks the optimum balance between the values that produce the greatest profit and the values that produce the smallest loss.

The problem is, of course, that today's price behavior may not resemble yesterday's price behavior at all. Factors that affect prices are almost countless and in constant change. The conditions that caused a $7/32$ box and five-box reversal to work well for T-bonds last month, for example, may not be repeated this month or ever again.

# Appendix C

## More about Moving Averages

### Weighted Moving Averages

All prices are not all of equal importance. Yesterday's price is likely to be a better indication of current market sentiment than last week's price, and last week's price more indicative than the price a month ago. On this thesis, some technicians weight the various closing prices, assigning higher values to more recent prices. A typical weighting system for a 5-day moving average would be:

$$1 \cdots 2 \cdots 3 \cdots 4 \cdots 5$$

That is, today's closing price would be multiplied by 5, the previous day's closing price multiplied by 4, the day before that multiplied by 3, and so on back to the 5 days ago. The totals are then summed and divided by the sum of the weights.

To take an example, suppose the "prices" for the last 5 days were 17, 20, 22, 23, and 24. The

simple average would be the sum of those
numbers (106) divided by 5, or 21.2. The
weighted average, using the weighting system
described before, would be:

| Day | Price | × | Weight | = | Weighted Daily Value |
|-----|-------|---|--------|---|----------------------|
| 5 | 24 | × | 5 | = | 120 |
| 4 | 23 | × | 4 | = | 92 |
| 3 | 22 | × | 3 | = | 66 |
| 2 | 20 | × | 2 | = | 40 |
| 1 | 17 | × | 1 | = | 17 |
| | | | 15 | | 335 ÷ 15 = 22.3 |

The weighted 5-day average (22.3) is higher
than the simple 5-day average (21.2) because the
more recent prices are higher, and by design
they have a greater influence on the outcome.

This is only one example. Weights may be
assigned to any number of days and in any
amounts.

The ultimate in weighting is called an
*exponential* moving average. The recent days
still get the most emphasis, but every day back
to the start of the calculations is given some
mathematical recognition. The technique was
developed for use in antiaircraft fire control
during World War II, to forecast the position of a
moving target.

To get an exponential moving average started,
you need an initial value. For this you could use
the simple average of closing prices over the
past several days, say 10 days. This value is
plugged into the formula:

$$MN = MO + C(P - MO)$$

where

MN = the new moving average
MO = yesterday's moving average
P  = today's closing price
C  = a smoothing constant

Each day the calculation is made again, using the previous day's exponential moving average for *MO*.

The key is C, the smoothing constant. It is always a number between 0 and 1. The smaller it is, the more days are included in the exponential moving average. For example, if a constant of .05 is used, the past 44 days have about 90 percent of the total weight. With a smoothing constant of .20, the past 10 days have about 90 percent of the total weight, and with a constant of .40 the past 4 days have 90 percent of the total weight. The value of the constant must be chosen by the technical analyst to fit the character of that particular market.

## Trading with Moving Averages

The simplest approach to trading with a single moving average is:

*When the daily closing price is above the moving average, be long.*

*When the daily closing price is above the moving average, be short.*

| Day | Closing Price | Three-Day Moving Average | Position |
|-----|---------------|--------------------------|----------|
| 1 | 89.50 | | |
| 2 | 88.70 | | |
| 3 | 87.25 | 88.50 | |
| 4 | 86.40 | 87.25 | Go short |
| 5 | 86.10 | 86.58 | Stay short |
| 6 | 85.90 | 86.13 | Stay short |
| 7 | 85.70 | 85.90 | Stay short |
| 8 | 86.30 | 85.97 | Stay short |
| 9 | 86.75 | 86.25 | Cover short; go long |
| 10 | 87.30 | 86.78 | Stay long |

For example, suppose you had just begun to keep a 3-day moving average, and the prices of the past several trading days were as shown in the table. On Day 3, the first day that you can calculate a value for the moving average, the closing price is below the moving averge value. Following the two rules previously mentioned, you take a short position on Day 4.

On Day 5 the closing price is still below the moving average, so you keep your short position. Ditto for Day 6 and 7. On Day 8, after the close, you see that a switch has occurred; the closing price has moved above the 3-day moving average. Following the rules, you close out your short position and take a new long position on Day 9. You keep the long position until the daily closing price drops back below the moving average.

These two simple trading rules keep you always in the market. There are other moving average methods that allow more time for the price trend to change. For example, some traders use two moving averages, one short-term (e.g., a 5-day moving average) and one long-term (e.g., a 20-day moving average). A long position is held when the price is above both moving averages. A short position is held when the price is below both moving averages. At all other times the trader is out of the market.

As with point-and-figure charts, technical analysts have identified the moving averages that worked best in certain markets in the past. Many have published their conclusions. These trading criteria suffer from a problem we have talked about before. They assume that today's markets will closely resemble yesterday's markets, and that may not be the case.

## ENDNOTES

1. *Economics of Futures Trading*, by Thomas A. Hieronymus. Commodity Research Bureau, New York City.
2. *Hedging Foreign Exchange*, by Eric T. Jones and Donald L. Jones. John Wiley & Sons, Inc., New York City.
3. *Futures Trading: Concepts and Strategies*, by Robert E. Fink and Robert B. Feduniak. New York Institute of Finance, New York City.

# Index